THE INTERNATIONAL CO-OPERATIVE ALLIANCE AND THE CONSUMER CO-OPERATIVE MOVEMENT IN NORTHERN EUROPE, c. 1860–1939

MANCHESTER
1824
Manchester University Press

The International Co-operative Alliance and the consumer co-operative movement in northern Europe, c. 1860–1939

Mary Hilson

Manchester University Press

Published by Manchester University Press
Altrincham Street, Manchester M1 7JA

www.manchesteruniversitypress.co.uk

British Library Cataloguing-in-Publication Data

A catalogue record for this book is available from the British Library

ISBN 978 1 5261 0080 1 hardback

First published 2018

Typeset
by Toppan Best-set Premedia Limited
Printed in Great Britain
by CPI Group (UK) Ltd, Croydon, CR0 4YY

Contents

List of tables — *page* vi
Acknowledgements — vii
Abbreviations — ix
Introduction: a transnational approach to co-operative history — 1
1 Co-operation in the Nordic countries before 1914: international networks and the transmission of ideas — 22
2 Co-operative internationalism in practice: the International Co-operative Alliance (ICA) before and after the First World War — 53
3 The politics of international co-operation: neutrality and crisis — 82
4 Nordisk Andelsforbund (NAF), co-operative trade and Nordic co-operation during the interwar period — 109
5 Co-operation and the emergence of the Nordic 'middle way' — 136
Conclusion — 162
Bibliography — 170
Index — 190

Tables

2.1 Subscriptions received from national members of the ICA, in amount and as percentage of total, 1902, 1913, 1922 and 1936 *page* 62

2.2 The social programme for the ICA meetings in London, October 1929 69

2.3 Väinö Tanner's journey to the ICA meetings in London, October 1929 71

4.1 Purchases from abroad by ICWS members, as percentage of total imports by co-operative societies, 1922, 1929 and 1930 114

4.2 Percentage shares of NAF annual turnover, by member, 1919–27 121

4.3 NAF annual trade as percentage of total, by member, 1928–40 122

C.1 Membership of consumer co-operative societies, as percentage of population in selected countries, 1935–39 163

Acknowledgements

I began the research for this book during a period I spent as a visiting researcher at NordForsk Centre of Excellence: The Nordic Welfare State – Historical Foundations and Future Challenges (NordWel) in 2009. I would like to thank Pauli Kettunen, Henrik Stenius and colleagues at NordWel Helsinki and the Centre for Nordic Studies (CENS) at Helsinki University. Grateful thanks also to the School of European Languages, Culture and Society (SELCS) at UCL for supporting several periods of research leave and the travel needed to undertake this research; and to Pirjo Markkola, Jari Ojala and colleagues at the Department of History and Ethnology, University of Jyväskylä, where I spent a period as a visiting researcher during the spring of 2014.

Thanks are due to staff at many libraries and archives, in particular Ulla Tapiovaara-Harpf and colleagues at the Finnish Labour Archives, Helsinki; Gillian Lonergan and colleagues at the National Co-operative Archives, Manchester; Michael Hagström and colleagues at KF's archives, Stockholm.

My work has benefited enormously from the comments and criticisms of colleagues across the Nordic region and beyond. Earlier drafts of different chapters were presented to seminars at the following institutions: EINO seminar, Centre for Nordic Studies, Helsinki University; NordWel Helsinki; Institute of Contemporary History, Södertörn University; Department of Economic History, Uppsala University; Department of History and Classical Studies, Aarhus University; Department of History and Ethnology, University of Jyväskylä; Swedish Labour Movement Archives and Library, Stockholm; and also at a session of the 28th Congress of Nordic Historians at the University of Eastern Finland in Joensuu in 2014. In particular, I would like to thank Tapio Bergholm, David Harvey and Silke Neunsinger for their helpful comments on the manuscript, and also the two anonymous referees for Manchester University Press. Many thanks also to everyone at Manchester University Press and especially to Joe Haining for his thorough copy-editing. It goes without saying that any remaining errors are my own. My thinking about co-operation has also been greatly influenced by what I have learned from working with colleagues on collaborative projects on co-operative history. I would like to thank Pirjo

Markkola and Ann-Catrin Östman, who co-edited a volume on co-operatives and the social question with me, and Silke Neunsinger, Greg Patmore and all the contributors to our project on the global history of consumer co-operation.

Finally, warmest thanks to my former colleagues at the Department of Scandinavian Studies, UCL, and my current ones at the Department of History and Classical Studies, Aarhus University; and to my partner David Harvey for his support and companionship in the UK, Finland and now most recently in Denmark.

Aarhus, July 2017

Abbreviations

CWS	Co-operative Wholesale Society
DkF	Det kooperative Fællesforbund
FDB	Fællesforeningen for Danmarks Brugsforeningerne
ICA	International Co-operative Alliance
ICWS	International Co-operative Wholesale Society
ILO	International Labour Organization
KF	Kooperativa Förbundet
KK	Kulutusosuuskuntien Keskusliitto
NAF	Nordisk Andelsforbund
NKL	Norges Kooperative Landsforening
OTK	Suomen Osuustukkukauppa
RACS	Royal Arsenal Co-operative Society
SOK	Suomen Osuuskauppojen Keskuskunta
YOL	Yleinen Osuuskauppojen Liitto

Introduction: a transnational approach to co-operative history

Co-operation means many different things. In its most basic sense of working together it is as old as humanity. Since the early nineteenth century, the term has been used more specifically to refer to economic organisations that variously process and sell agricultural products, supply banking and credit, manufacture different commodities and distribute essential goods to consumers. It is this last form of distributive or consumer co-operation – specifically in relation to the international co-operative movement during the decades either side of the First World War – that is the focus of this book.

By 1939 consumer co-operation had become a mass movement. The co-operative store, or 'Co-op', was an essential part of everyday life for millions across Europe and beyond. It had become the main source of staples such as bread, tea, coffee, milk and potatoes. Although some co-operators tried to argue that the consumers' movement was the only true form of co-operation, this view was always contested and in many respects it is impossible to consider consumer co-operation in isolation from other types of co-operative, whether producer, agricultural or credit. This is especially relevant in relation to the fundamental questions with which this book is concerned: what was co-operation? Was it an economic system or a social movement? Did it aspire to challenge capitalism or to reform it? Did it contain at its heart a political vision for the transformation of society, or was it simply a practical guide for organising a business?

Most co-operatives define themselves by the organisational principles that they have in common. Co-operatives differ from other forms of economic enterprise, such as the limited joint stock company, in several fundamental ways. The most important of these are the commitment to member ownership and control, and a mechanism for redistributing the trading surplus among the members in proportion to patronage, rather than paying it as a return on capital investment.[1] Beyond these basic principles, however, co-operation itself was often hard to define. Lacking its own political programme, the co-operative movement has been open to varying and sometimes even contradictory interpretations. It has been seen as a radical alternative to capitalism and a means to make capitalism function more effectively; as a tool of working-class emancipation and an elite strategy to soothe revolutionary tensions and promote social harmony; as a practical business model and a utopian vision. At different times co-operation has been aligned with political visions on both the left and the right. And it has provoked varying responses from political elites in different places, ranging from outright repression, to indifference, to official recognition and incorporation in government policy.

The history of co-operation can be approached in many different ways. From a business history perspective studying co-operatives can illuminate important changes in retailing and commerce, while for social historians co-operation is relevant to the history of consumption and consumerism. My own interest in co-operation arose from a local study of popular politics in the southern English naval city of Plymouth during the early twentieth century. Here, the labour movement, organised around the politics of production, was relatively weak, but there was a very large and vibrant co-operative society. During the First World War this society was at the centre of local struggles over food rationing and price control and it played an important, though contested, role in the emergence of a Labour challenge to established political alignments in Plymouth.[2] Subsequent comparative work indicated how these struggles were not confined to Plymouth, but were repeated across Europe, even in non-belligerent countries such as Sweden.[3] This was apparent to contemporary co-operators as well, and after 1918 they devoted much time to the question of how to apply co-operative principles to the re-organisation of trade, not only locally and nationally but also internationally.

This book is concerned with the transnational history of co-operation, an area which has hitherto been relatively little researched.[4] From its beginnings co-operation was shaped by the transfer and exchange of ideas across national boundaries, and from 1895 it also had its own international organisation, the International Co-operative Alliance (ICA). The book focuses on co-operation in the Nordic countries – Denmark, Finland, Norway and Sweden – where the movement has often been perceived as unusually strong by contemporary observers and historians alike. Representatives of the Nordic co-operative organisations played an active role within the ICA and sometimes worked together to adopt common positions on matters of co-operative policy.[5]

In the 1930s co-operation became part of emerging ideas of the Scandinavian 'middle way', most famously in the work of Marquis Childs. Studying it can therefore offer a new perspective on the roots of the Scandinavian or Nordic model.[6] But the politics of co-operation in the region could also be deeply controversial. An examination of the debates and conflicts over co-operation, both at home and abroad, casts further light on the social and political history of a turbulent period.

Co-operative history

Until recently consumer co-operation was not well served by academic historians, at least in comparison to other social movements such as the labour movement.[7] Its relative neglect was all the more remarkable given the importance of co-operation in Europe during the first half of the twentieth century. By 1940 membership of the British consumers' co-operative movement, the largest in Europe, amounted to over 8.7 million, or about 18 per cent of the population.[8] Nonetheless, co-operation has often been ignored by labour historians, who were more interested in conflicts in the sphere of production and the organisations that emerged from these such as trade unions and socialist labour parties. They were often quite dismissive of the co-operative movement, which they regarded as being devoid of ideological aspirations and undermining class consciousness.[9] In Britain, for example, the emergence of consumer co-operative societies during the 1840s and after was seen as symptomatic of the defeat of working-class radicalism in the mid-nineteenth century, marking a gulf between the utopian and community-building aspirations of earlier co-operation and the more prosaic emphasis on shopkeeping and the dividend after 1844.[10]

The relationship between co-operation and the organised labour movement was complicated, however, and fluctuated in different times and places. Worker or producer co-operatives formed part of the challenge to capitalism in France during the 1830s and 1840s, in the form of workshops organised by small groups of skilled artisans.[11] Similar associations were also found in Britain, but according to Peter Gurney they gradually lost their distinctively working-class character from the 1870s, and what became known as co-partnership was regarded with derision by many within the labour movement.[12] But the idea of the workers' producer co-operative never disappeared completely.[13] It was debated widely within the Finnish labour movement, for example, and also in Denmark where the ambition to form producer co-operatives was part of the first social democratic party programme agreed in 1876.[14]

Labour movement attitudes towards consumer co-operation were also sceptical. Like many of its counterparts, the German Social Democratic Party (SPD) was initially hostile to co-operation, influenced by Lassalle's theory of the iron law of wages.[15] During the debate on revisionism during the 1890s this stance began to shift, and in 1910 the Second International agreed a resolution formally recognising the role of consumer co-operation in improving the living standards of the working class. The success of the socialist co-operative Vooruit in Ghent was also influential in persuading many socialists to overcome their suspicions and acknowledge co-operation as a 'third pillar' of the working-class movement alongside trade unions and socialist parties, even though for many it remained a subordinate pillar.[16] Although most consumer co-operatives were reluctant to commit themselves to formal political alliances, in the early twentieth century they were widely perceived to be part of the labour movement. Indeed, in some cases they can be argued to have had a decisive impact on the consolidation of the reformist social democratic wing of the labour movement after the First World War.[17]

The growth of interest in the history of consumption and consumer politics since the late 1980s triggered a re-examination of co-operative history, emphasising the continuities from earlier nineteenth-century radicalism.[18] To name a few examples: Peter Gurney's influential study portrayed British co-operation as a movement with its own distinctive ideology and culture, which offered its followers an alternative to mass capitalist consumption during the second half of the nineteenth century and the first half of the twentieth.[19] Ellen Furlough examined French co-operation against the background of changes in capitalist retailing and the emergence of a modern consumer society in the second half of the nineteenth century, while also drawing attention to the continuities between the earlier associations and later consumer co-operatives.[20] Peder Aléx explored how the Swedish co-operative union educated consumer-citizens in rational consumption as part of the development of the welfare state during the twentieth century.[21] Similar perspectives also shaped Ellen Furlough and Carl Strikwerda's collection of essays on co-operative history in Europe, North America and Japan, which showed how studies in the history of co-operation could also shed light on the evolution of capitalist consumption and especially the ways in which it was gendered.[22]

Despite their emphasis on the radical roots of co-operation, these studies often expressed scepticism about the ability of the co-operative movement to sustain its opposition to capitalist consumerism. By the 1990s once-powerful co-operative businesses appeared to be in decline in most of the global north, experiencing loss of market share or even collapse in the cases of Germany and Austria.[23] The hegemony of neo-liberalism and the decline of the industrial working-class communities in which co-operation was often rooted all served to undermine interest in the movement and meant that in a long-term perspective it was invariably viewed through the pessimistic lens of decline.[24] Furlough suggests that even during the 1920s French co-operators were already imitating the commercial strategies of their capitalist competitors rather than challenging them.[25] The main problems came after 1950, however, as consumer co-operatives struggled to respond to new trends in mass consumption and the related changes in retailing.[26]

Since the turn of the millennium there have been some signs of revival, both in the fortunes of co-operative businesses and in scholarly interest. The United Nations proclaimed 2012 to be International Year of Co-operatives, in recognition of the sector's resilience to the global financial crisis that began in 2007 and of its importance especially in the global south.[27] New historical studies of co-operative organisations have also been inspired by milestones such as centenaries or other anniversaries.[28] As Anthony Webster and John K. Walton pointed out in the introduction to a special themed issue of *Business History* on co-operatives, the challenge is now to 'mainstream' co-operative history and to place it in a wider context.[29]

As Lawrence Black and Nicole Robertson note in their introduction to a collection of essays on the British co-operative movement, 'taking stock' of co-operative history can help to illuminate many other aspects of twentieth-century social and economic history.[30] The distinctive management and commercial strategies of co-operatives are of interest to business historians. In many countries co-operatives led the way in the introduction of new forms of retailing, in the organisation of wholesale and production, in the design of their brands and buildings, and in their practical and theoretical attempts to link production, distribution and consumption.[31] As Robertson's research has shown, larger co-operative societies often provided extensive educational and leisure activities for their members, contributing to the development of distinctive working-class cultures.[32] They were also widely discussed as a potential solution to the 'social question' in the early twentieth century.[33] In many parts of Europe co-operatives mobilised the working-class women who formed the majority of their customers, and the Women's Co-operative Guild became one of the largest and most radical women's organisations in early twentieth-century Britain, campaigning on issues such as suffrage, divorce reform and peace.[34]

Studying the consumer co-operative movement can also shed light on the political conflicts that have arisen over consumption. These conflicts were not confined within national boundaries. Frank Trentmann's research on the politics of free trade in nineteenth-century Britain shows that working-class consumers were well aware of their dependence on the global food trade and willing to take action in support of free trade.[35] This awareness was further heightened by the disruptions to international trade during the First World War, when serious food shortages caused political unrest across Europe.[36] Trentmann shows that the concept of fair trade is not a recent phenomenon, but one which has historical roots, for example in the 'buying for Empire' campaigns in Britain of the 1920s and 1930s which mobilised housewives in support of imperial trade.[37]

Many co-operators could be described as liberal internationalists, motivated by the conviction that the re-organisation of international trade according to co-operative principles would also help to secure peace. Such convictions were never purely theoretical, as from the early 1920s the ICA sought to co-ordinate trade between the co-operative wholesale societies of different countries and assist its members in securing access to imported goods at favourable prices.[38] Trying to establish the extent to which these co-operative moral economies permeated to the members every time they 'opened the larder door', in Gurney's phrase, is notoriously difficult of course. But the ordinary material goods that the co-operative stores supplied could have a powerful symbolic message. As this book will try to show, the story of international co-operation was as much about commodities such as coffee, raisins, matches and lightbulbs as it was about political resolutions and sophisticated analyses of international political economy.

Finally, examining these struggles within the co-operative movement can help to suggest a more integrated approach to the history of consumption, which recognises the relationship between consumption and production rather than seeing them as oppositional categories.[39] The ICA was never exclusively an organisation of consumers, despite the aspirations of some of its members to make it so. The early years of the Alliance were shaped by struggles between the French and British supporters of profit-sharing producer co-operatives on the one hand, and powerful consumer co-operatives on the other. The domination of the latter group was consolidated in 1904 when the representatives of the German agricultural and credit co-operatives withdrew, but membership of the Alliance remained open to all types of co-operative.[40] The struggles over food shortages in many countries during the First World War strengthened the position of the consumer co-operatives, but their dominance was never complete. The mixed agricultural and rural consumer co-operative unions of Finland and Denmark were prominent members of the ICA during the interwar period, and the expansion of the Alliance beyond Europe led to the admission of many more producer co-operatives. From the early 1930s co-operators were increasingly likely to speak of the mutually dependent interests of producers and consumers, and how co-operation could help to promote these.

Transnational history and internationalism

Interest in transnational history – also under designations including global history, world history, entangled history and *histoire croisée* – grew enormously during the 1990s and afterwards, as demonstrated by the number of conferences and special journal issues devoted to this theme.[41] The twin trends of globalisation and (in Europe) a new dynamic phase of European integration during the early 1990s stimulated a heightened awareness of the interconnected and entangled nature of the world in which we live, which in turn generated new interest in exploring the historical roots of these connections.[42] Some scholars have pointed out that transnational history is not so very new. The term itself has a nineteenth-century pedigree and generations of historians have written transnational studies without necessarily acknowledging them as such.[43] Nonetheless, there is no doubt that the current boom has been stimulated by contemporary developments in communications technology and academic mobility, and in many cases it has been connected to an explicit agenda of internationalisation promoted by universities and research councils.[44]

There are as many ways to write transnational history as there are historians seeking to do so.[45] The field is broad, and criticisms of imprecision in the ways in which the term 'transnational' is used are probably justified.[46] Nonetheless, most historians would probably agree that transnational history is not a distinctive method so much as a perspective: a 'way of seeing'.[47] What seems to define transnational history, above all, is scepticism towards the nation state as the dominant frame for historical enquiry: 'the conviction that historical and social processes cannot be apprehended and understood exclusively within customary, delineated spaces or containers, might they be states, nations, empires or regions'.[48] Transnational historians, therefore, are interested in links, flows and connections; 'contacts, coalitions and inter-actions across state boundaries'; people and communities 'in between' nation states.[49] These connections may be studied in many different ways and using different methods as appropriate to the phenomenon under study. Studies of the transfer of people, ideas or things between two national contexts need not necessarily be incompatible with comparisons of the same phenomenon in two or more nations; indeed, transnational history often rests on a fruitful combination of both approaches.[50]

As noted above, the boom in transnational history is connected to an awareness of the impact of globalisation on our own times, even though historians disagree about the novelty of late twentieth-century transnationalism.[51] However, most scholars accept that certain periods have witnessed an intensification of transnational activity, and that one such period was the second half of the nineteenth century. The hegemony of economic liberalism in the most powerful European state of the era (Britain) stimulated global flows of capital, goods and labour, and led to what is often described as the 'first era of globalisation'. This was accompanied by an 'extraordinarily rapid growth' in the number of international organisations, made possible by revolutionary developments in transport and communications.[52]

The new international organisations concerned themselves with tasks such as the collection and sharing of information and the agreement of standard values, definitions, weights and measures. Many also espoused an explicit commitment to internationalism, defined in Magaly Rodríguez García's words as:

> all types of initiatives (both formal and informal) that transcended (or aimed to transcend) national borders, for example the promotion of 'universal' values and calls for free trade, conferences involving individuals of different nationalities for the promotion of international law and peace, and the establishment of international organizations.[53]

Writing of the international women's movement, Leila Rupp suggests that internationalism was 'a spirit rather than a formal ideology'; a description that seems apt.[54] It was not necessarily opposed to nationalism but rather stimulated by its rise. Internationalists aspired to transcend national borders, but their thinking was usually influenced by national categories and the desire to forge a new internationalist 'imagined community' out of the 'notion of [national] differences'.[55] For this reason, Kevin Callahan has suggested that the term 'inter-nationalism' more accurately captures the ideology and practices of the Socialist International, a designation that would certainly apply to many other international organisations of the early twentieth century.[56]

As this suggests, and as many have been quick to point out, transnational history does not necessarily imply an outright rejection of the nation state as an irrelevance. On the contrary, it is acknowledged that nations and nation states have been immensely important in shaping how we have understood the world.[57] No nation developed in a vacuum but nation states were themselves shaped by transnational historical processes.[58] Transnational history is thus not associated with any particular spatial scale; rather it requires historians to think carefully about space and scale. It implies, to use Jürgen Osterhammel's term, a 'polycentric' analysis which requires the historian to 'begin from both ends at the same time', combining micro and macro levels of enquiry.[59] A further dimension is added by a focus on a particular historical meso-region or *Geschichtsregion*, such as *Norden* or Scandinavia, which is the focus of this book.[60] As Philipp Ther has pointed out, such studies may offer a particularly fruitful means to move beyond national histories and contribute to a new understanding of Europe 'as a space of communication and interaction' rather than as an inflexible 'territorial container'.[61] The porous borders and shared linguistic, legal, social and cultural traditions of such regions demand but also facilitate a transnational approach. For citizens of the Nordic countries the most important contacts and connections have often been those with their closest neighbours, though these could never be taken for granted and were also sometimes sources of tension.[62]

This study is guided, therefore, by a multi-layered approach in its ambition to examine the connections and transfers that shaped the development of the co-operative movement in a number of different countries in the late nineteenth and early twentieth centuries. The co-operative movement was international – and indeed internationalist – from its beginnings.[63] The ICA, founded in London in 1895, was in many ways typical of the international organisations of the late nineteenth and early twentieth centuries. It grew out of networks of personal and informal contacts established between mostly British and French co-operators in the 1870s and 1880s, and during its early years it was dominated by the representatives of a few key national organisations, principally those of Britain.[64] Although it aspired from its foundation to be a truly global organisation – the opening congress was attended by delegates from Australia, India, Argentina and the USA – it remained dominated by Europeans throughout the interwar period and did not develop non-European regional sub-organisations until after the Second World War.[65]

As with other international organisations, the original aims of the ICA included the sharing of information between members and the standardisation of co-operative principles. There was also an aspiration to establish commercial relations between members.[66] By the outbreak of the First World War it had established the bureaucratic structures to enable it to do this. Delegates at its 1913 congress also agreed a resolution articulating their commitment to pacifism and expressing the hope that 'the reasons for ... international conflicts will disappear as the social and economic life of every nation becomes organised according to co-operative principles'.[67] Their idealism soon turned to bitter disappointment, of course, but recent research has shown that the First World War should not be seen as a defeat for internationalist aspirations. Rather, as Daniel Gorman has argued, internationalism 'came of age' in the 1920s, stimulated not only by reactions to the horrors of the war but also the new possibilities created by the Treaty of Versailles.[68]

In 1929 the League of Nations listed the existence of 478 international organisations.[69] Again the ICA was in many ways typical of these, claiming by 1930 to represent the interests of 100 million co-operators in Europe, the Americas and Asia. It had acquired most of the trappings of the internationalist 'imagined community' with its flag, its trilingual publications, its International Co-operative Day and the performances and rituals associated with the triennial congress, held in a succession of different European cities until 1937. During the 1920s and 1930s it also took concrete steps to develop an internationalist co-operative ideology and strategy.[70]

Despite the size of its membership, the ICA is largely conspicuous by its absence from the histories of interwar internationalism.[71] Nor has it been studied in any detail by historians of the co-operative movement, who have more usually focused on co-operation in one country. Two book-length accounts of the ICA's history do exist, both based on sources from the ICA's own archives. The first, from 1970, was written by former ICA director W. P. Watkins. It has the status of an official history and is more descriptive than analytical, but it is also empirically detailed and forms a useful supplement to the primary sources that were available for the present study.[72] The same level of detail also characterises Rita Rhodes' book on the ICA during the period 1910–50, which was published by the Alliance as part of its centenary celebrations in 1995.[73] Rhodes argues that the ICA was a remarkable institution, for, unlike other international organisations such as the Second International, it avoided splitting into social democratic and communist camps after 1917 and retained the membership of the USSR even into the Cold War period. Rhodes attributes this to the flexibility of the ICA's ideology and organisation, while arguing that its constitution provided a solid basis for cohesion. Like Watkins, Rhodes' perspective is that of an insider and is largely celebratory in tone, though again the book is a useful source of empirical detail.

Rhodes suggests that the ICA's 'co-operative spirit' meant that it was also less prone to fractures along national lines than other organisations, though she argues that the dominant influence on its development, at least during the first half of the twentieth century, came from Britain. This can be challenged on two counts. First, I have argued elsewhere that debates on co-operative principles during the 1930s did indeed split the Alliance into informal internal blocs: a social democratic group including Britain, Belgium and Austria, which saw co-operation as the 'third pillar' of the labour movement; and another group insisting on the political neutrality and social inclusiveness of co-operation. This latter group came increasingly to be dominated by the Nordic co-operative movements.[74] Additionally, there were the consumer co-operative movements that were incorporated into authoritarian regimes in Italy and Germany, which ceased to be members of the Alliance from 1926 and 1934, respectively. Second, although the powerful British consumer co-operatives were indeed influential in terms of membership and resources, they could not take this position for granted. The balance of power within the Alliance was shaped by many factors and was constantly in flux. British resources were undoubtedly important to the ICA, but their dominance could also act as a brake on the development of international co-operation. This was to be especially relevant in the efforts to develop international trade, which are examined further in chapter 4 of this book.

Nordic co-operation and the ICA

This book examines the development of co-operative internationalism in the ICA and some of its member organisations during the late nineteenth century and the interwar period. The aim is not to provide a comprehensive history of the ICA. The study is broader in that it is concerned not only with the ICA as an organisation, but that it attempts to adopt a transnational approach to the history of the ICA and the links and connections that shaped it and its member organisations.[75] It seeks to compare co-operative theories and practices in different national contexts and to understand how these were shaped by transnational transfers, contacts and exchanges, between individuals and between organisations. It also seeks to understand how co-operators conceived of their movement as an international one, how they tried to theorise internationalism and to put it into practice in the crisis-ridden years of the 1920s and 1930s.

The study is also narrower than would be required for a history of the ICA, as it focuses on the co-operative movement in one region of Europe only, namely the Nordic countries of Denmark, Finland, Norway and Sweden. There are several reasons why this apparently rather small and peripheral part of Europe is extremely interesting and illuminating in the context of the international co-operative movement. Firstly, co-operation was very strong in the region. The co-operative movement grew very rapidly from the establishment of the first permanent societies in the 1890s (earlier in Denmark), and by the 1920s its importance in terms of both membership and trade was widely acknowledged.[76] This meant that the influence of the Nordic co-operative organisations within the ICA was as great as or even greater than that of many more populous countries. Secondly, some of the leaders of these movements – such as Anders Örne and Albin Johansson – played an active and prominent role in international debates. From 1920 the Swedes held one of the positions on the ICA's Executive Committee, and from 1927 the Alliance's president was the Finn Väinö Tanner.

Thirdly, the book aims to shed further light on the reputation of the small Nordic countries for transnational regional co-operation and internationalism. Daniel Gorman reminds us that internationalism was never monolithic, but that international institutions were shaped by different national traditions: Anglo-American influences on the League of Nations, for example, French influences on the International Labour Organization (ILO) or Soviet internationalism in the Comintern.[77] As Daniel Laqua points out, it is important to look beyond the larger states. Participation in international organisations was an important strategy for small, neutral countries such as Belgium, the Netherlands and Switzerland.[78] The Nordic countries were not French-speaking – as Switzerland and Belgium were – nor were they situated at the heart of the European railway network, which Laqua notes as being significant for the decision to locate international organisations in Belgium.[79] Nonetheless, Norbert Götz has pointed to the emergence of a distinctively Nordic tradition of internationalism during the early twentieth century, motivated by a small-state consciousness and expressed in the development of joint Nordic initiatives at the League of Nations.[80] At the same time, international organisations such as the League of Nations also became important forums for the development of Nordic regional co-operation, though this is an area which has been little researched until recently.[81]

This book argues for the importance of a distinctively Nordic contribution to the shaping of international co-operation and the ICA, while at the same time also examining the ICA itself as a site for Nordic regional co-operation. Rita Rhodes, as noted, has argued that the dominant influence in the ICA was the British consumer co-operative movement. The British never had it all their own way, however, and during the interwar period they were challenged on a number of issues by representatives of the Nordic co-operative organisations, who were moreover also prepared to collaborate with one another to present a joint position. Indeed, Rhodes suggests that the Nordic delegates' joint action to secure the election of Väinö Tanner as ICA president in 1927 marks the emergence of 'the first geographical pressure group within the ICA'.[82]

Co-operation has certainly become a part of the national 'story' of the four Nordic nations, albeit in slightly different ways in each case. During the first half of the twentieth century the Nordic co-operative movements also attracted favourable international attention, as examples of the region's successful economic modernisation and its resistance to political extremism. At the turn of the twentieth century the Danish agricultural co-operative societies were already attracting praise from international commentators as a model for the successful organisation of agriculture.[83] By the 1930s attention had shifted towards Sweden, where the co-operative movement's successful struggles against monopoly capitalism was famously extolled by the American journalist Marquis Childs and helped persuade President Roosevelt to commission a study of European co-operation as part of his plans for the New Deal.[84] Childs and other writers saw the co-operative emphasis on social harmony and the reconciliation of the interests of producers and consumers as a distinctive Nordic 'middle way' between communism and capitalism, a characterisation which has become very influential in shaping images of the Nordic region during the twentieth century. Studying the Nordic co-operative movements in a transnational perspective may thus help shed further light on the roots of the Nordic model during the first half of the twentieth century.

Outline of the book

The book is organised chronologically, starting with the introduction of co-operative ideas to the Nordic countries and the establishment of co-operative organisations. Particular attention is paid to the importance of transnational and inter-regional networks, and the transfer and exchange of co-operative ideas. The foundation and early history of co-operation in the Nordic region is compared in chapter 1. As discussed there, the development of co-operation did not take place in a vacuum, but was shaped by contemporary European debates and the transfer of ideas from other contexts. An important reference point for all the Nordic countries was the Rochdale Society of Equitable Pioneers, founded in northern England in 1844, but this was never the only source of co-operative ideas: equally significant were influences from other European countries, including Germany and France. Chapter 1 also outlines the organisation of the consumer co-operative movement in each of the Nordic countries, acknowledging its diversity and the range of relationships between different types of co-operative society.

In chapter 2 the focus switches to the formalisation of these transnational contacts through the ICA, from its establishment in 1895 until the 1920s.

The chapter asks how the ICA functioned and evolved as an international organisation: what did 'internationalism' mean and how was this practised? Chapter 3 follows the debates within the ICA through the difficult years of the 1920s and 1930s, examining how co-operators sought to respond to political and economic crises, and their attempts to establish a coherent ideology for the movement. Again, the emphasis is on the particular contributions of the Nordic representatives, and indeed on the emergence of this group as a distinctive bloc within the ICA, despite its diversity. Chapter 4 deals with attempts to develop structures for international co-operative trade, and considers the reasons for the rather modest achievements of the International Co-operative Wholesale Society (ICWS) in contrast to the success of the Nordic co-operative wholesale Nordisk Andelsforbund (NAF). Finally, in chapter 5 the focus is on international interest in the Nordic co-operative movements in the context of the region's emerging image as a beacon of stability and modernity in the late 1930s.

The bulk of the source material for the interwar period is drawn from the ICA papers preserved in the Finnish Labour Archives in Helsinki. It seems likely that these were Väinö Tanner's personal papers, since they correspond to his time as president of the Alliance, and they also occasionally include handwritten notes on the meetings that he chaired. Where there are gaps, these have been supplemented by ICA materials from Kooperativa Förbundet's archive in Stockholm and reports on meetings from national co-operative journals. I have also consulted the published ICA congress reports and the ICA's official journal, *International Co-operative Bulletin* (from the 1928 *Review of International Co-operation*), which are available in the UK National Co-operative Archives in Manchester. The ICA was a tri-lingual organisation and produced all its materials in English, French and German; most, though not all, of the ICA material I have used is in English. I have only rarely had the opportunity to compare different versions of the texts, which would possibly be interesting as there were occasionally semantic discussions arising from disagreements over translation. Many of the Executive and Central Committee meetings were not only minuted but also transcribed more or less verbatim, and these records give an extremely detailed and valuable account of the proceedings.

It has not been possible to undertake a systematic examination of archive records for the co-operative organisations of all four Nordic countries within the scope of this study. However, I have consulted the co-operative press in each case, especially with reference to international contacts. I have also referred to the published writings of the region's leading co-operators, and some unpublished correspondence, especially that of Hannes Gebhard, deposited in the Finnish National Archives in Helsinki. As far as the ICWS is concerned I have used sources, mostly minutes, from both Helsinki and Stockholm. The bulk of the NAF archive is held by the Danish National Archives, but this is mostly made up of commercial correspondence, and the board meeting minutes do not seem to have survived. The sections on the NAF are thus drawn together from a variety of sources, including correspondence in the archives of both Sweden's KF and the Finnish wholesale OTK, and also the archive of the Norwegian co-operative union NKL, held in the Norwegian National Archives.

Notes

1 The International Co-operative Alliance (ICA) lists seven fundamental principles of co-operation, as follows: voluntary and open membership, democratic member control, member economic participation, autonomy and independence, a commitment to education and training, a commitment to work with other co-operatives and a concern for community. These principles were agreed in 1995 but were based on earlier formulations adopted in 1966 and 1937. See: ICA, 'Co-operative Identity, Values and Principles', available at http://ica.coop/en/whats-co-op/co-operative-identity-values-principles, accessed 29 January 2016. See also: J. Birchall, *People-Centred Businesses: Co-operatives, Mutuals and the Idea of Membership* (Basingstoke: Palgrave Macmillan, 2011), pp. 3–9; E. Furlough and C. Strikwerda, 'Economics, Consumer Culture and Gender: An Introduction to the Politics of Consumer Co-operation', in E. Furlough and C. Strikwerda (eds), *Consumers against Capitalism? Consumer Co-operation in Europe, North America and Japan, 1840–1990* (Lanham: Rowman and Littlefield, 1999), p. 27. For a discussion of co-operation in a broader sense, see: R. Sennett, *Together: The Rituals, Pleasures and Politics of Co-operation* (London: Allen Lane, 2012).

2 M. K. Hilson, 'Working-Class Politics in Plymouth, c. 1890–1920' (PhD dissertation, University of Exeter, 1998); M. Hilson, 'Consumers and Politics: The Co-operative Movement in Plymouth, 1890–1920', *Labour History Review*, 67:1 (2002), 7–27.

3 M. Hilson, 'Co-operation and Consumer Politics in Comparative Perspective: Britain and Sweden during the First World War', in P. Verbruggen and L. Soubry (eds), *Consumerism versus Capitalism? Co-operatives Seen from an International Comparative Perspective* (Ghent: Amsab-Institute of Social History, 2003).

4 See, however: J. Birchall, *The International Co-operative Movement* (Manchester: Manchester University Press, 1997); Furlough and Strikwerda (eds), *Consumers Against Capitalism?*; E. Furlough, 'Consumer Cooperation', in A. Iriye and P.-Y. Saunier (eds), *The Palgrave Dictionary of Transnational History: From the Mid-19th-Century to the Present Day* (Basingstoke: Palgrave Macmillan, 2009); M. Hilson, S. Neunsinger and G. Patmore (eds), *A Global History of Consumer Co-operation since 1850: Movements and Businesses* (Leiden: Brill, 2017).

5 M. Hilson, 'A Consumers' International? The International Cooperative Alliance and Cooperative Internationalism, 1918–1939: A Nordic Perspective', *International Review of Social History*, 56:2 (2011), 203–33.

6 K. Musiał, *Roots of the Scandinavian Model: Images of Progress in the Era of Modernisation* (Baden-Baden: Nomos Verlagsgesellschaft, 2002), esp. pp. 196–201; M. Hilson, 'Consumer Co-operation and Economic Crisis: The 1936 Roosevelt

Inquiry on Co-operative Enterprise and the Emergence of the Nordic "Middle Way"', *Contemporary European History*, 22:2 (2013), 181–98.

7 See: E. Furlough, *Consumer Cooperation in France: The Politics of Consumption 1834–1930* (Ithaca and London: Cornell University Press), pp. 7–8; C. Wrigley, 'The Co-operative Movement', *Mitteilungsblatt des Instituts für soziale Bewegungen*, 27 (2002), 103–16; L. Black and N. Robertson, 'Taking Stock: An Introduction', in L. Black and N. Robertson (eds), *Consumerism and the Co-operative Movement in Modern British History: Taking Stock* (Manchester: Manchester University Press, 2009), p. 1.

8 A. Bonner, *British Co-operation: The History, Principles and Organisation of the British Co-operative Movement* (Manchester: Co-operative Union, 1961), p. 160.

9 The debate is summarised in P. Gurney, *Co-operative Culture and the Politics of Consumption in England, 1870–1930* (Manchester: Manchester University Press, 1996), pp. 3–11. See also: N. Balnave and G. Patmore, 'The Politics of Consumption and Co-operation: An Overview', *Labour History*, 91 (2006), 1–12: 3–4.

10 S. Pollard, 'Nineteenth-Century Co-operation: From Community Building to Shop-keeping', in A. Briggs and J. Saville (eds), *Essays in Labour History, 1886–1923* (London: Macmillan, 1960). For discussion of this point, see: B. Lancaster and P. Maguire, 'The Cooperative Movement in Historical Perspective', in B. Lancaster and P. Maguire (eds), *Towards the Co-operative Commonwealth: Essays in the History of Co-operation* (Manchester: Co-operative College/History Workshop Trust, 1996), p. 6.

11 Furlough, *Consumer Cooperation in France*, pp. 15–16.

12 Gurney, *Co-operative Culture*, pp. 148–50.

13 For an overview of producer co-operatives, see: M. van der Linden, *Workers of the World: Essays Towards a Global Labour History* (Leiden: Brill, 2011), ch. 8.

14 On Finland, see: H. Stenius, *Frivilligt, jämlikt, samfällt: Föreningsväsendets utveckling i Finland fram till 1900-talets början med speciell hänsyn till mass-organisationsprincipens genombrott* (Helsinki: Svenska litteratursällskapet i Finland, 1987), pp. 320–7; J. von Schoultz, *Bidrag till belysande av Finlands socialdemokratiska partis history, del 1: Tiden före representationsreformen år 1906* (Helsinki: Söderström, 1924), pp. 194–5. For an example of worker co-operatives in Finland, see: T. Bergholm, 'Masculinity, Violence and Disunity: Waterfront Strikes and Strikebreakers in Finnish Ports in the 1920s and 1930s', *International Journal of Maritime History*, 8:1 (1996), 23–42: 26–8. On Denmark, see: H. Grelle, *Det kooperative alternativ: Arbejderkooperationen i Danmark 1852–2012* (Copenhagen: Arbejdermuseet/ABA, 2012), pp. 41–2.

15 B. Fairbairn, 'The Rise and Fall of Consumer Co-operation in Germany', in Furlough and Strikwerda (eds), *Consumers Against Capitalism?*, p. 283.

16 On the influence of Vooruit, see: H. Defoort, 'The Strongest Socialist Party in the World? The Influence of Belgian Social Democracy in International Socialism prior to 1914 as a Means to Study the Relations between Socialism and Co-operation', in P. Verbruggen and L. Soubry (eds), *Consumerism versus Capitalism? Co-operatives Seen from an International Comparative Perspective* (Ghent: Amsab-Institute of Social History, 2003).

17 For example, in Finland, see: P. Kettunen and T. Tuomisto, 'Från enhetlighet till inre kamp. Revolutionära och reformistiska tendenser i den finländska arbetarrörelsen på 1910- och 1920-talet', in J. Christensen (ed.), *Nordisk arbejderbevægelse i mellemkrigstiden. Stat, parti og fagbevægelse* (Copenhagen: SFAH, 1980), p. 182. I would like to thank an anonymous referee for bringing this point to my attention.

18 For examples of continuity, see the essays in S. Yeo (ed.), *New Views of Co-operation* (London: Routledge, 1988).

19 Gurney, *Co-operative Culture.*

20 Furlough, *Consumer Cooperation in France.*

21 P. Aléx, *Den rationella konsumenten. KF som folkuppfostrare 1899–1939* (Stockholm/Stehag: Brutus Östlings Bokförlag Symposion, 1994).

22 Furlough and Strikwerda, 'Economics, Consumer Culture and Gender', pp. 1–6; 43–52.

23 For a comparative perspective on co-operative problems in Europe in the 1980s, see: J. Brazda and R. Schediwy (eds), *A Time of Crises: Consumer Co-operatives and Their Problems Around 1990* (Vienna: Fachbereich für Genossenschaftswesen, Universität Wien, 2011; first published 1989), available at https://genos.univie.ac.at/veroeffentlichungen/, accessed 10 August 2016. See also: Hilson, Neunsinger and Patmore (eds), *Global History*, esp. section 3.

24 A. Webster and J. K. Walton, 'Introduction', in 'The Business of Co-operation: National and International Dimensions since the Nineteenth Century', *Business History*, 54:6 (2012), 825–32: 825; Lancaster and Maguire, 'Cooperative Movement', p. 3; Black and Robertson, 'Taking Stock', p. 2.

25 Furlough, *Consumer Cooperation in France.*

26 Furlough and Strikwerda, 'Economics, Consumer Culture and Gender', p. 33; see also: E. Ekberg, 'Confronting Three Revolutions: Western European Consumer Co-operatives and Their Divergent Development', *Business History*, 54:6 (2012), 1004–21; Hilson, Neunsinger and Patmore (eds), *Global History.*

27 See: M. Hilson, S. Neunsinger and G. Patmore, 'A Global History of Consumer Co-operation', in Hilson, Neunsinger and Patmore (eds), *Global History.*

28 Examples include histories of the Norwegian co-operative union NKL, the UK's Co-operative Group and the Danish consumer co-operatives. See: E. Lange (ed.), *Organisert kjøpekraft: Forbrukersamvirkets historie i Norge* (Oslo: Pax forlag, 2006); J. F. Wilson, A. Webster and R. Vorberg-Rugh, *Building Co-operation: A Business History of the Co-operative Group, 1863–2013* (Oxford: Oxford University Press, 2013); K. Jensen (ed.), *Brugsen – en anderledes forretning? 1866–2016: Dansk brugsbevægelse fra pastor Sonne til det moderne Coop* (Albertslund: Samvirke, 2016).

29 Webster and Walton, 'Introduction', 826. 'Mainstreaming Co-operation' was the title of a conference on co-operation held in Manchester in 2012; see: Co-operative College (2012), 'Mainstreaming Co-operation', available at www.co-op.ac.uk/2012/07/mainstreaming-co-operation/, accessed 10 August 2016.

30 Black and Robertson, 'Taking Stock'.

31 For examples, see: G. Shaw and A. Alexander, 'British Co-operative Societies as Retail Innovators: Interpreting the Early Stages of the Self-Service Revolution',

Business History, 50:1 (2008), 62–78; P. Jonsson, 'From Commercial Trickery to Social Responsibility: Marketing in the Swedish Co-operative Movement in the Early Twentieth Century', in Hilson, Neunsinger and Patmore (eds), *Global History*.

32 N. Robertson, *The Co-operative Movement and Communities in Britain 1914–1960: Minding Their Own Business* (Farnham: Ashgate, 2010).

33 M. Hilson, P. Markkola and A.-C. Östman (eds), *Co-operatives and the Social Question: The Co-operative Movement in Northern and Eastern Europe (1880–1950)* (Cardiff: Welsh Academic Press, 2012).

34 N. Black, 'The Mothers' International: The Women's Co-operative Guild and Feminist Pacifism', *Women's Studies International Forum*, 7:6 (1984), 467–76; G. Scott, *Feminism and the Politics of Working Women: The Women's Co-operative Guild 1880s to the Second World War* (London: UCL Press, 1998).

35 F. Trentmann, *Free Trade Nation: Commerce, Consumption and Civil Society in Modern Britain* (Oxford: Oxford University Press, 2008).

36 A. Nützenadel and F. Trentmann, 'Introduction: Mapping Food and Globalization', in A. Nützenadel and F. Trentmann (eds), *Food and Globalization: Consumption, Markets and Politics in the Modern World* (Oxford: Berg, 2008), p. 11.

37 F. Trentmann, 'Before Fair Trade: Empire, Free Trade and the Moral Economies of Food in the Modern World', in Nützenadel and Trentmann (eds), *Food and Globalization*.

38 See chapter 4; also: K. Friberg, 'A Co-operative Take on Free Trade – International Ambitions and Regional Initiatives in International Co-operative Trade', in Hilson, Neunsinger and Patmore (eds), *Global History*.

39 F. Trentmann, 'Beyond Consumerism: New Historical Perspectives on Consumption', *Journal of Contemporary History*, 39:3 (2004), 373–401: 387; M. Hilton and M. Daunton, 'Material Politics: An Introduction', in M. Hilton and M. Daunton (eds), *The Politics of Consumption: Material Culture and Citizenship in Europe and America* (Oxford: Berg, 2011), p. 10.

40 On the early history of the ICA, see: W. P. Watkins, *The International Co-operative Alliance 1895–1970* (London: ICA, 1970).

41 For a discussion of the terminology of transnational history, see: C. A. Bayly et al., 'AHR Conversation: On Transnational History', *American Historical Review*, 111:5 (2006), 1440–64.

42 Bayly et al., 'AHR Conversation', 1442; P. Ther, 'Comparisons, Cultural Transfers and the Study of Networks: Toward a Transnational History of Europe', in J. Kocka and H.-G. Haupt (eds), *Comparative and Transnational History: Central European Approaches and New Perspectives* (New York: Berghahn Books, 2009), pp. 209–10; M. G. Müller and C. Torp, 'Conceptualising Transnational Spaces in History', *European Review of History*, 16:5 (2009), 609–17: 610; B. Struck, K. Ferris and J. Revel, 'Introduction: Space and Scale in Transnational History', *International History Review*, 33:4 (2011), 573–84: 574–5.

43 P.-Y. Saunier, 'Learning by Doing: Notes about the Making of the *Palgrave Dictionary of Transnational History*', *Journal of Modern European History*, 6:2 (2008), 159–72: 159–62; Struck, Ferris and Revel, 'Introduction', 573. Others

have argued, however, that a distinctively 'new' global history has emerged in response to globalisation after 1945; see: B. Mazlish, *The New Global History* (New York: Routledge, 2006).

44 Struck, Ferris and Revel, 'Introduction', 575; Bayly et al., 'AHR Conversation', 1455. This book is in its own way the product of academic mobility and international exchange, as explained in the acknowledgements.

45 The claim that the theoretical-methodological debate has outstripped actual empirical research does not seem to be valid any longer; see, however: H. Kaeble, 'Between Comparison and Transfers – and What Now? A French-German Debate', in Kocka and Haupt (eds), *Comparative and Transnational History*, p. 37; Müller and Torp, 'Conceptualising Transnational Spaces', 611. For a useful review of recent work, see: S. Macdonald, 'Transnational History: A Review of Past and Present Scholarship' (working paper, UCL Centre for Transnational History, 2013), available at http://www.ucl.ac.uk/centre-transnational-history/objectives/simon_macdonald_tns_review, accessed 10 August 2016.

46 P. Clavin, 'Defining Transnationalism', *Contemporary European History*, 14:4 (2005), 421–39: 433; J. Osterhammel, 'A "Transnational" History of Society: Continuity or New Departure?' in Kocka and Haupt (eds), *Comparative and Transnational History*, p. 44.

47 See comments by S. Beckert in Bayly et al., 'AHR Conversation', 1454, 1460.

48 Struck, Ferris and Revel, 'Introduction', 573–4. See also: D. Cohen and M. O'Connor, 'Introduction: Comparative History, Cross-National History, Transnational History – Definitions', in D. Cohen and M. O'Connor (eds), *Comparison and History: Europe in Cross-National Perspective* (Abingdon and New York: Routledge, 2004), p. ix; S. Conrad, 'Double Marginalization: A Plea for a Transnational Perspective on German History', in Kocka and Haupt (eds), *Comparative and Transnational History*. For further discussion of the critique of 'methodological nationalism', see: M. Hilson and S. Neunsinger, 'Samarbete over gränser. Reflektioner och erfarenheter från ett kollektivt forskningsprojekt om konsumentkooperationens globala historia', *Historisk Tidskrift*, 133:3 (2013), 450–71: 452, n. 5. Philipp Ther points out that the national perspective is rarely supported openly but rather is implicit in much history writing, while transnational history has always been explicit in the need to challenge the national paradigm. See: Ther, 'Comparisons, Cultural Transfers', pp. 210–11.

49 R. O. Keohane and J. S. Nye, *Transnational Relations and World Politics* (Cambridge, MA: Harvard University Press, 1981), cited in Clavin, 'Defining Transnationalism', 425. Clavin uses the metaphor of the honeycomb to describe transnationalism as 'in between' spaces. See also: Osterhammel, '"Transnational" History', p. 45.

50 This is in contrast to earlier debates during the 1990s when historians of transfer criticised comparative historians for entrenching rather than challenging national differences. See: Osterhammel, '"Transnational" History'; J. Kocka and H.-G. Haupt, 'Comparison and Beyond: Traditions, Scope and Perspective of Comparative History', in Kocka and Haupt (eds), *Comparative and Transnational History*; P. Jonsson and S. Neunsinger, 'Comparison and Transfer – A Fruitful Approach to National History?', *Scandinavian Journal of History*, 32:3 (2007), 258–80.

51 See: Mazlish, *New Global History.*
52 F. S. L. Lyons, *Internationalism in Europe 1815–1914* (Leyden: A. W. Sythoff, 1963), pp. 14–15.
53 M. Rodríguez García, 'Early Views on Internationalism: Marxist Socialists vs Liberals', *Revue belge de philology et d'histoire – Belgisch Tijdschrift voor filologie en geschiednis*, 84:4 (2006), 1049–73: 1051.
54 L. J. Rupp, *Worlds of Women: The Making of an International Women's Movement* (Princeton: Princeton University Press, 1997), p. 108.
55 Rupp, *Worlds of Women*, p. 109. Internationalism was therefore not necessarily the same as cosmopolitanism: 'an embrace of diversity and difference'. See: D. Laqua, 'Transnational Intellectual Cooperation, the League of Nations and the Problem of Order', *Journal of Global History*, 6:2 (2011), 223–47: 232.
56 K. Callahan, 'Performing "Inter-Nationalism" in Stuttgart in 1907: French and German Socialist Nationalism and the Political Culture of an International Socialist Congress', *International Review of Social History*, 45:1 (2000), 51–87; also: K. Callahan, *Demonstration Culture: European Socialism and the Second International, 1889–1914* (Leicester: Troubadour Publishing Ltd, 2010), p. xviii.
57 Osterhammel, '"Transnational" History', p. 47; Struck, Ferris and Revel, 'Introduction', 576.
58 Patricia Clavin points out a paradox of transnationalist studies that 'transnational ties can dissolve some national barriers while simultaneously strengthening or creating others'. See: Clavin, 'Defining Transnationalism', 431; also: Conrad, 'Double Marginalization', p. 53.
59 Osterhammel, '"Transnational" History', p. 43. See also: Struck, Ferris and Revel, 'Introduction', 576; Müller and Torp, 'Conceptualising Transnational Spaces'.
60 On the concept of historical region or *Geschichtsregion*, see: S. Troebst, 'Introduction: What's in a Historical Region?', *European Review of History – Revue européene d'histoire*, 10:2 (2003), 173–88.
61 Ther, 'Comparisons, Cultural Transfers', especially pp. 214–15; see also: M. Berg, 'Global History: Approaches and New Directions', in M. Berg (ed.), *Writing the History of the Global: Challenges for the Twenty-first Century* (Oxford: Oxford University Press/British Academy, 2013), p. 10.
62 On transnational voluntary association co-operation in the Nordic region, see: N. Götz, H. Haggrén and M. Hilson, 'Nordic Cooperation in the Voluntary Sector', in J. Strang (ed.), *Nordic Cooperation: A European Region in Transition* (London: Routledge, 2016).
63 I. MacPherson, 'The International Co-operative Movement and Peace: Questions Drawn from Its Early History', in J. Emmanuel and I. MacPherson (eds), *Co-operatives and the Pursuit of Peace* (Victoria: British Colombia Institute for Co-operative Studies, 2007).
64 Lyons, *Internationalism*, p. 191; Watkins, *International Co-operative Alliance.*
65 This parallels developments in the international women's movement during the interwar period; see: M. Sandell, 'Regional versus International: Women's Activism and Organizational Spaces in the Inter-war Period', *International History Review*,

33:4 (2011), 607–25. For the ICA after the Second World War, see: Watkins, *International Co-operative Alliance.*

66 Birchall, *International Co-operative Movement*, p. 44.

67 *Report of the Proceedings of the Ninth Congress of the ICA, held at Glasgow, 25–28 August 1913* (London: ICA, 1913), pp. 39–48; also cited in: Birchall, *International Co-operative Movement*, p. 47.

68 D. Gorman, *The Emergence of International Society in the 1920s* (Cambridge: Cambridge University Press, 2012); also: A. Iriye, *Global Community: The Role of International Organizations in the Making of the Contemporary World* (Berkeley: University of California Press, 2002); Rupp, *Worlds of Women*, p. 34; Clavin, 'Defining Transnationalism', 429; A. Arsan, S. L. Lewis and A.-I. Richard, 'Editorial – The Roots of Global Civil Society and the Interwar Moment', *Journal of Global History*, 7:2 (2012), 157–65: 163; R. Boyce, *The Great Interwar Crisis and the Collapse of Globalization* (Basingstoke: Palgrave Macmillan, 2009).

69 Iriye, *Global Community*, p. 28.

70 Hilson, 'Consumers' International?'.

71 It is not mentioned, for example, in Bob Reinalda's massive *Routledge History of International Organizations: From 1815 to the Present* (New York: Routledge, 2009), and is also overlooked in histories of the Second International, such as J. Braunthal, *History of the International 1864–1914*, trans. H. Collins and K. Mitchell (London and Edinburgh: Thomas Nelson and Sons Ltd, 1966), despite the links between the two organisations. An exception is: Lyons, *Internationalism*, pp. 191–200.

72 Watkins, *International Co-operative Alliance.*

73 R. Rhodes, *The International Co-operative Alliance during War and Peace 1910–1950* (Geneva: ICA, 1995).

74 Hilson, 'Consumers' International?'.

75 See: G. Sluga, 'Editorial – the Transnational History of International Institutions', *Journal of Global History*, 6:2 (2011), 219–22; also: P. Duedahl and K. Gram-Skjoldager, 'De international organisationers Danmarkshistorie: En introduktion', *Temp*, 10 (2015), 5–15: 7.

76 For an overview, see: M. Hilson, 'The Nordic Consumer Co-operative Movements in International Perspective, 1890–1939', in R. Alapuro and H. Stenius (eds), *Nordic Associations in a European Perspective* (Baden-Baden: Nomos, 2010), pp. 215–17.

77 Gorman, *International Society*, pp. 3–6.

78 D. Laqua, *The Age of Internationalism and Belgium 1880–1930: Peace, Progress and Prestige* (Manchester: Manchester University Press, 2013), pp. 8–9.

79 Laqua, *Age of Internationalism*, p. 9.

80 N. Götz, 'On the Origins of Parliamentary Diplomacy: Scandinavian "Bloc Politics" and Delegation Policy in the League of Nations', *Cooperation and Conflict*, 40:3 (2005), 263–79; N. Götz, 'Blue-Eyed Angels at the League of Nations: The Genevese Construction of Norden', in N. Götz and H. Haggrén (eds), *Regional Cooperation and International Organizations: The Nordic Model in Transnational Alignment* (London: Routledge, 2009); N. Götz, 'Parliamentary Democracy Going Global:

The Fading Nordic Model', in J. Kurunmäki and J. Strang (eds), *Rhetorics of Nordic Democracy* (Helsinki: Finnish Literature Society, 2010).

81 N. Götz and H. Haggrén, 'Introduction: Transnational Nordic Alignment in Stormy Waters', in N. Götz and H. Haggrén (eds), *Regional Cooperation and International Organizations: The Nordic Model in Transnational Alignment* (London: Routledge, 2009), p. 5.

82 Rhodes, *International Co-operative Alliance*, pp. 147–8.

83 Musiał, *Scandinavian Model*, pp. 196–201.

84 P. Teeboom, 'Searching for the Middle Way: Consumer Co-operation and the Co-operative Movement in New Deal America' (PhD dissertation, University of Amsterdam, 2009); Hilson, 'Consumer Co-operation and Economic Crisis', 181–98.

1

Co-operation in the Nordic countries before 1914: international networks and the transmission of ideas

Nordic co-operative societies emerged during the nineteenth century as part of the wave of popular associations that included the free churches, the folk high schools, the temperance movement, voluntary fire brigades and civil defence corps, and the labour movement.[1] There is a broad historical consensus that, aided by a relatively benign and tolerant state, the nineteenth century popular movements were a means to channel popular dissent and avoid violent conflict. They thus helped to guarantee the relatively smooth evolution of the Nordic societies into peaceful, consensual democracies.[2]

Although it has attracted less attention from historians than some of the other popular movements – notably the labour movement – the co-operative movement has a recognised place in narratives of the Nordic 'paths to modernity'. It has been acknowledged as an example of the 'schools for democracy' provided by the popular movements, which helped to shape the consensual and pragmatic traditions of the Nordic democracies.[3] Co-operation has also been ascribed a prominent role in the region's economic development. In Denmark (above all) and Finland it was seen as a major influence on the development of a modern, export-orientated agricultural sector, while throughout the region it also came to be associated with important innovations in retail and distribution.[4]

Until recently at least, it is probably fair to say that most accounts of co-operation were produced within the movement itself, written either to chronicle the history and achievements of co-operative societies for internal purposes, or as a response to international interest in the success of Nordic co-operatives. Not surprisingly, these accounts have tended to shape understandings of the origins of co-operation in the Nordic countries, albeit in contradictory ways. On the one hand, co-operation has often been described as an essential characteristic of Nordic peasant societies, born out of the need for hard work and mutual support in a cold climate. The directors of the Finnish co-operative organisation Pellervo, for example, writing in the forward to the English translation of Pellervo's centenary history, suggested: 'In a country like Finland, sparsely populated with a short summer and a long hard winter, the idea of people working together in their common interest comes naturally.'[5]

On the other hand, while the *potential* for successful co-operation was deep-rooted in peasant traditions, early attempts to found co-operative societies were, according to the traditional narrative, often short-lived, because they were based on inadequate organisational principles. In the late nineteenth century a small group of enlightened individuals encountered successful examples of co-operation while travelling abroad, and transplanted these ideas to their own countries as the basis for permanent national co-operative organisations. Traditional co-operative historiography in the Nordic countries has thus tended to emphasise the influence of these individuals as the 'founding fathers' of modern co-operation. In common with many other European countries, moreover, co-operative history has often been told as a story of progression from the local co-operative store to the national federation (*Norges* Kooperative Landsforening; *Suomen* Osuuskauppojen Keskuskunta).

Inevitably, however, the story is more complicated than this. As societies that were rapidly modernising in the late nineteenth century, the Nordic countries shared an openness to new ideas from abroad: what historian Pauli Kettunen has described as 'the avant-gardism of the intellectual elite of a peripheral country'.[6] The transfer and adaptation of these ideas was also shaped by cross-border collaboration and exchange within the Nordic region, especially from the 1860s.[7] But there was no simple linear process of diffusion from co-operative centres like Britain and Germany to the Nordic periphery. The Rochdale model of consumer co-operation became a common reference point throughout the Nordic countries, but it was never the only one. Instead, like elsewhere, the formative years of the co-operative movement were marked by prolonged and sometimes bitter struggles over the meanings of co-operation, which in Finland and Denmark eventually resulted in formal and enduring splits.

Co-operation in the Nordic region was thus remarkably diverse. It included the co-operative dairies and slaughterhouses of Denmark and the credit societies of Finland; large consumer societies in the big cities and small shops in the countryside. Its membership ranged from the social democratic workers of cities like Malmö and Tampere to the conservative farmers of Ostrobothnia. This diversity was also expressed in different terminology. In Sweden the imported term *kooperation* was most commonly used in the consumer movement, as in the name of the Swedish co-operative union Kooperativa Förbundet (KF). In Denmark, co-operative societies were known as *andelsselskaber*, based on the term *andel*— (meaning 'share'), though consumer co-operatives were usually known as *brugsforeninger* or simply *brugsen*.[8] In Norway, co-operative societies were known as *samvirkelag*, while in Swedish-speaking Finland the term *andel*— was used for both agricultural and consumer co-operation, as in *andelslag* or *andelsaffär* (co-operative store). The equivalent term in Finnish is *osuus*— (for example, *osuuskauppa*, meaning co-operative store).

Not surprisingly, this diversity has also spawned quite distinct historiographical traditions in all the countries of the region. Yet, despite the differences, there were some common characteristics. The movement was certainly popular: on the eve of the Second World War, membership of consumer co-operative societies in Sweden and Denmark was estimated to amount to over 10 per cent of the entire population, and in Finland over 16 per cent.[9] It has been estimated that a quarter of all Norwegians lived in a household with co-operative membership, given that usually only one member of a family joined a co-operative society.[10] There was also some common ground, as from the 1920s representatives of the Nordic co-operative movements worked together in the ICA to defend the principle of co-operative political neutrality.[11]

This chapter examines the early history of the co-operative movement in Denmark, Norway, Finland and Sweden in the context of international developments and the transfer of ideas. Although the national historiographies are reasonably well developed, less attention has been paid to the transnational dimensions of co-operation.[12] The chapter examines the main influences on the development of co-operation in the Nordic countries, and asks how co-operative ideas were transferred and adapted to specific national contexts. It begins with a brief survey of the history of co-operation in each country in turn before considering the main similarities and differences in the region's co-operative organisations. Particular attention is paid to the role of individuals during the formative years of the movement (until about 1910), and the personal networks that shaped the development of co-operation within the Nordic region and also beyond.

The early history of the Nordic co-operative movements, 1860s to 1914

Denmark: farmers and workers

There can be few other countries where co-operation has been as important in national narratives as it has been in Denmark.[13] The agricultural co-operative movement has been ascribed a central role in the modernisation of the Danish economy in response to the global agricultural depression of the 1870s. Mads Mordhorst has written that co-operation is seen as 'a specific Danish democratic model of doing business … decentralised and locally anchored', in contrast to large-scale globalised industry.[14] The term 'co-operative liberalism' has been coined to describe the combination of self-help and solidarity with the liberal commitment to free trade that is assumed to characterise Danish capitalism.[15] With its emphasis on the role of farmers as the main agents in the transition to modernity, co-operation thus belongs to the so-called 'farmer narrative' (*gårdmandslinien*) which has dominated Danish history writing for much of the twentieth century.[16]

The agricultural co-operative movement certainly grew very rapidly after the foundation of the first co-operative dairy in 1882: by 1903 there were over a thousand co-operatives in Denmark, processing the products of over 80 per cent of the country's cows and over 50 per cent of its pigs.[17] Economic historians have sought to explain this success with reference to Denmark's political and cultural homogeneity after 1864, in comparison to other more fractured European societies. It was also a response to the economic opportunities presented by the availability of new technology (such as the milk separator) and facilitated by the relatively high levels of education among Danish farmers.[18] Thus, the co-operatives were linked to another important Danish rural institution: the folk high schools (*folkehøjskoler*) – although the Danish co-operator J. Th. Arnfred suggested, in an account of Danish co-operation first published in 1929, that foreign visitors to Denmark often tended to over-estimate the impact of the folk high schools on the co-operative movement.[19] There were, in fact, no formal links between the two, even though many co-operative leaders had been educated through the folk high schools. Nonetheless, both institutions came to be indelibly bound up with the status of the free farmers as the main bearers of nineteenth-century Danish national identity.

The roots of the consumer co-operative movement (*brugsbevægelsen*) were different, however. As Poul Thestrup has suggested, the foundation of the Thisted Workers' Association (Thisted Kjøbstads Arbeiderforening) in 1866 has taken on 'an almost mythical status' in the history of Danish consumer co-operation.[20] The society is generally cited as the first successful consumer co-operative in Denmark, and its story has much in common with similar foundation stories in the other Nordic countries. According to this narrative, the society was formed after the local pastor, Hans Christian Sonne, encountered the co-operative idea abroad and successfully transplanted it as a means to alleviate the poverty of his parishioners, in the form of a consumer society based on the Rochdale principles.[21] Thus, it was not the farmers who were initially the main beneficiaries of consumer co-operation but the artisans and labourers of the provincial market towns.[22]

Not surprisingly, the early history of Danish consumer co-operation was more complex than this suggests. As Thestrup has shown, there was a lively interest in English and German models of co-operation in Denmark in the 1850s, resulting in several attempts to found consumer co-operatives in Copenhagen before the mid-1860s.[23] These efforts were part of several related developments: firstly, the debates in liberal circles about social reform, self-help and moral education; secondly, the trade law (*næringsloven*) in force from 1862, which broke the towns' monopoly on trade and stimulated the development of the retailing sector; and thirdly, the rises in the price of grain – and thus of essential provisions – during the 1850s and after 1865.[24] '[England] should stand as our model and tutor,' wrote Sonne in his 1867 book on the

Thisted society.[25] But it was by no means inevitable that this should be the case. German cultural influences remained strong in Denmark throughout the nineteenth century, even after the military defeat by Prussia in 1864 and despite the growing export trade with Britain.[26] Among his countrymen, Sonne may be considered unusual in his good command of English, though there is no evidence that he had actually visited England.[27] Nonetheless, his efforts to communicate the success of the Thisted society meant that it became significant in helping to spread interest in Rochdale consumer co-operation in Denmark.[28]

Although the North Jutland market town of Thisted thus formed the model, it was actually in the countryside that consumer co-operative societies (*brugsforeninger*) expanded most rapidly during the last three decades of the nineteenth century. They were greatly assisted by an amendment to the trade law from 1873, which exempted them from a prohibition on the establishment of retailing businesses in the immediate hinterland of market towns, an exemption granted on the grounds that they traded only with their own members.[29] A report to the ICA's journal, *International Co-operative Bulletin*, in 1909 noted the rural character of the Danish consumer movement as one of its most distinctive features. The societies were numerous, but generally very small, with an average of only 141 members (compared to 950 for Germany, and 1,726 for Britain). The majority operated only one shop and over 80 per cent of them were located more than one Danish mile (7.5 kilometres) from the nearest town.[30] By the turn of the century, consumer co-operative societies had become an established feature of rural life alongside the co-operative dairies. From the 1890s, they had also come to be regarded as part of an integrated co-operative movement – *andelsbevægelsen* – that included societies of producers and consumers. This was reflected in the establishment of a joint committee (Andelsudvalget) for the entire movement in 1899.[31]

At the same time, the possibilities of co-operation were also debated among workers in the larger cities. The social democratic labour movement was initially sceptical towards consumer co-operation, partly on ideological grounds but also because it regarded small shopkeepers as part of its natural constituency in the major cities. Despite this, co-operative bakeries were established in Aarhus and Copenhagen during the mid-1880s and these were followed by consumer societies serving the interests of the urban working class.[32] These societies acknowledged their legacy to the Rochdale principles and indeed to Thisted, but strongly asserted their independence from the farmers' co-operative movement. The difference is also reflected in the terms used for the two movements: *andelsbevægelsen* for rural co-operation and *bykooperation* for the urban workers' societies. Worker co-operation (*arbejderkooperation*) in Denmark came to mean primarily the establishment of joint stock companies owned and managed by trade unions, of which the best-known example was the brewery Stjernen, founded in 1902.[33]

This division reflected one of the principal cleavages in late nineteenth-century Danish society, between self-owning farmers in the countryside and the waged workers in the cities.[34] It was not a division that was watertight, however, and Kristoffer Jensen has described consumer co-operation as an unusual institution, precisely for its ability to span the two traditions.[35] Common ground was provided by the co-operative wholesale society Fællesforeningen for Danmarks Brugsforeningerne (FDB), which was founded in 1896 as a merger of two regional wholesales.[36] FDB supplied goods to farmers' co-operatives in the countryside and workers' co-operatives in the towns, though some in the labour movement remained sceptical of its close ties to the farmers' movement and their political party Venstre.[37] Poul Thestrup writes that for its part FDB was forced to abandon the principle of only admitting societies based on collective liability (*solidarisk ansvar*) in order to accommodate the workers' societies, requiring them instead to purchase their orders with cash.[38] When the Copenhagen consumer societies merged in 1916, the new society Hovedstadens Brugsforening was allowed 16 votes in FDB in recognition of its size, thus avoiding the split over the very same issue that took place in the Finnish consumer co-operative movement that same year (see below).[39] There was a formal institutional division nonetheless, with the foundation of a co-operative union for the workers' co-operatives, Det kooperative Fællesforbund (DkF), in 1922. The new organisation sought membership of the ICA, though there is no evidence that it played a particularly active role, either here or in the Nordic context.[40]

Taken as a whole, the Danish consumer co-operative movement could certainly hold its own in international comparisons. A report to the ICA's Central Committee in 1926 ranked FDB fifth in terms of national wholesale trade for 1924, smaller only than the acknowledged giants: the English and Scottish Co-operative Wholesale Societies, the Soviet Union's Tsentrosoiuz and the German Grosseinkaufsverband.[41] It was not the strength of Danish consumer co-operative societies that came to define Denmark's role in the ICA, however, so much as the perception of Denmark as an example of a successfully integrated co-operative movement, one that united societies of consumers and producers under the same central organisation.[42] Andelsudvalget, through its leaders, such as Severin Jørgensen, the founder of FDB, and later A. Axelsen Drejer, the editor of its journal *Andelsbladet*, acted as the main voice of Danish co-operation within the ICA. After 1918 relations with the other Nordic countries were also handled through FDB and its membership of the Scandinavian Co-operative Wholesale Society, or Nordisk Andelsforbund (NAF).[43]

Norway: local loyalties

The traditional narrative of the beginnings of Norwegian co-operation bore many resemblances to that of Denmark. According to this account, there were efforts to organise local co-operative societies in the 1850s and 1860s, but these made little lasting impact. The first permanent organisations were established in the 1890s, largely as a result of the efforts of the Kristiania lawyer O. Dehli (1851–1924). Dehli had encountered co-operation while on a state-financed study trip to Britain and America in the early 1890s, and on his return he introduced the Rochdale Principles as the basis for financially sound and permanent co-operative organisations. Dehli was also the driving force behind the establishment of the Norwegian co-operative union (Norges Kooperative Landsforening, NKL) in 1906, and therefore has an undisputed position as the 'founding father' of Norwegian consumer co-operation.[44]

As in the Danish case, however, the early history of Norwegian co-operation is more complex than this story suggests. The authors of NKL's centenary history noted important continuities between the earlier co-operative societies and the later wave of organisation during the 1890s.[45] As elsewhere in Europe, such efforts must be seen in the context of economic and social developments in the second half of the nineteenth century. The Kristiania workers' society (Kristiania Arbeidersamfund), founded in 1864, took Rochdale co-operation as its model, but it was part of a broader wave of new liberal organisations, especially in the towns. As Even Lange suggests, these societies were partly an expression of paternalist efforts to integrate the emerging working class in a rapidly changing society, but they were also part of the struggle for free trade and the decline of the historical privileges of the towns and their merchants.[46] Moreover, although Rochdale co-operation was important as a model for the new wave of co-operative organisations founded in the 1890s, and indeed for NKL itself, so too were the experiences of other countries.[47] Speaking to NKL's founding congress in 1906, Dehli referred to examples from England, Germany, Switzerland and Sweden, but made a special reference to Denmark, which he argued 'should be our ideal with regard to unity and collaboration'.[48]

The cleavages fracturing the co-operative movement in Norway were indeed similar to those in Denmark: between the town and countryside; between Kristiania (later Oslo) and the periphery; between bourgeois liberalism and the social democratic labour movement. But it proved much more difficult to overcome these difficulties and establish a co-operative union. NKL was founded in 1906 after more than a decade of effort, and functioned both as a national union for consumer co-operative societies and, from 1907, as the national wholesale society.[49] Even after it was established, NKL continued to grow relatively slowly in comparison to co-operative unions elsewhere during this period, and the majority of local co-operative societies remained unaffiliated before the First World War.[50]

In contrast to Denmark, Norway had no equivalent of Andelsudvalget, a joint committee representing both the consumers' and the agricultural producers' movements. This difference reflected the more disparate nature of the agricultural co-operative movement in Norway. From the mid-nineteenth century Norwegian agriculture underwent a similar transition to that experienced in Denmark, marked by a switch from grain production to dairy produce and meat.[51] Unlike Denmark, however, most of this production supplied the domestic market, as rising real wages produced a substantial growth in the consumption of dairy produce and meat during the period 1850–1920.[52] Co-operative dairies were influential in this transition and spread rapidly after 1870, so that by 1905 there were 694 supplier-owned dairies throughout Norway, many of them supported by the agricultural improvement society Selskapet for Norges vel.[53] As Harald Espeli has pointed out, these societies were not covered by specific legislation, and they thus took a variety of forms, not all of them co-operative.[54] There was very little influence from Denmark, though one Norwegian historian has pointed to the importance of Swiss organisational forms.[55] Although farmers' co-operatives co-existed harmoniously with consumer societies in many rural districts, the scepticism of the latter towards the labour movement prevented many of them from affiliating to NKL.[56]

The main challenge for the founders of NKL, however, was the need to reconcile their ambitions for a centralised, national organisation based in Kristiania, with the diverse needs of co-operative societies in different regions.[57] Despite its rapid growth, the Norwegian co-operative movement was fractured by local and regional loyalties, and for this reason NKL remained relatively small in comparison to its Nordic sister organisations. An ICA report on the relative positions of national co-operative wholesales in 1910 placed NKL a long way down the list, with an annual turnover that was estimated to be a fifth of the Swedish co-operative union's and less than 2 per cent of that of the Danish FDB.[58] This did not prevent NKL from participating in the ICA, however. Dehli attended the 1904 congress as a member of the Comité de Patronage and submitted reports on the state of the Norwegian movement, while delegates representing NKL and other Norwegian societies attended the 1910 congress.[59] But NKL was the least visible of all the Nordic co-operative organisations in the ICA, not only before the First World War but throughout the period covered by this book.

Finland: 'neutral' and 'progressive'

Of all the Nordic countries, it was Finland where the social and political cleavages within the co-operative movement were strongest. Like in Denmark, the differences between the large working-class consumer co-operatives in the towns and the smaller societies in the countryside became so great that they could not be contained within one organisation, and this resulted in a formal and lasting split between the two branches of the consumer co-operative movement in 1916. There was also a high level of integration between the rural distributive co-operatives – or one group of them at least – and the agricultural producer co-operatives.[60] But there was also an important difference between Finland and Denmark. Where Danish co-operation was to a large extent a decentralised movement, in Finland there was much more control over local societies from the centre, and in this respect Finland had more in common with Sweden.[61]

Because of the centralisation of the Finnish co-operative movement, traditional accounts of co-operative history placed great weight on the role of the lone pioneer, who discovered co-operation abroad and successfully transplanted it to his own country. This was Hannes Gebhard (1864–1933), widely regarded as the 'father of Finnish co-operation' both at home and abroad.[62] Gebhard was a university agronomist who, according to his biographers, first encountered the co-operative idea during a period studying agricultural statistics in Germany and Austria. In Berlin he attended Professor Max Sering's lecture series on agrarian economics and policy, including the Raiffeisen system of credit co-operatives.[63] This inspired him to undertake further studies in co-operation, and his travels in Scandinavia, Germany, Britain and France in 1898–99 resulted in a book on agricultural co-operative societies abroad, *Maanviljelijäin yhteistoiminnasta ulkomailla* (1899).[64] Gebhard was part of a small group that in 1899 established the Pellervo society to spread knowledge about co-operation in Finland, and he was also instrumental in the drafting of national legislation for co-operative societies in 1901.[65]

In founding Pellervo, Gebhard referred to his knowledge of agricultural co-operation outside Finland, but his examples were carefully chosen. In a lecture series delivered to university students in 1899 he described in some detail both the German Raiffeisen co-operatives and the French agricultural societies. However, his main source of inspiration came not from these 'civilised nations' (*kulturländer*), but from Ireland and Hungary. In Ireland's 'tragic history' Gebhard saw direct parallels with the Finnish nationalists' struggles against Russia, as well as with the problems of rural poverty and mass emigration.[66] As a means to tackle these problems, Gebhard turned to the example of the Irish Agricultural Organisation Society (IAOS), founded in 1894 by Horace Plunkett, which became a direct model for Pellervo. Gebhard corresponded with IAOS leaders for the exchange of information, publications and practical advice, and his own account of the foundation of Pellervo was published in the IAOS' own journal, *The Irish Homestead*, in December 1899.[67]

Pellervo was not a co-operative itself, and it did not share with other co-operative societies the principle of democratic member control, even if its work was intended to lead to the establishment of organisations that did. Gebhard explicitly rejected the Danish tradition of grassroots organisation as a suitable model for Finland, on the grounds that the general population was simply not as advanced educationally as it was in Denmark.[68] Instead, Pellervo would rely on a small group of enlightened individuals who would spread knowledge about co-operation in the Finnish countryside and thereby contribute not only to improving the economic situation of the farmers but also to raising their 'moral strength'.[69] Co-operation was thus a means to self-help, giving farmers the material and moral resources they needed to improve their own situation. Writing in the ICA's journal in 1912, Gebhard suggested that Pellervo's original aim had been 'not so much to contribute to the development of Co-operation as to further the development of agriculture, and [Pellervo's founders] considered Co-operation as a means to be employed in order to accomplish their aim'.[70]

Initially, Gebhard and the founders of Pellervo were sceptical towards consumer co-operation, based on the assumption derived from 'the large European countries' that consumer co-operatives would adopt a different ideological course to the agricultural movement and become associated with the social democratic labour movement.[71] But when Pellervo was founded in 1899 there was already a thriving consumer co-operative movement in Finland. Rochdale co-operation had been discussed in the press at least from the 1860s, but, as elsewhere in the Nordic region, the foundation of consumer societies was also stimulated by the decline of rural self-sufficiency and the gradual liberalisation of trading laws.[72]

In the absence of legal recognition for co-operatives before 1901 these societies were usually organised as joint stock companies. The first permanent co-operative societies were established in the early 1880s by groups of industrial workers in the cities of Viipuri (Vyborg) and Tampere, followed by similar initiatives in Helsinki, Turku and elsewhere.[73] Henrik Stenius writes that there were 79 co-operative societies registered in Finland before the turn of the century, of which two thirds were founded in the 1890s.[74] Their growth was also stimulated by the improving material living standards of Finnish workers as the country experienced rapid economic change at the end of the nineteenth century.[75]

As this suggests, it is therefore possible to distinguish two quite separate traditions of co-operation in Finland: the consumer co-operatives associated with the urban working class, and the rural co-operatives stimulated by Pellervo. However, relations between the consumer co-operatives and Pellervo proved to be closer than anticipated. The co-operative law of 1901 applied to all types of co-operative society and triggered an explosive growth in consumer co-operatives during the first decade of the twentieth century: from 66 societies in 1903 to 463 societies in 1908, operating over 800 co-operative stores.[76] Moreover, these consumer societies were just as likely to seek advice from Pellervo as the agricultural societies were, at least during the early days.[77]

A further point of connection was Hedvig Gebhard, who made significant contributions to her husband Hannes' work on agricultural co-operation but also pursued her own interests in consumer societies, especially as a means to improve the lives of women.[78] Gebhard corresponded with the influential secretary of the English Women's Co-operative Guild, Margaret Llewellyn Davies, though she had to decline invitations to attend the Guild's annual congresses.[79] She was also a founding member of the management board of the Helsinki consumer co-operative Elanto. An article series on women and consumer co-operation written for the journal *Nutid* in 1905 demonstrates Gebhard's familiarity with consumer societies elsewhere in Europe, as well as reference to Charles Gide's writings. What is most striking here is the emphasis on the moral purpose of consumer co-operation, as a counterweight to the evils of credit trading, food adulteration and profiteering, and as a means to promote the education and moral improvement of its customer-members, especially women of limited means.[80]

The national co-operative wholesale organisation, Suomen Osuuskauppojen Keskuskunta (SOK), founded in 1904, brought together two rather different branches of the consumer co-operative movement. The initiative united the small rural co-operative societies influenced by Pellervo with the larger consumer co-operatives in the major cities. An important figure in the latter group was Väinö Tanner, who had not long previously returned from a period working at the headquarters of the German co-operative wholesale in Hamburg and was also to become a founder member of Elanto.[81] From 1905 SOK also began publishing its own journal, *Yhteishyvä*, and a division of labour was agreed with another central organisation, Hankkija, which would confine itself to agricultural requisites while SOK supplied goods to consumer societies.[82]

The directors of SOK sought to maintain the unity and political neutrality of their organisation, but even before the outbreak of the First World War it was quite clear that there were tensions within it.[83] What eventually brought matters to a head was the question of how the local societies should be represented at SOK congresses. The larger urban societies demanded voting rights in proportion to membership while the smaller rural ones insisted on the principle of 'one member one vote'. The split came to be described in terms of 'progressive' (*edistysmielinen/framstegsvänlig*) societies versus 'neutral' or bourgeois co-operatives. The representation question dominated the national meetings of SOK in 1915 and 1916, and eventually led to a walkout by the progressives, who founded a new organisation, Kulutusosuuskuntien Keskusliitto (KK), to serve the propaganda, educational and organisational needs of their societies.

By the end of 1916 societies representing 78,000 members remained in the old organisation, 70,000 had joined the new, 28,000 belonged to both and 13,000 to neither.[84] Many on the progressive side initially hoped to maintain SOK as a neutral wholesale organisation for both wings of the movement, but this proved impossible. The new wholesale Suomen Osuustukkukauppa (OTK) held its first meeting in Helsinki in December 1917 and began operations early in 1918 amid the very difficult conditions of the civil war. Following a difficult early period, OTK's wholesale business grew rapidly, and like SOK it also developed its own production, although the split between the two wholesales was often acknowledged to be a hindrance in this respect.[85] Both organisations also continued to insist on their political neutrality. KK-OTK rejected formal ties with the labour movement, even though in practice there were often strong overlaps. Politics continued to be debated within KK, but according to its historian Aaltonen, the majority remained firmly concerned with practicalities rather than 'radical' and 'utopian' visions.[86]

There were some parallels between the situation in Finland and that in Denmark; though in Finland the split also reflected the very bitter social and political divisions that were to flare up in the 1918 civil war. Pellervo remained the kernel of the 'neutral' movement, though the agricultural co-operatives were fractured again in 1919 with the foundation of a separate union for the Swedish-speaking societies, Finlands Svenska Andelsförbund.[87] A further parallel with Denmark lies in the extent to which the 'neutral' consumer co-operatives were integrated with the agricultural societies through Pellervo. The Finnish agricultural co-operatives were as influential as their Danish counterparts in helping to promote the modernisation of Finnish agriculture and ease its late nineteenth-century transition from grain production to animal and dairy products. By improving and controlling standards, the agricultural organisations also helped to support a flourishing export industry, especially in butter. Whereas the Danish movement was largely regarded as a self-help strategy pursued by the free farmers, Finnish agricultural co-operation was much more top-down and patrician in its approach: its aim was to help promote social reform and to improve the conditions of the small farmers.[88]

Sweden: rational consumption[89]

The Swedish co-operative movement avoided the open conflicts seen in Finland, but there were nonetheless stark divisions between consumer and agricultural co-operation. What is striking here, however, is the dominance of consumer co-operation. From the 1870s there were attempts to organise agricultural co-operatives, including dairies and joint purchasing organisations, but these never achieved anything like the success and importance of the Danish societies.[90] According to Olof Brandesten, this was also reflected in the dominance of consumer co-operation in the historiography, where the agricultural movement was long overlooked.[91]

The dominance and undoubted success of the Swedish co-operative union KF, together with its strong reputation within the international co-operative movement, has imparted a rather teleological quality to Swedish co-operative history.[92] This is not unusual in co-operative history writing more generally, but the portrayal of KF as the main bearer of the Rochdale tradition after 1918 was perhaps stronger in Sweden than anywhere else in the Nordic region. In the accounts of the movement's own historians, earlier experiments with co-operative societies formed an acknowledged part of the pre-history of co-operation, but were doomed to failure without the guidance of a strong central organisation and its model rules based on the Rochdale principles.[93] Thus, although co-operation was discussed in Sweden during the 1860s and even before – according to one historian over 300 consumer societies were founded during the period 1867–79 – these were mostly short-lived and disappeared again after a few years of activity.[94]

The KF historian Axel Gjöres, writing in the 1920s, attributed these failures to 'the participants' poor economic understanding, inadequate methods of administration and the lack of organized collaboration between societies'.[95] He was particularly scathing about the shortcomings of the so-called 'ring movement' (*ringrörelsen*) founded by L. O. Smith during the 1880s, which attempted to organise workers into local buying clubs to negotiate supply agreements with wholesalers, financed by a specially established central bank. After an initial wave of enthusiasm in 1883, the promised agreements turned out in most cases to be non-existent and the rings swiftly collapsed. The reasons for the subsequent stagnation of co-operation were all too obvious from the perspective of the 1920s: the nascent co-operatives 'lacked the support of a central organisation that could provide guidance and advice on business planning and management, and they also lacked a wholesale business that they could trust with their purchases'.[96]

In Sweden, as in Finland, the co-operative movement is thus an outstanding example of what Henrik Stenius has described as '[t]he preparedness to accept standardized, statutory norms', in contrast to the more grassroots, bottom-up traditions of organising that were more prevalent in Denmark and Norway.[97] Unlike in Finland, however, the functions of co-operative rule-setting and propagandising and those of the wholesale were not separated but combined into one organisation. Like Pellervo, KF was founded in 1899. One of its most important early tasks was the devising of a set of model rules, derived from the Rochdale Principles, which could be adopted by all local co-operative societies and audited by the central union.[98] Attempts to establish a wholesale organisation followed from 1903, inspired partly by the example of the Danish FDB.[99]

This centralising tendency within the Swedish co-operative movement should not be allowed to obscure the diversity within the movement and the varied influences on co-operative thinking in nineteenth-century Sweden and indeed within KF itself during its early years. As elsewhere in the region, the co-operative idea attracted the attention of middle-class reformers interested in the 'social question', with the first texts on co-operation appearing in the mid-nineteenth century.[100] Holyoake's history of the Rochdale Pioneers was an important influence, but so too were the Schulze-Delitzsch societies of Germany.[101] By the 1890s, however, the British consumer co-operative movement was at the forefront of Swedish thinking. A translation of a British pamphlet on workers' consumer co-operation appeared in 1894, financed by a Stockholm factory director who also wrote the foreword.[102]

The British co-operative movement was also influential on the establishment of KF, largely through the agency of its first secretary Gerhard Halfred von Koch (1872–1948).[103] The co-operative career of von Koch was in many ways similar to those of his Nordic contemporaries such as Dehli and Gebhard (and he also corresponded with the latter), but like these, it illustrates the heterogeneous roots of late nineteenth-century co-operation. Von Koch was born into a liberal family, and like Gebhard trained as an agronomist, developing his own interest in the social question while working as a farm steward in Skåne. In 1897 he took leave of absence from his employment in order to study social reform in England, where his relatives – his paternal grandmother was from Kent – helped to introduce him to liberal circles in London. Von Koch later described how he came across the Co-operative Wholesale Society (CWS) warehouses while out walking in the East End of London and was directed from there to the impressive premises of the Royal Arsenal Co-operative Society (RACS). Convinced he had found the big idea he had been searching for, von Koch abandoned his agricultural work and devoted himself to an in depth study of the English co-operative movement, influenced by his new contacts at RACS and later James Dean of the Scottish CWS.[104] In June 1898 he returned to Sweden and embarked on a lecture tour extolling the virtues of the English co-operative model. In this enterprise he relied at least partly on private means, as letters to his mother included several direct requests for funds.[105]

At the same time, and quite independently of von Koch's efforts, there were also signs of a shift in labour movement attitudes to consumer co-operation during the 1890s. The leadership of the Swedish Social Democratic Labour Party (SAP), founded in 1889, was typical among its European contemporaries in its indifference or even hostility towards co-operation. The social democratic journal *Arbetet* wrote disparagingly in 1891 of 'the myth of the paradisial consumer society of Rochdale', while according to co-operative historian Karl Nilsson the pioneering socialist agitator August Palm was a 'decided opponent' of consumer co-operation.[106] Three influences seem to have triggered the shift in attitudes: firstly, the rising prices of basic consumer goods after the tariff reform of 1888; secondly, the growing prominence of the revisionist debate in international socialism; and thirdly, the success and growing fame of the socialist consumer co-operative movement in Belgium.[107] Co-operation began to be taken seriously in labour movement circles and by the end of the

1890s working-class consumer co-operative societies had been established in Sweden's three largest cities.[108]

The 1899 meeting that constituted KF thus brought together at least two different strands of thinking on co-operation that had developed on parallel lines during the 1890s: a liberal social reform tradition associated with von Koch, and the labour movement strand which was represented by social democrats including Axel Rylander, Axel Danielsson and A. C. Lindblad, the editor of the Gothenburg socialist journal *Ny Tid*.[109] The consensus among historians is that von Koch's vision won out over the socialist one, notably in the decision to abandon the reference to working-class struggle in the new organisation's rules in favour of a more inclusive commitment to 'spread the general improvement of citizens and raise the condition of the population both morally and economically'.[110] Against the 'wild competition' of the retail trade, consumer co-operative societies would help to promote harmony between social groups. In its broadest sense, co-operation (*samvärkan*) would 'unite people in brotherly collaboration (*samarbete*) and bring about a more just division of common gains'.[111] By educating the worker in his political and social responsibilities, co-operation would also be a vital tool in hindering the development of a revolutionary labour movement, as von Koch suggested in a private letter:

> for one [thing] is certain: the worker will soon gain power and he will then need to be educated; he will then need to have sufficient interest in economic matters to prevent violent disturbances. We may well have a social revolution, but it must happen peacefully.[112]

Yet the two groups were perhaps closer in their vision of co-operation than some of their rhetoric implied. In his lecture tours during the late 1890s von Koch responded pragmatically to labour movement interest in co-operation. Conscious of his own class background, he seems to have deliberately tried to avoid the possibility of conflict by drawing on his knowledge of English co-operation rather than commenting on Swedish conditions. Commenting on his experiences in his letters, he was pleased when this tactic seemed to have worked and a meeting of trade unionists near Gävle voted almost unanimously to establish a co-operative society.[113]

Although the main reference point for von Koch was always Rochdale, he was not averse to including a report on the achievements of the socialist Belgian co-operatives in *Social Tidskrift*, the journal that he owned and edited.[114] At the same time the co-operative vision of Axel Rylander, expressed in a series of articles for *Social-Demokraten* in 1894, did not differ greatly from von Koch's in his emphasis on both the practical economic advantages and the moral and educative (*uppfostrande*) benefits of the co-operative movement.[115] As Katarina

Friberg has pointed out, however, von Koch's interest in co-operation was always a means to the wider end of social reform.[116] Although he devoted much of his energy and his personal resources to KF during its early years – including placing *Social Tidskrift* at the disposal of the new organisation – von Koch disappeared from Swedish co-operative history after 1905 when he resigned as KF's secretary in order to serve on a public enquiry.

Von Koch's successor, Martin Sundell, was influential in cementing KF's status at the apex of a highly centralised movement, notably through his insistence on the adoption of model rules for co-operative societies. Sundell also steered Swedish consumer co-operation more firmly towards links with the labour movement, so that the KF executive was dominated by social democrats until at least 1920, even though it remained formally neutral.[117] As an anarchist, however, Sundell had an eclectic vision of co-operation. Like von Koch, he was open-minded about the types of co-operation that could be accommodated within KF, including agricultural and productive societies, and he was also drawn to the Georgist idea of establishing model co-operative communities.[118]

KF's commitment to agricultural co-operation was thus reaffirmed at its 1903 congress; but despite this, it failed to attract agricultural members.[119] From the 1890s attempts had been made to establish co-operative dairies modelled on both the Finnish and especially the Danish experiences, but Swedish agricultural co-operation largely lacked its own central organisations until the 1930s.[120] Nor did the rural farming population show much interest in consumer co-operation. Olof Ruin estimated that only 8 per cent of the membership of KF-affiliated societies were farmers in 1910, in stark contrast to the situation in Finland and Denmark, and although the proportion grew steadily there remained strong social differences.[121] More than in any of the other Nordic countries, consumer co-operation in Sweden must be seen as a response to the problems of urban industrial capitalism, and was thus largely a movement of the working class.[122] Consumer co-operation had first emerged in the context of the falling real wages of the 1890s, and KF's advance in the first decade of the twentieth century was profoundly shaped by its struggles against the monopoly suppliers of basic consumer commodities, notably margarine.[123]

The KF leadership continued to insist on co-operation's political neutrality, however, and in the hands of a new generation of leaders after the First World War they were to become very active internationally in campaigning for the maintenance of co-operative political neutrality.[124] As a counterweight to this, KF was perhaps also to become the most influential of the Nordic organisations in propagandising for a distinctively *co-operativist* vision that emphasised co-operation as an end in itself, rather than as an adjunct to other social currents such as the labour movement. This was, however, a consumerist vision above all else. As Peder Aléx has suggested, KF's ideology can best be summed up in its commitment to promoting rational consumption through the education of consumers, the pursuit of modernity and efficiency in its business model, and action to defeat cartels through establishing its own production.[125]

Nordic networks: was there a Nordic co-operative movement?

It is clear that co-operation in the Nordic countries was extremely diverse. With some justification we may ask whether, for example, the Jutland farmer delivering milk to the co-operative dairy and the working-class housewife shopping at the co-operative stores in Malmö could really be said to belong to the same movement. Even if we narrow the focus to the consumer co-operative movement, there was still a world of difference between the small local stores of rural Denmark or Finland, and the working-class societies of major cities like Helsinki or Copenhagen. For all their professions of unity and aspirations to overcome social divisions, the Nordic co-operative movements were fractured along familiar fault lines: town and country, worker and farmer, socialist and liberal. In some cases these generated separate vocabularies and historiographical traditions. Moreover, there is plenty of anecdotal evidence at least that these divisions endured until quite late in the twentieth century, with many Nordic consumers continuing to assert their class and political identities by the choice of where they bought their groceries.

At the same time, we should not overlook the fact that co-operation *did* have a common reference point throughout the Nordic countries in its insistence on the Rochdale legacy. Although this was interpreted in different ways, knowledge about Rochdale and other co-operative models was shared and transmitted through regional Nordic networks. The co-operative movement was part of what historian Ruth Hemstad has called the 'Indian summer' of Nordic co-operation (co-operation here in the sense of cross-border collaboration, or *nordiskt samarbete*). After Prussia's defeat of Denmark in 1864, aspirations to found a pan-Scandinavian state gradually gave way to the more modest ambitions of promoting inter-Nordic contacts at the level of civil society. Collaboration in the scientific, educational and cultural spheres flourished in the late nineteenth century as professional associations, students and academics, civil servants and voluntary associations developed regional networks. These were forged, for example, through pan-Nordic congresses, journals and also more informal contacts, developed in order to exchange information and discuss new ideas.[126]

During the late nineteenth century, in the absence of formal structures, personal networks were important in the exchange of ideas across national borders. In each of the Nordic countries, as we have seen, the dissemination of knowledge about co-operation was associated with a handful of co-operative pioneers: Pastor Sonne and later Severin Jørgensen in Denmark; Ole Dehli in Norway; G. H. von Koch in Sweden; Hannes and Hedvig Gebhard in Finland. Their role as the national 'fathers [*sic*] of co-operation' was enhanced by the reliance of the ICA on a network of individual correspondents during its early years, at least outside its core membership countries.[127] Hannes and Hedvig Gebhard, for example, were in regular correspondence with the ICA office on behalf of Pellervo during the early years of the twentieth century, and Hannes Gebhard attended the ICA's 1904 congress to report on co-operative developments in Finland.[128]

For G. H. von Koch, as for other members of the pioneer generation, interest in co-operation was a means to an end, shaped by his broader interests in social reform.[129] Von Koch was initially interested in all branches of co-operation, but, influenced by his British contacts, he reported to his mother in March 1898 that he had decided to devote himself purely to consumer co-operation.[130] By contrast, agronomist Hannes Gebhard's primary interests were in agriculture and land reform, and his travels abroad were motivated by his academic studies in this field.[131] As Riitta Mäkinen has noted, Nordic networks were important for Finnish agronomists and Gebhard corresponded regularly with representatives of agricultural societies in Denmark and Norway, as well as attending at least one Nordic agricultural conference in 1907.[132] The Pellervo Society's journal of the same name was never exclusively about co-operation, but also provided more general coverage of agricultural questions. The same was true of von Koch's journal *Social Tidskrift*, which served as the main organ not only of KF during its early years but also of a number of other societies for popular education and social reform.[133] Like Gebhard, von Koch was assisted in his work by the contribution of his wife, Carola von Koch née Sahl, whose language skills were particularly valuable in mediating knowledge about developments abroad. Hedvig Gebhard and Carola von Koch acted as unpaid research assistants to their husbands, assisting with the collection of information and especially with translating and editing texts.[134]

The connection between co-operatives and the 'social question' also meant that much of the work of these pioneers was undertaken in an official or quasi-official state capacity, often supported by public funds. Gebhard and Dehli both encountered co-operation while taking up grants for overseas study trips, while Axel Granström's 1898 book on co-operation was based on his official report to the Finnish Senate on economic societies abroad.[135] After the turn of the century, these broader networks began to give way to more distinctively co-operative ones. The practice of sending fraternal delegates to co-operative congresses quickly became well established, especially within the Nordic region.

The co-operative press of all four countries regularly carried reports on co-operative developments and activities in neighbouring countries, as well as in the rest of Europe. The mutual intelligibility of the Scandinavian languages was also important in facilitating the exchange of co-operative journals across the region and meant that editors were able easily to reproduce articles appearing elsewhere. The production of a Swedish edition of *Pellervo* was particularly important in this respect, even though the journal was produced for Swedish-speaking readers in Finland.[136] The writings of leading members of the different national co-operative organisations were also disseminated across the region. In turn this facilitated the emergence of a new *professional* network of co-operators, who were educated and worked within the movement, and most importantly also developed their international connections under its auspices. Such relationships were significant for the foundation of the joint Nordic co-operative wholesale NAF in 1918, and for the participation of the Nordic federations within the ICA.[137]

As with the spread of other contemporary ideas such as social democracy, Denmark has to be regarded as a Nordic pioneer in the development of co-operation. The example of Denmark and FDB was cited as an inspiration and a source of practical advice by the founders of NKL and KF. The Danish co-operator P. Eskesen told the KF congress in 1900 that 'the figures from England are almost incomprehensibly large, so perhaps the Danish situation was more interesting, and by relating the history of the movement in Denmark [he] hoped to be able to answer many questions'.[138] KF's decision to locate its wholesale business in Malmö was influenced partly by its proximity to FDB's facilities and advice in Copenhagen, and Dehli reported to NKL's founding meeting in 1906 that the Danish wholesale would be assisting the new organisation by supplying goods.[139] Gebhard, as we have seen, rejected Denmark as a model for Finland. But Finnish co-operation was cited as a model for the rest of the region: for example Martin Sundell's plan for a KF department to monitor local society finances was inspired by similar practices in Finland, and by the 1920s the Helsinki co-operative Elanto was referred to as one of the leading examples of urban consumer co-operation in the Nordic region.[140]

In turn, the emergence of a working-class co-operative movement in Denmark was influenced by developments in the rest of the Nordic region. Whereas in Sweden and Norway the parallel lines of interest in consumer co-operation from socialists and liberals, respectively, eventually merged into the foundation of the central organisations KF and NKL, the Danish labour movement remained more sceptical. Working-class co-operative bakeries and stores were founded in Aarhus and Copenhagen during the 1880s, but the social democratic party leadership was at best lukewarm in its reaction to these developments.[141] A shift in these attitudes was triggered partly by the 1907 Scandinavian labour congress, where a Swedish resolution recognising consumer co-operation as part of the labour movement gained majority support despite the scepticism of the Danish delegates.[142]

Conclusion

It is possible to speak of *two* consumer co-operative movements in the Nordic countries: the *andelslag* of the countryside, which were closely linked to the farmers' co-operative societies, and the *konsumtionsföreningar* of the towns, which were much more closely aligned, culturally at least, with the social democratic labour movement, even if they eschewed formal ties. These two movements developed more or less in parallel during the 1890s and early twentieth century, although there were important overlaps in ideas and also in personnel. Contemporaries also tended to understand co-operation in terms of this division, which they traced to models elsewhere in Europe. The entry on consumer co-operation in a 1922 Finnish dictionary of political science and administration distinguished between the 'co-operativism' (*ko-operatistinen osuustoiminta*) of the Nîmes school associated with Charles Gide among others, and the socialist co-operative model of Belgium, with its roots in the ideas of Owen and Fourier.[143]

The author of this article did, however, acknowledge that the two movements had much in common, and it should not be assumed that the boundaries between these different currents were watertight. Although the movements developed separate organisations, they also shared common ideas. These can be summarised as follows: firstly, co-operation was widely understood as a response to the 'social question', and thus a means to tackle the problems arising from rapid social and economic change. It was conceived not only as a means to tackle the social problems arising from the experience of modernisation but also as a way to promote modernisation. In Norway and Finland in particular this was linked explicitly to national mobilisation, but this applied to some extent to Denmark and Sweden too. Thus, co-operation has subsequently come to be understood as an essential element of the Nordic 'paths to modernity', in its contribution both to the economic infrastructure and to the development of the consensual Nordic model of democracy. In the 1920s and 1930s this translated into an emphasis on rational, efficient and modern methods of production, distribution and supply.[144]

Secondly, co-operation in all its forms shared with the other nineteenth-century popular movements an emphasis on education and self-improvement. This could be practical – co-operative societies offered their members education in modern book-keeping methods or the latest animal husbandry techniques

– but such efforts were also linked to a wider moral purpose. Cultivation of the 'co-operative spirit' (*den kooperativa andan*) was an essential part of co-operative activities. Both KF in Sweden and NKL in Norway fought hard against what they regarded as the evil of credit during the 1920s and 1930s.[145] As Peder Aléx has suggested, KF sought to create 'rational consumers' (*rationella konsumenter*) who were taught through co-operation how to manage their household budgets effectively and become well-nourished, productive citizens.[146]

Thirdly, despite the clear divisions discussed above, the Nordic co-operative movements avoided formal political alignments. That said, the relationship between co-operation and other political movements was always fluid, whether in the Nordic countries or elsewhere. For middle-class reformers like Dehli, von Koch and Gebhard, co-operation was a means to keep the 'little people' (*småfolket*) away from socialism, but co-operation's political neutrality was inevitably challenged by the organisation of predominantly working-class societies among urban consumers. At a local level in particular there was often a very big overlap in personnel between the social democratic labour movement and the co-operative movement, especially in the large urban co-operative societies such as Elanto in Helsinki.

The labour movement, for its part, was initially ambivalent or even hostile, but gradually overcame this after the turn of the century and, as we have seen, regional links through the Scandinavian labour congresses were influential in securing this change of attitude. In some cases, the labour movement was prepared to commit itself to supporting consumer co-operation, for example in Finland where the Social Democratic Party agreed a resolution to this effect at its 1903 congress.[147] But without exception the Nordic co-operative federations refused to follow the examples of consumer co-operative societies elsewhere in Belgium, Austria and Britain and formally align themselves with political parties. Instead, they came to regard the British decisions as a betrayal of the Rochdale principles, and from the 1920s KF's leaders in particular increasingly came to see themselves as the self-appointed guardians of the true Rochdale heritage, defending political neutrality within the ICA.[148]

Thus, rather than regarding the co-operative movement as a branch of other social movements – such as the farmers' movement or the labour movement – it seems to make most sense, as several historians have indeed suggested, to insist on its distinctiveness as a movement in its own right, with its own ideological trajectory and own particular institutional culture. After the First World War, some Nordic co-operators came to play a leading role in attempts to articulate this co-operativism in the context of the ICA. To some extent then, the unity of the movement was also achieved through the development of its relations with international institutions, notably the ICA.

Notes

1 J. Michelsen, 'Nordiske landbrugskooperativer i politiske og økonomiske omgivelser under forandring', in K. K. Klausen and P. Selle (eds), *Frivillig organisering i Norden* (Oslo: Tano, 1995), p. 173.

2 N. Kayser Nielsen, *Bonde, stat og hjem. Nordisk demokrati og nationalisme – fra pietismen til 2. verdenskrig* (Aarhus: Aarhus Universitetsforlag, 2009), ch. 7; N. Kayser Nielsen and J. Bale, 'Associations and Democracy: Sport and Popular Mobilization in Nordic Societies c.1850–1900', *Scandinavian Journal of History*, 37:1 (2012), 69–86: 74; H. Stenius, 'Nordic Associational Life in a European and an Inter-Nordic Perspective', in R. Alapuro and H. Stenius (eds), *Nordic Associations in a European Perspective* (Baden-Baden: Nomos Verlag, 2010), p. 31. For a critical view of the consensual interpretation of Nordic democracy, see, for example: S. Nyzell, *'Striden ägde rum i Malmö': Möllevångskravallerna 1926. En studie av politiskt våld i mellankrigstidens Sverige* (Malmö: Malmö högskola, Skrifter med historiska perspektiv, 10, 2010), pp. 350–97.

3 G. R. Nelson et al. (eds), *Freedom and Welfare: Social Patterns in The Northern Countries of Europe* (Copenhagen: Ministries of Social Affairs of Denmark, Finland, Iceland, Norway, Sweden, 1953), p. 234.

4 On co-operation and economic development in Denmark, see: M. J. Iversen and S. Andersen, 'Co-operative Liberalism: Denmark from 1857 to 2007'; M. Mordhorst, 'Arla: From a Decentralized Co-operation to an MNE'; on Finland: S. Fellman, 'Growth and Investment: Finnish Capitalism, 1850s-2005'; all in S. Fellman et al. (eds), *Creating Nordic Capitalism: The Business History of a Competitive Periphery* (Basingstoke: Palgrave Macmillan, 2008). On Nordic consumer co-operation and retailing innovations see E. Ekberg, 'Against the Tide: Understanding the Commercial Success of Nordic Consumer Co-operatives, 1950–2010', in M. Hilson, S. Neunsinger and G. Patmore (eds), *A Global History of Consumer Co-operation since 1850: Movements and Businesses* (Leiden: Brill, 2017).

5 M. Kuisma et al., *The Pellervo Story: A Century of Finnish Co-operation, 1899–1999*, trans. M. Wynne-Ellis (Helsinki: Pellervo/Kirjayhtymä, 1999), p. 5.

6 P. Kettunen, 'The Transnational Construction of National Challenges: The Ambiguous Nordic Model of Welfare and Competitiveness', in P. Kettunen and K. Petersen (eds), *Beyond Welfare State Models: Transnational Historical Perspectives on Social Policy* (Cheltenham: Edward Elgar, 2011), p. 22.

7 R. Hemstad, *Fra Indian Summer til nordisk vinter. Skandinavisk samarbeid, skandinavisme og unionsoppløsningen* (Oslo: Akademisk Publisering, 2008).

8 For a discussion of the Danish terminology, see: N. F. Christiansen, 'Denmark's Road to Modernity and Welfare: The Co-operative Way', in M. Hilson, P. Markkola and A.-C. Östman (eds), *Co-operatives and the Social Question: The Co-operative Movement in Northern and Eastern Europe (1880–1950)* (Cardiff: Welsh Academic Press, 2012), pp. 26–7.

9 H. Gebhard and I. Rahola, *Huvuddraget av andelsrörelsen i Finland*, trans. Allan Lagus (Helsinki: Sällskapet Pellervo, 1939), p. 36.

10 E. Lange (ed.), *Organisert kjøpekraft. Forbrukersamvirkets historie i Norge* (Oslo: Pax forlag, 2006), pp. 129–30.

11 M. Hilson, 'A Consumers' International? The International Cooperative Alliance and Cooperative Internationalism, 1918–1939: A Nordic Perspective', *International Review of Social History*, 56:2 (2011), 203–33.

12 See, however: M. Hilson, 'The Nordic Consumer Co-operative Movements in International Perspective, 1890–1939', in R. Alapuro and H. Stenius (eds), *Nordic Associations in a European Perspective* (Baden-Baden: Nomos Verlag, 2010); M. Hilson, 'Consumer Co-operation in the Nordic Countries, c. 1860–1939', in Hilson, Neunsinger and Patmore (eds), *Global History.*

13 Mordhorst, 'Decentralized Co-operation', p. 340. There were also references to the co-operative movement in the debate on a Danish cultural canon instigated by the Ministry of Culture in 2016; see: Danmarkskanon, available at www.danmarks-kanon.dk, accessed 17 August 2016. See also: Kayser Nielsen, *Bonde, stat og hjem*, p. 267.

14 M. Mordhorst, 'Arla and Danish National Identity: Business History as Cultural History', *Business History*, 56:1 (2014), 116–33: 129.

15 Iversen and Andersen, 'Co-operative Liberalism', p. 266.

16 Mordhorst, 'Danish National Identity', 125–9; T. Kjærgaard, 'Gårdmandslinien i dansk historieskrivning', in C. Bjørn (ed.), *Fra fortid og nutid: En antologi* (Copenhagen: Dansk historisk fællesforening, 1984).

17 I. Henriksen, 'Avoiding Lock-In: Co-operative Creameries in Denmark 1882–1903', *European Review of Economic History*, 3:1 (1999), 57–78: 58.

18 Henriksen, 'Avoiding Lock-In'; K. H. O'Rourke, 'Late Nineteenth Century Denmark in an Irish Mirror: Land Tenure, Homogeneity and the Roots of Danish Success', in J. L. Campbell, J. A. Hall and O. Pedersen (eds), *National Identity and the Varieties of Capitalism: The Danish Experience* (Montreal: McGill-Queen's University Press, 2006).

19 J. Th. Arnfred, 'Dansk Andelsbevægelse', in A. Axelsen Drejer (ed.), *Den danske Andelsbevægelse* (3rd edn, Copenhagen: Martins forlag, 1934), p. 22.

20 P. Thestrup, *Nærbutik og næringslovs-omgåelse: En undersøgelse af brugsforeningerne og deres placering i innovationsprocessen i Danmark mellem 1850 og 1919* (Odense: Odense Universitetsforlag, 1986), p. 138.

21 Christiansen, 'Denmark's Road', p. 25.

22 K. Jensen (ed.), *Brugsen – en anderledes forretning? 1866–2016: Dansk brugsbevægelse fra pastor Sonne til det moderne Coop* (Albertslund: Samvirke, 2016), p. 30.

23 Thestrup, *Nærbutik og næringslovs-omgåelse*, pp. 110–15, 134.

24 Thestrup, *Nærbutik og næringslovs-omgåelse*, pp. 125–6, 155, 161, 168; E. H. Pedersen, 'Svenske og danske andelsorganisationer og deres virksomhed til 1930'ernes begyndelse', *Historisk Tidsskrift* (DK), 82 (1982–3), 305–21: 305. Thestrup describes the trade law as the most radical change since the Middle Ages as far as rural trade was concerned.

25 '[England] maa staae for os som Forbillede og Læremester.' H. Chr. Sonne, *Om Arbeiderforeninger. Til Oplysning og Veiledning* (Copenhagen: H. Hagerups Boghandel, 1867), p. 2.

26 J. R. Rasmussen, *Modernitet eller åndsdannelse? Engelsk i skole og samfund 1800–1935* (Copenhagen: Museum Tusculanums Forlag, 2003), pp. 22–9.

27 Thestrup, *Nærbutik og næringslovs-omgåelse*, pp. 137–9.
28 Thestrup, *Nærbutik og næringslovs-omgåelse*, pp. 143–4; Jensen, *Brugsen*, pp. 29–30.
29 Jensen, *Brugsen*, pp. 38–9, 58.
30 *International Co-operative Bulletin*, 14 January 1911, pp. 20–1. Even by the early 1950s the average number of members in a Danish consumer society was only 230; see: Nelson, *Freedom and Welfare*, p. 200.
31 C. Bjørn, *Anders Nielsen Svejstrup Østergaard* (Odense: Landbohistorisk selskab, 1993), pp. 56–60.
32 H. Grelle, *Det kooperative alternative. Arbejderkooperationen i Danmark 1852–2012* (Copenhagen: Arbejdermuseet/ABA, 2012), pp. 40–4; C. Bryld, 'Kooperationen – et stridspunkt i den socialdemokratiske strategiudvikling 1871–1923', *Arbejderhistorie*, 4 (December 2003), 3–22; Christiansen, 'Denmark's Road', pp. 27–9.
33 K. Månsson, 'Stjernen – arbejderbevægelsens bryggeri', *Arbejderhistorie*, 4 (2003), 23–37; Grelle, *Det kooperative alternative*.
34 Bjørn describes it as a difference 'mellem Højskolesangbogen og Arbejdersangbogen', which is difficult to translate but refers to the cultural traditions – here expressed in communal singing – of rural and urban institutions. C. Bjørn, *Fortid med fremtid: Danske Andelsselskaber 100 år 1899–1999* (Copenhagen: Danske Andelsselskaber, 1999), p. 44.
35 'Brugsbevægelsen har som en af få organisationer kunnet trække på og hente legitimitet fra begge fortællinger [om dansk modernitet] … både i "gårdmands-fortællingen" og i "byfortællingen".' ('The consumer co-operative movement is one of the few organisations that has been able to draw its legitimacy from both narratives [of Danish modernity] … both the "farmer narrative" and the "urban narrative".'), Jensen, *Brugsen*, p. 19.
36 Bjørn, *Fortid med fremtid*, p. 20.
37 For the debates among Copenhagen trade unionists on FDB, see: Grelle, *Det kooperative alternative*, pp. 73–4.
38 Thestrup, *Nærbutik og næringslovs-omgåelse*, p. 432. On collective liability (*solidarisk ansvar*), see: Arnfred, 'Dansk Andelsbevægelse', pp. 25–7.
39 Thestrup, *Nærbutik og næringslovs-omgåelse*, p. 449.
40 Rigsarkivet, Aarhus (now in Viborg) (hereafter DRA): 06156 Andelsudvalget, 1910–64 Mødereferater mv vedr deltagelsen i ICA 1910 mm: Axel Drejer to Henry May, 14 July 1924.
41 Työväen arkisto, Helsinki (hereafter TA): 334.5 Kansainvälinen Osuustoimintaliitto (KOL), Box 0.2: Reports to Central Committee: Trade of national wholesale societies 1924 and 1925; papers for October 1926 meetings of ICA committees.
42 TA: 334.5 KOL, Box 0.3: Paper on the Federation of Danish Co-operative Societies (De samvirkende danske Andelsselskaber), in papers for November 1927 meeting of ICA Executive. The movement's own standard work on Danish co-operation, published by Andelsudvalget, also included a chapter on urban co-operation and Det kooperative Fællesforbund. A. Axelsen Drejer (ed.), *Den danske Andelsbevægelse* (3rd edn, Copenhagen: Martins Forlag, 1934).
43 See chapter 4. On the role of Severin Jørgensen, see: Ellen Mølgaard Korsager, 'Severin Jørgensen', in Jensen, *Brugsen*.

44 R. Arnesen, *Co-operation in Norway* (Oslo: Norges Kooperative Landsforenings Forlag, 1937), p. 3; on Dehli's influence, see also the entry on Dehli in Edv. Bull and E. Jansen (eds), *Norsk Biografisk Leksikon*, vol. 3 (Oslo: H. Aschehoug, 1926), pp. 293–5.
45 Lange, *Organisert kjøpekraft*, pp. 58–63.
46 Lange, *Organisert kjøpekraft*, pp. 33–40.
47 Lange, *Organisert kjøpekraft*, pp. 78, 91–2.
48 'Danmark bør staa for oss som et ideal m.h. til sammenslutning og samarbeide.' Riksarkivet, Oslo (hereafter NRA): PA 1394 Coop/NKL BA: Aaa L0001 Kongressprotokoller 1906–52: Det kooperative landsmøde, 26–27 June 1906, pp. 11–16. See also: Lange, *Organisert kjøpekraft*, pp. 91–2.
49 Lange, *Organisert kjøpekraft*, pp. 64–77.
50 Lange, *Organisert kjøpekraft*, p. 88.
51 O. H. Grytten and K. B. Minde, 'The Demand for Consumer Goods in the Modernisation of the Norwegian Economy, 1850–1920', *Scandinavian Economic History Review*, 46:1 (1998), 57; H. Espeli, T. Bergh and A. Rønning, *Melkens pris. Perspektiver på meierisamvirkets historie* (Oslo: Tun Forlag, 2006), p. 20.
52 Grytten and Minde, 'Consumer Goods', 55.
53 Espeli, Bergh and Rønning, *Melkens pris*, pp. 21, 24, 27.
54 Espeli, Bergh and Rønning, *Melkens pris*, p. 22.
55 Stein Treite, cited in Espeli, Bergh and Rønning, *Melkens pris*, p. 22.
56 Lange, *Organisert kjøpekraft*, pp. 107–8.
57 Lange, *Organisert kjøpekraft*, p. 92.
58 'Relative positions of co-operative wholesales, 1910', *International Co-operative Bulletin*, April 1911, p. 109.
59 *Report of Proceedings at the Sixth Congress of the International Co-operative Alliance, held at Budapest, 5–8 September 1904* (London: ICA, 1905); *Report of the Proceedings of the Eighth Congress of the International Co-operative Alliance, held at Hamburg, 5–7 September 1910* (London: ICA, 1911).
60 Notably, this is how it was portrayed, and seen, externally. See, for example: H. Gebhard, 'Report on the Collaboration of the Various Branches of Co-operation in Finland', *International Co-operative Bulletin*, January 1912, pp. 1–8; T. Odhe, 'En finsk förgrundsgestalt ur tiden', *Kooperatören*, 1933, pp. 61–6.
61 Stenius, 'Nordic Associational Life', pp. 54–5; H. Stenius, *Frivilligt, jämlikt, samfällt. Föreningsväsendets utveckling i Finland fram till 1900-talets början med speciell hänsyn till massorganisationsprincipens genombrott* (Helsinki: Skrifter utgivna av Svenska litteratursällskapet i Finland, 1987), p. 335.
62 He was described as such in obituaries in the international co-operative press; see: *Andelsbladet*, 3 March 1933; *Uhistegelised Uudised*, 4 March 1933; *Konsumentbladet*, 11 March 1933; *Konsumgenossenschaftlichen Rundschau*, 11 March 1933; *Kooperatøren*, 15 March 1933. All in: Pellervo-seuran arkisto, Helsinki (hereafter Pellervo): Lehtileikk. ulkom. leht. kirjoituksia. The designation 'father of co-operation' was also reported to be engraved on his official memorial: 'Professor Hannes Gebhards minne hedres', *Kooperatøren*, 24, 1934, p. 258. The following discussion of Gebhard and Pellervo draws on M. Hilson, 'Transnational Networks in the Development

of the Co-operative Movement in the Early Twentieth Century: Finland in the Nordic Context', in Hilson, Markkola and Östman (eds), *Co-operatives and the Social Question*.

63 A.-L. Sysiharju, 'Gebhard, Hannes', *Kansallisbiografia-verkkojulkaisu, Studia Biographica 4* (Helsinki: Suomalaisen Kirjallisuuden Seura, 1997), available at www.kansallisbiografia.fi/kansallisbiografia/henkilo/4278, accessed 6 July 2017; see also: R. Mäkinen and A.-L. Sysiharju, *Eteenpäin ja ylöspäin. Hedvig Gebhardin osuus ja toiminta* (Helsinki: Otava, 2006).

64 Sysiharju, 'Gebhard, Hannes'.

65 For the early history of Pellervo, see: Kuisma et al., *The Pellervo Story*.

66 H. Gebhard, *Andelsvärksamhet bland jordbrukarna! Tre föredrag* (Helsinki: Otava, 1899), pp. 8–9. See also Hilson, 'Transnational Networks', p. 94.

67 Kansallisarkisto, Helsinki (hereafter KA): Hannes Gebhardin arkisto: Saapuneet kirjeet I 1882–1932: R. A. Anderson to Hannes Gebhard, 27 November 1899; G. Russell to Hannes Gebhard, 11 January 1900; 16 January 1900; *Irish Homestead*, 30 December 1899; Lionel Smith-Gordon, preface to Hannes Gebhard, *Co-operation in Finland* (London: Williams and Norgate, 1916), p. viii. See also: M. Hilson, '"A Model Co-operative Country": Irish-Finnish Contacts at the Turn of the Twentieth Century', *Irish Historical Studies*, 41:160 (2017), 227–43.

68 Gebhard, *Andelsvärksamhet*, p. 54.

69 'höjandet af vårt folks sedliga kraft.' Wäinö Axelsson, lecture to founding meeting of Pellervo; Pellervo: Pellervon päiväkirja, 18 October 1899; Gebhard, *Andelsvärksamhet*, pp. 54–6.

70 Hannes Gebhard, 'Report on the Collaboration of the Various Branches of Co-operation in Finland', *International Co-operative Bulletin*, January 1912, pp. 1–2; also cited in Hilson, 'Transnational Networks', p. 90.

71 Gebhard, 'Report on the Collaboration', p. 3.

72 A search of the digitised newspaper collections of the Finnish National Library suggests that the first reference to the Rochdale Pioneers is from 1861; see: 'Verkliga välgörenhets anstalter', *Wiborg*, 38 (17 May 1861). Searched for term 'Rochdale' at http://digi.kansalliskirjasto.fi/sanomalehti/search, accessed 12 December 2016. Also: 'Konsumtionsföreningar', *Finlands Allmänna Tidning*, 198 (28 August 1865). See also: E. Aaltonen, *Finlands konsumenter i samarbete*, trans. S. Malmström (Helsinki: KK, 1954), p. 10. On the liberalisation of trade in Finland, see: V. Rasila, 'Kauppa ja rahaliike', in J. Ahvenainen, E. Pihkala and V. Rasila (eds), *Suomen taloushistoria 2: Teollistuva Suomi* (Helsinki: Tammi, 1982), pp. 89–90.

73 Aaltonen, *Finlands konsumenter*, pp. 11–13; Rasila, 'Kauppa ja rahaliike', p. 94.

74 Stenius, *Frivilligt, jämlikt, samfällt*, p. 320.

75 S. Heikkinen, 'Major necessities and minor luxuries: Workers as consumers in Finland at the turn of the twentieth century', *Scandinavian Economic History Review*, 46:1 (1998), 59–70.

76 Rasila, 'Kauppa ja rahaliike', p. 94; on the rapid growth of co-operation after 1901, see also: Stenius, *Frivilligt, jämlikt, samfällt*, pp. 323–4; Aaltonen, *Finlands konsumenter*, p. 26.

77 Gebhard, 'Report on the Collaboration'.

78 On Hedvig Gebhard, see: A.-L. Sysiharju, 'Gebhard, Hedvig (1867–1961)', *Biografiskt Lexikon för Finland 2: Ryskatiden* (2009), available at www.blf.fi/index.php, last accessed 12 December 2016; Mäkinen and Sysiharju, *Eteenpäin ja ylöspäin*.
79 KA: Hedvig Gebhardin arkisto: Hedvig Gebhard to Margaret Llewellyn Davies, 10 August 1904, 19 October 1904, 17 November 1905, 5 October 1910; MLD to HG, 26 August 1904, 17 May 1906.
80 Hedvig Gebhard, 'Kooperationen. En social rörelse, som står kvinnorna nära', *Nutid: Tidskrift för sociala frågor och hemmets intressen*, 3 (March 1905), 89–97, and 4 (April 1905), 129–42.
81 On Tanner's stay in Germany, see: J. Paavolainen, *Nuori Tanner menestyvä sosialisti. Elämäkerta vuoteen 1911* (Helsinki: Tammi, 1977), pp. 123–34. Tanner was mentored in Hamburg by the leading German co-operator Heinrich Kaufmann, who was to have an important influence on his career.
82 Aaltonen, *Finlands konsumenter*, pp. 40–7; T. Odhe, *Finland: A Nation of Co-operators*, trans. John Downie (London: Williams & Norgate, 1931), p. 43.
83 KA: Hannes Gebhardin arkisto: Hannes Gebhard to Hans Müller, 24 November 1910; Aaltonen, *Finlands konsumenter*, pp. 67–72.
84 The split is covered in detail in Aaltonen, *Finlands konsumenter*, pp. 81–114; figures on membership of SOK and KK from p. 102.
85 Odhe, *Finland*, p. 49.
86 Aaltonen, *Finlands konsumenter*, p. 141.
87 See: B. Wallén, *Enighet ger styrka. Finlands Svenska Andelsförbund 80 år* (Helsinki: Finlands Svenska Andelsförbund, 1999).
88 A.-C. Östman, 'Civilising and Mobilising the Peasantry: Co-operative Organisation and Understandings of Progress and Gender in Finland, c. 1899–1918', in Hilson, Markkola and Östman (eds), *Co-operatives and the Social Question*.
89 P. Aléx, *Den rationella konsumenten. KF som folkuppfostrare 1899–1939* (Stockholm/Stehag: Brutus Östlings Bokförlag Symposion, 1994).
90 O. Brandesten, *Lantbrukarnas organisationer. Agrart och kooperativt 1830–1930* (Stockholm: Kungliga Skogs- och Lantbruksakademien, 2005), pp. 394–400. On agricultural co-operation in Sweden, see also: F. Eriksson, 'Swedish Agrarian Press: Co-operatives and the Social Question c.1880–1917', in Hilson, Markkola and Östman (eds), *Co-operatives and the Social Question*.
91 Brandesten, *Lantbrukarnas organisationer*, pp. 17–22.
92 For example, KF was highly praised in M. W. Childs, *Sweden – the Middle Way* (revised edn, New York: Penguin Books, 1948; first published 1936). For a later example, see: J. W. Ames, *Co-operative Sweden Today* (Manchester: Co-operative Union, 1956).
93 For example: K. Nilsson, *Stockholms kooperation 1900–1915* (Stockholm: Kooperativa Förbundets bokförlag, 1952), pp. 6–8.
94 Aléx, *Den rationella konsumenten*, pp. 49–57; A. Påhlman, *Pionjärerna* (Stockholm: Kooperativa Förbundets bokförlag, 1944), pp. 223–35; on organisation from 1867, see: O. Ruin, *Kooperativa Förbundet 1899–1929: En organisationsstudie* (Lund: Rabén & Sjögren, 1960), p. 4.

95 'ringa ekonomiska insikter hos deltagarna, bristfälliga förvaltningsmetoder samt frånvaro av organiserad samverkan mellan föreningarna'. A. Gjöres, *Konsumentkooperationen i Sverige* (Stockholm: Tidens förlag, 1925), p. 7.

96 'saknade stödet av en centralorganisation, som kunde vägleda och råda via verksamhetens planläggning och ledning, och de saknade också ett eget partihandelsföretag att anlita vid inköpen'. Gjöres, *Konsumentkooperationen*, pp. 7–8, quote p. 10. On the ring movement, see also: Aléx, *Den rationella konsumenten*, pp. 56–7; Påhlman, *Pionjärerna*, pp. 232–3; for a local example, see: A. Påhlman and W. Sjölin, *Kooperationen i Karlskrona 1869–1939* (Stockholm: Tiden, 1940), pp. 12–14.

97 Stenius, 'Nordic Associational Life', p. 55.

98 On the development of the KF model rules, see: K. Friberg, 'Visions and Organisation: Kooperativa Förbundet and the Social Question in Sweden', in Hilson, Markkola and Östman (eds), *Co-operatives and the Social Question.*

99 On the development of KF's wholesale business, see: H. Kylebäck, *Konsumentkooperation och industrikarteller* (Stockholm: Rabén & Sjögren, 1974), pp. 35ff.

100 Frederika Bremer described English co-operative stores in an article series for *Aftonbladet* in 1852; see: F. Bremer, *England om hösten 1851. Utgiven och kommenterad av Klara Johanson* (Stockholm: Norstedt, 1922); Påhlman, *Pionjärerna*, pp. 223–4; also: Friberg, 'Visions and Organisation', pp. 58–62.

101 On the influence of Schulze-Delitzsch in Sweden, see: Aléx, *Den rationella konsumenten*, pp. 52–4, who cites works by G. K. Hamilton and C. E. Ljungberg from 1864 and 1865, respectively; also: Påhlman, *Pionjärerna*, pp. 224–30; M. Hilson, 'The Consumer Co-operative Movement in Cross-National Perspective: Britain and Sweden, c. 1860–1939', in L. Black and N. Robertson (eds), *Consumerism and the Co-operative Movement in Modern British History* (Manchester: Manchester University Press, 2009). Katarina Friberg suggests rightly that we still know little about the impact of discussions of foreign co-operative models in 1860s; see: Friberg, 'Visions and Organisation', p. 60.

102 A. H. Dyke Acland and B. Jones, *Arbetarnes cooperations-föreningar i Storbritannien – hvad de uträttat och hvad de åsyfta*, trans. P. D., foreword by O. Lamm (Stockholm: Nordin & Josephson, 1894); Påhlman, *Pionjärerna*, pp. 232–5.

103 On von Koch, see: A. Wirén, *G. H. von Koch: Banbrytare i svensk socialvård* (Stockholm: Rabén & Sjögren, 1980), pp. 58–60.

104 Wirén, *G. H. von Koch*, pp. 58–62; Påhlman, *Pionjärerna*, pp. 234–5; Hilson, 'Transnational Networks', p. 93.

105 KB, Acc. 1980/8:2: G. H. von Koch to Agathe von Koch, 20 December 1898; 11 September 1899.

106 'myten om Rochdales paradisiska konsumtionsförening'; cited in H. Tingsten, *Den svenska socialdemokratins idéutveckling* (Stockholm: Tidens förlag, 1941), p. 375; Nilson, *Stockholms kooperation*, p. 9.

107 I. Millbourn, 'Kooperatismen – ett alternativ till kapitalismen och socialdemokrati 1900–1920', *Scandia*, 57:1 (1991), 89–112: 93–6; Tingsten, *Den svenska socialsocialdemokratins idéutveckling*, pp. 376–7; Aléx, *Den rationella konsumenten*, pp. 65–7.

108 These were: Andelsbolaget Arbetarnas konsumtionsförening, founded November 1894 in Stockholm; Fram, founded 1895–6 in Göteborg after the Belgian model; Pan, founded January 1898 in Malmö. Tingsten, *Den svenska socialsocialdemokratins idéutveckling*, pp. 376–8; Aléx, *Den rationella konsumenten*, pp. 66–7. On the early years of co-operation in Malmö, see: K. Friberg, *The Workings of Co-operation: A Comparative Study of Consumer Co-operative Organisation in Britain and Sweden 1860 to 1970* (Växjö: Växjö University Press, 2005), pp. 155–6.

109 See: Ruin, *Kooperativa Förbundet*, pp. 142–4.

110 'sprida allmän medborgerlig uppfostran och höja befolkningens ställning i såväl moraliskt som ekonomiskt avseende'. Cited in Ruin, *Kooperativa Förbundet*, p. 145.

111 'förena människor i broderligt samarbete och åstadkomma en rättvis fördelning af den gemensamma vinsten'. G. H. von Koch, 'Om arbetarnas konsumtionsföreningar i England', *Studentföreningen Verdandis småskrifter*, 78 (Stockholm: Albert Bonniers förlag, 1899), p. 23.

112 'Ty ett är säkert: arbetaren får mycket snart makten och då bör han vara bildad; och då bör han ega sådant intresse i ekonomiskt afseende att våldsamma störningar förhindras. Social revolution får det gärna bli, men den skall ske fredligt.' Kungliga Biblioteket (hereafter KB), Acc. 1980/8:2: G. H. von Koch to Agathe von Koch née Wrede, 31 August 1898.

113 KB, Acc. 1980/8:2: G. H. von Koch to Agathe von Koch, 26 October 1898; 31 October 1898.

114 'Den kooperativa rörelsen. Från det kooperativa Belgien', *Social Tidskrift*, 11 May 1902.

115 A. Rylander, 'Kunna konsumtions och produktionsföreningar gagna arbetarrörelsen?', *Social-Demokraten*, 8 October 1894; 16 October 1894; 22 October 1894.

116 Friberg, 'Visions and Organisation', pp. 66–7.

117 Friberg, 'Visions and Organisation', pp. 67–70; Aléx, *Den rationella konsumenten*, pp. 97–100; Ruin, *Kooperativa Förbundet*, pp. 137–8.

118 On Sundell's co-operative vision, see also: B. Sundin, 'Kooperationen som utopi: Martin Sundell och den kooperativa rörelsen', *Lychnos* (1991), 77–109.

119 Ruin, *Kooperativa Förbundet*, pp. 223–4.

120 F. Eriksson, 'Modernity, Rationality and Citizenship: Swedish Agrarian Organisations as Seen through the Lens of the Agrarian Press, circa 1880–1917', in P. Wawrzeniuk (ed.), *Societal Change and Ideological Formation among the Rural Population of the Baltic Area 1880–1939* (Huddinge: Södertörns Högskola, 2008), pp. 163–5; Ruin, *Kooperativa Förbundet*, p. 196.

121 Ruin, *Kooperativa Förbundet*, pp. 197–9.

122 On this point, see also: Pedersen, 'Svenske og danske andelsorganisationer', 305–21: 306.

123 See: Millbourn, 'Kooperatismen', pp. 105–6; see also chapter 5.

124 See chapter 3.

125 Aléx, *Den rationella konsumenten*.

126 Hemstad, *Fra Indian Summer til nordisk vinter*; N. Götz, H. Haggrén and M. Hilson, 'Nordic Cooperation in the Voluntary Sector', in J. Strang (ed.), *Nordic Cooperation: A European Region in Transition* (London: Routledge, 2016).

127 See chapter 2.

128 KA: Hannes Gebhardin arkisto: ICA congress proceedings 1904, pp. 316, 413–16.

129 Friberg, 'Visions and Organisation'; on Dehli, see: G. Roalkvam, 'Ole Dehli', *Norsk biografisk leksikon* (2009), available at http://nbl.snl.no/Ole_Dehli, accessed 14 January 2014.

130 KB, Acc. 1980/8:2: G. H. von Koch to Agathe von Koch, 20 March 1898.

131 These included study trips to Germany and Austria in 1893–94 and to Scandinavia, Germany, Paris and London in 1898–99. T. Carpelan and L. O. Th. Tudeer, *Helsingfors universitet. Lärare och tjänstemän från år 1828* (Helsinki: Söderström, 1925), pp. 246–50. I am grateful to Stefan Nygård for bringing this source to my attention.

132 R. Mäkinen, 'Finska agronomers skandinaviska kontakter, deras alternative och bondens nationella roll', in H. Haggrén, R. Hemstad and J. Marjanen (eds), *Civilsamhällets Norden* (Helsinki: CENS, 2005); KA: Hannes Gebhardin arkisto: Saapuneet kirjeet I 1882–1932.

133 Wirén, *G. H. von Koch*, p. 90.

134 Wirén, *G. H. von Koch*, p. 233.

135 A. Granström, *Om kooperativa självhjälpsföreningar* (Mariehamn: Förf., 1898); Carpelan and Tudeer, *Helsingfors universitet*; Sysiharju, 'Gebhard, Hannes'; Roalkvam, 'Ole Dehli'.

136 Pellervo: Pellervo-Seura ulkomaankirjeenvaihtoa 1911–25: Pellervo to FSA (n.d.); Pellervo to KF and SLR (n.d.); Pellervo to KF, 29 September 1920; KF to Pellervo, 4 October 1920.

137 See chapters 3 and 4.

138 'Siffrorna från England voro för oss nästan ofattligt stora, måhända vore de danske förhållandena mer inträsserande, och genom att berätta rörelsens historia i Danmark hoppades talaren kunde ge svar på många frågor.' Kooperativa Förbundets arkiv, Stockholm: Berättelser över Kooperativa Förbundets kongresser, åren 1899–1906: 1900.

139 NRA: PA 1394 Coop/NKL BA: Det kooperative landsmøde, 26–27 June 1906, pp. 11–16.

140 H. Stolpe and S. Stolpe, *Boken om Albin Johansson I* (Stockholm: Rabén & Sjögren, 1969), pp. 110–11; on Elanto, see: T. Odhe, *Kooperationen i Finland* (Stockholm:' Kooperativa Förbundets bokförlag, 1929), pp. 180–200, where it is described as a 'model co-operative society'.

141 Grelle, *Det kooperative alternative*, pp. 46–8; 73–4.

142 Grelle, *Det kooperative alternative*, pp. 81–3; Bryld, 'Kooperationen'; I. Theien, 'Two Phases of Consumer Co-operation in Scandinavia: Pre-war Pluralism and Post-war Unification under Social Democracy', in P. Verbruggen and L. Soubry (eds), *Consumerism versus Capitalism? Co-operatives seen from an International Comparative Perspective* (Ghent: Amsab-Institute of Social History, 2003), pp. 78–81.

143 K. J. Wedenoja, 'Osuuskaupat', in L. Harmaja et al. (eds), *Valtiotieteiden käsikirja. Aakkosellinen tietoteos*, vol. 2 (Helsinki: Tietosanakirja Osakeyhtiö, 1922), pp. 640–1.

144 See chapter 5.
145 Lange, *Organisert kjøpekraft*, pp. 150–3; Aléx, *Den rationella konsumenten*, pp. 126–44.
146 Aléx, *Den rationella konsumenten*.
147 J. von Schoultz, *Bidrag till belysande av Finlands socialdemokratiska partis historia* (Helsinki: Söderström, 1924), pp. 201–2.
148 See chapter 3.

2

Co-operative internationalism in practice: the International Co-operative Alliance (ICA) before and after the First World War

Like other international organisations of the late nineteenth and early twentieth centuries, the ICA did not emerge in a vacuum, but was rooted in the personal international networks that had developed among co-operators during the second half of the nineteenth century.[1] These networks originated in northern and western Europe. The first ICA congresses were essentially bipartite collaborations between French and British co-operators, and although early attempts were made to widen the geographical reach, the Alliance's affairs and activities continued to be dominated by the representatives of a core group of countries: France, Germany, Britain, Belgium, the Netherlands and Switzerland.[2] After the First World War this was widened to include Austria, Czechoslovakia and the Nordic countries, but southern and eastern Europe – and beyond – remained rather remote.

In his classic study of nineteenth-century internationalism, F. S. L. Lyons suggested that there were three common features shared by all international organisations: the periodic international congress; the permanent committee; and a bureau or secretariat.[3] The ICA had all three, but the balance between these institutions altered considerably during the first years of its existence, away from the congress and in favour of the committees and the secretariat as the main decision-making bodies. This was not a straightforward evolution, but was marked by conflicts over the aims and meanings of co-operation and the relationship between the representatives of its different branches: consumer, agricultural and producer. Most contemporaries agreed that consumer co-operation had achieved a position of dominance within the Alliance by the outbreak of the First World War, but its hegemony was never complete and alternative forms of co-operation were debated throughout the period covered in this book. Like other internationalist organisations of the same period, the ICA also faced the difficulty of reconciling the idealistic belief in internationalism with the national interests of its members, which at times threatened to overwhelm it.

This chapter analyses the performance and practice of co-operative internationalism through an examination of the ICA from its foundation in 1895 until the outbreak of the Second World War in 1939. The first section of the chapter surveys the origins and early history of the ICA. Following this, the nationalities question is discussed: in what ways did the Alliance's internationalism serve to reinforce national differences, as has been noted for other organisations?[4] In the third section, I consider more closely the international co-operative congress. As Kevin Callahan has noted of the Second International, congresses were an important part of the 'demonstration culture' of international organisations, and after 1900 were 'increasingly transformed into mass public spectacles of demonstration designed to promote unity within the [socialist] movement while displaying international socialist solidarity to external audiences'.[5]

The International Co-operative Congress, held triennially in a succession of European cities, also underwent a similar shift. What do we know about how international co-operative congresses were organised and the experiences of those who attended them? In general, we can note a decline in the importance of the political function of the congress as a place to debate and agree co-operative policy, and a growing emphasis on its symbolic role as a demonstration of co-operative internationalism both internally and externally. The Alliance's decision-making machinery is dealt with in the fourth section of the chapter, which also examines the internal geography of the ICA.

The ICA's beginnings and early development

The idea of an international co-operative congress had been discussed from the mid-nineteenth century, without concrete results. A French attempt to convene such a meeting in 1867 failed when the authorities refused to give their permission, evidence perhaps of the extent to which co-operation was still regarded as dangerously radical in some quarters.[6] During the 1880s the idea was taken up by co-operators in Britain and France. Two influential individuals were the bilingual Nîmes co-operator Edouard de Boyve, who had addressed the British Co-operative Union's 1886 congress on the need to formalise international co-operative relations, and the veteran British co-operator Edward Vansittart Neale, who was also well-connected internationally.[7] For both men, the cultivation of international contacts has to be seen within the context of ideological struggles within their respective national co-operative movements.[8]

Neale was a fervent supporter of co-partnership or profit-sharing, a form of co-operation which was rapidly losing ground to the consumer societies in the Co-operative Union during the late nineteenth century.[9] After Neale's death in 1892, at the age of 82, his colleague and supporter of co-partnership Edward Owen Greening took up the initiative, but lacking international networks of his own, he recruited Henry Wolff to help establish an international co-operative alliance. Wolff, who was to become the new Alliance's first president, brought with him extensive knowledge of the agricultural and credit co-operative societies in Germany and toured the continent at his own expense to galvanise support among co-operators in Belgium, the Netherlands and Italy, before the ICA was formally launched at a congress in London in 1895.[10]

This is not the place to re-tell the early history of the ICA in detail.[11] Nonetheless, some summary points may be made. To start with, we should note the roots of the Alliance in the personal networks developed among a relatively small group of mostly middle- or upper-class men. This helps to explain the ambivalence later co-operative historians sometimes showed towards the Alliance's early history, where the initiatives of the 1890s were seen as a necessary prologue to the business of establishing a 'proper' international as a federation of national co-operative unions after the turn of the century. Writing in the mid-1920s, for example, the Finnish author K. E. Primus-Nyman noted the dominance of 'lords, bishops, statesmen, parliamentarians and other notables, whose names, opinions and life's work stood in glaring contrast to those of the 28 poor flannel weavers in Rochdale'.[12] Although the French co-operator Charles Gide described the years leading up to 1895 as the 'bourgeois period' of the ICA's history,[13] its founders also drew on their contacts with the aristocracy to ensure that the Alliance's meetings were marked with the dignity and formalities that they felt appropriate. The English aristocrat Earl Grey hosted a formal reception to mark the Alliance's launch in 1895, as well as chairing the conference sessions, while those attending meetings in 1900 and 1904 were entertained at sumptuous banquets provided by noblemen and attended by the French president and Hungarian prime minister, respectively, in the latter case at an event held in Archduke Joseph's palace on the banks of the Danube.[14]

The congresses of 1895 and 1896 established a rudimentary structure based on the congress and a central committee as the main decision-making bodies, but for its first five years or so at least, the Alliance had little existence outside its congress meetings. Beyond the core group in Britain, France and the Low Countries, it relied on a network of individuals appointed or self-appointed as the representatives of their nation. Hannes and Hedwig Gebhard were asked regularly to report on co-operative developments in Finland, for example, and in preparation for the 1904 Budapest congress, Wolff commissioned a series of reports from prominent social reformers on the state of co-operation in the 'backward' regions of central and Eastern Europe.[15]

The first decade of the twentieth century saw a gradual shift away from these individuals, and their rather ad hoc approach to international relations based on personal networks, towards the establishment of a more formal and bureaucratic organisation. Several developments hastened this change. First, there was a generational shift as the founders of the Alliance withdrew from international activism due to death or old age.[16] Second, the co-operative movement grew very rapidly after 1900, which resulted in an expansion of the Alliance's membership away from the original Anglo-French core. Explaining the necessity of rule changes to the 1910 congress, the Central Committee noted: 'The international co-operative movement of to-day is a living reality, whereas, fifteen years ago it was scarcely more than a beautiful dream.'[17]

Third, as a consequence of this growth, consumer co-operation was gaining an ever greater influence on the ICA during the first decade of the twentieth century. Although initially hostile to an initiative that seemed intended to support co-partnership, soon after the Alliance's foundation the British Co-operative Union changed tack and decide to support the new organisation. It contributed nearly three quarters of the Alliance's subscriptions and donations in the financial year 1901/2, and although that proportion declined over the following years, it was openly acknowledged that the Alliance would be unable to function without this support.[18] When the fourth ICA congress was held in Manchester in 1902, the Co-operative Union was able to consolidate its control of the Alliance by defeating a proposal to create a separate sub-section for co-partnership within the ICA.[19]

In Budapest two years later, delegates voted down a proposal sanctioning the tolerance of state aid to co-operative societies, and in doing so precipitated the withdrawal of a large number of agricultural and credit societies from German-speaking parts of central Europe.[20] Distributive co-operation, according to the presenter of the proposal, the Frenchman Count de Rocquigny, was 'the simplest, the easiest to practise' form of co-operation. It required very little capital, and thus had no need for subventions from the state. Productive and credit associations were different, however, and had benefited from state assistance in many parts of Europe.[21] The proposal to allow the acceptance of state aid was strongly opposed by representatives of consumer societies from Britain and Germany. 'Are there really two distinct classes of citizens in the State?' asked an Austrian delegate. 'Why on earth should the distributive society of industrial working men be treated so much worse than the distributive society of agricultural labourers, or than agrarian organisations?'[22]

The growing dominance of consumer co-operation precipitated moves to formalise the Alliance's bureaucratic structures, a process which was completed over several stages at the congresses held in Hamburg in 1910, Glasgow in 1913 and Basle in 1921. Following a decision taken at the Cremona congress in 1907, a Special Committee was established to prepare a comprehensive revision of the rules, and a draft version was agreed at the Hamburg congress three years later.[23] The rules were presented to the congress delegates as a clean break for the Alliance, replacing the 'little more than makeshift' document agreed in 1896.[24] The draft confirmed the decision made in 1902 that only co-operative societies and central unions could be admitted to membership, with individuals relegated to the status of honorary observers. It removed the reference to co-partnership and self-help in the Alliance's objects, while also asserting its openness 'to co-operators of all shades of opinion' and its political and religious neutrality.[25]

The draft also attempted to formalise the Alliance's finances by requiring members to pay subscriptions on a sliding scale in proportion to membership, and it provided for a thorough overhaul of the decision-making machinery. The triennial congresses, which hitherto had been conducted 'more in the nature of meetings for academic discussion', would now become 'an International Co-operative Parliament really competent to decide on rules of conduct'. To that end, the congress would consist only of accredited delegates, allocated to members in proportion to size.[26] Representation on the Central Committee would be determined by the size of national subscriptions, though delegates were assured that this proposal was 'very far removed from the capitalistic principle that "he who pays the piper chooses the tune"'.[27]

Finally, the draft provided for the creation of a permanent bureau in London, and the appointment of a full-time salaried general secretary.[28] All this was intended to realise the ambition that the Alliance should become 'an international centre for co-operative propaganda, literature and statistics, and … a sort of central exchange between the co-operative organisations of all nations'.[29] From January 1909 the *International Co-operative Bulletin* appeared monthly in three languages (French, English and German), edited by Hans Müller from his base in Switzerland.[30]

Nationalism and internationalism: the ICA and the nationalities question

With the adoption of the draft rules at the Hamburg congress, by what was described as an overwhelming majority, the ICA had come of age. It had gained, in the words of one of its historians, a 'definitive constitution', and it had established a structure for its activities which was to endure, with only a few minor adaptations, throughout the interwar period.[31] Inevitably, such a profound change could not be free from controversy. As the drafters of the rules had predicted, there were some objections to the principle that entitlement to Central Committee representation would be in proportion to the size of subscription.[32] The summaries of the comments in the European co-operative press that were published in the *Bulletin* also indicate some dissatisfaction with the short time allowed for debating the proposals. The French co-operator Albert Thomas suggested that the formalisation of the congress proceedings had contributed to stifling debate, rather than fostering it. '[A]s a matter of fact the International Co-operative Congresses are conducted by the Central Committee with a high hand,' he wrote. 'Almost no discussion follows. A series of declarations are made and Congress is asked to confirm them.'[33]

Like most other international organisations of the period, the ICA was organised on the principle of 'inter-nationalism', or what historian Henrik Stenius has referred to as the 'Olympic Games principle'.[34] Internationalism was conceived not as an alternative to nationalism but as an extension of it, with participation conditional upon membership of a national organisation.[35] Co-operative internationalism was also shaped by the racial-national categories that were ubiquitous in early twentieth-century thinking.[36] For example, Charles Gide noted the growing influence of German co-operators before 1914, which he described with reference to some established stereotypes: he wrote that they brought to the ICA 'the spirit of discipline … the gregarious instinct … [and] the cult of organisation'.[37] Had the war not intervened, he suggested, they would most likely have taken over leadership of the Alliance from the British.[38]

In many parts of central and Eastern Europe in particular, co-operatives were intimately bound up in contemporary struggles over national self-determination and mobilised in the defence of ethnic or national interests.[39] The diversity of ethnic groups in the Austrian Empire had hindered the formation of united co-operative organisations before 1918, for example.[40] The conflicts that this induced sometimes spilled over into the ICA, partly because the principle of nation-state representation was not applied consistently. Gide acknowledged that the Alliance had failed to deal adequately with the 'embarrassing question' of national claims to representation when it allowed separate representation to Finland despite its status as a Grand Duchy of the Russian Empire, but not to Bohemia or Poland.[41] After the rule changes of 1910, the Polish co-operative union Odrodzenie used the pages of the *International Co-operative Bulletin* to argue that it was entitled to separate representation, pointing out that similar claims were made by representatives of Czech and Ruthenian co-operatives, but all were rejected by the Austrian union.[42]

The nationalities question was brought to a head, as for so many other international organisations, by the experiences of the First World War. Inevitably, the ICA found its activities severely disrupted by the outbreak of war in 1914 and the subsequent four years were summed up as 'the greatest trial to which such an organisation has ever been subjected'.[43] Pride in the Alliance's survival was tempered by disappointment at the apparent emptiness of the aspirations contained in the peace resolution passed at the 1913 congress.[44] At the same time, the post-war state of the co-operative movement seemed to offer grounds for optimism. In many countries co-operative societies had played a leading role in the implementation of state rationing schemes. A further acknowledgement of the movement's importance came with the decision of the Allied governments, in January 1919, to channel the resumption of trade with Russia through the co-operative movement.[45]

The outbreak of the war disrupted the process begun at the Hamburg and Glasgow congresses to re-organise the Alliance and to develop its internal machinery so that it could function as a truly international organisation. Largely on the initiative of the powerful German consumer co-operatives, led by Heinrich Kaufmann, the Glasgow congress had agreed to end the British dominance of the Alliance's Executive. The war made this impossible, and for the duration of hostilities the Alliance operated through the bi-monthly meetings of an exclusively British Executive Committee. The British representatives insisted that they had done their best to keep the internationalist spirit alive. The ICA's General Secretary Henry May became a member of the London Emergency Committee founded by the Society of Friends to raise funds to assist German, Austrian and Hungarian families affected by the war, and British co-operative societies not only responded to this appeal but also contributed to relief efforts for Belgium and Serbia.[46]

Regular communications were maintained with France and with co-operators in neutral nations. G. J. D. C. Goedhart of the Netherlands was able to act as an intermediary for communications with Germany and to assist with the efforts to continue publishing and circulating the Alliance's monthly trilingual periodical, *International Co-operative Bulletin*.[47] The Alliance's offices in London provided temporary asylum for two German nationals, who were employed to assist with German language matters. The Alliance took pride in claiming that its *Bulletin* was probably the only journal to continue circulating throughout the war in English, French and German, and it must be assumed that the Executive minutes were also scrupulously recorded in all three languages.[48]

As the war progressed, the Executive had to confront the question of resuming formal international contacts. The initiative was taken up by the French co-operative union, which announced plans to convene a meeting of representatives of co-operators in the Allied states in 1916. The Executive decided that the ICA could not be officially represented without compromising its neutrality, but agreed to cover expenses so that two of its officials could attend the French national congress, timed to coincide with the international meeting. After a lengthy discussion, it was also narrowly agreed to sanction their participation in the international conference, albeit in a purely personal capacity.[49] The conference, reported in the *Bulletin*, raised the possibility of reviving the international co-operative congress during 1917, but members of the Executive Committee remained cautious.[50]

As discussions on the revival of contacts continued after the cessation of hostilities, the first post-war meeting of the Central Committee came to be seen as a highly significant event, and it was felt that convening it prematurely, while many members were still unable to attend, would risk damaging the long-term future of the Alliance. Likewise, the Executive argued that participation at the post-war peace conference would risk the co-operative movement's reputation as a promoter of peace. 'Men's minds will necessarily be full of war bitterness', they argued, 'and very difficult questions with regard to territory, nationality, annexations or no annexations, indemnities or no indemnities, will have to be decided. These questions do not directly concern the Alliance.'[51]

These questions did concern co-operators in one important respect, however. The creation of new nation states under the Treaty of Versailles precipitated an expansion in the number of organisations eligible for membership, and one of the Alliance's most urgent post-war tasks was thus to amend the rules to take account of the new states. Representatives of co-operative unions in the successor states were invited to the inter-allied co-operative congress in 1919, and in 1920 it was reported that new members had been admitted from Armenia, Czechoslovakia, Georgia, Latvia, Lithuania, Poland and Ukraine.[52] The Alliance's officials tried to avoid becoming involved in difficulties arising from these new admissions, for example in 1921 when the Central Committee refused to intervene in a dispute over the allegiances of local co-operative societies in the Czechoslovak-Hungarian border region.[53]

By 1921 the ICA was able to hold its first full congress since the war, organised in Basle in neutral Switzerland. The proposals for rule changes approved at this congress were seen as a consolidation of the reforms begun at Hamburg, aiming to transform the ICA from 'a loose federation of organisations and individuals … into a closely knit alliance of national organisations', in the words of its president.[54] The Central Committee was confirmed as the main organ of the Alliance, with delegates elected by national federations in proportion to the size of their financial contributions. It was now very large, with over 30 countries eligible to nominate delegates by 1924, though not all of them attended. The Executive Committee, meanwhile, lost its exclusively British composition and became a truly international body, with seven members drawn from the most significant organisations in the Alliance.

Some problems remained, however. A French proposal to make the Alliance exclusively a union of national federations was rejected, meaning over 400 local co-operative societies from Britain retained separate membership – and with it, the right to appoint one Congress delegate for every 25,000 members.[55] Partly for this reason, although the financial dominance of the British organisations was not as overwhelming as it had been during the pre-war period, British contributions continued to account for just under a third of the Alliance's total subscription income during the 1920s. During the early 1920s the situation was also exacerbated by the currency crises in central Europe, which made it difficult for many members to pay their subscriptions (see table 2.1).

Even though the distribution of votes was not in strict proportion to these contributions, the financial dominance of the British organisations allowed them to exercise a strong influence over the Alliance, most controversially over the decision to endorse the membership of the Soviet co-operative organisation Tsentrosoiuz.[56] At the Basle congress, according to one of the Norwegian representatives, the British delegation got their resolution to accept Tsentrosoiuz passed, even though most of the rest of the delegations voted against, thanks to the 'peculiar voting rules'.[57] The admission of the Soviet organisations created a new problem: on paper at least, the Soviet Union was now by far the largest member of the ICA, though statistics on co-operative membership were impossible to verify. Aware of this, the Soviet delegates argued that not only Russia but also Ukraine should be formally represented on the ICA's Executive, and, moreover, that their named representatives should be allowed to nominate a proxy in case they were unable to attend meetings. This was rejected on the grounds that the Central Committee, not the Executive, was the forum for the representation of national interests; members of the Executive served in a personal capacity.[58] Discussions on these points dominated the agenda of Executive meetings for much of the 1920s and indicate the rather fluid and pragmatic nature of the way in which international representation was organised.

Performing internationalism: the international co-operative congress

During the early twentieth century, the international congress became established as the most important and visible manifestation of internationalism.[59] The ICA was no exception in this respect, and the arrangements for congresses and other international meetings became increasingly elaborate during the interwar period, while at the same time the formal role of the congress in deciding policy and conducting business declined. Organised every three years, the congresses served as milestones in the evolution of co-operation and the ICA, while also serving to affirm the achievements of co-operation to the delegates attending the congress and to a succession of European cities that hosted them.[60] The 1921 congress, held at Basle in neutral Switzerland, had immense significance as a reunion of co-operators from nations that had recently been at war, while the 1924 Ghent congress was seen as important in re-focusing the activities of the ICA on internal co-operative matters, as the post-war situation had stabilised.[61] The 1927 Stockholm congress was billed in advance as the biggest yet, 'a definite stage in the progress of International Co-operation', according to the Alliance's general secretary.[62] This was followed by an even grander congress in Vienna in 1930, which was attended by 554 delegates from 35 countries and could justifiably be described as the high point of co-operative internationalism in the interwar period, its optimism reflected in President Väinö Tanner's upbeat opening address.[63] Only three years later, however, the momentous decision was taken to postpone the congress planned for

Table 2.1 Subscriptions received from national members of the ICA, in amount and as percentage of total, 1902, 1913, 1922 and 1936

Country	1902		1913		1922		1936	
	contribution	% of total	contribution	% of total	contribution	% of total	contribution	% of total
Great Britain	£241. 12s., plus £52. from societies	76.24	£669.	40.60	£1,391. 0s. 10d.	48.05	£3,291. 16s. 3d.	32.37
Russia/USSR	£0. 15s.	0.19	£23. 18s.	1.45	£200.	7.26	£2,750.[a]	27.04
Germany	£17. 14s. 9d.	4.61	£304. 12s.	18.49	£100.	3.45		
France	£20. 2s. 9d.	5.23	£87. 17s. 6d.	5.33	£206. 5s. 5d.	7.13	£851. 13d. 4s.	8.37
Finland			£30. 16s. 6d.	1.87	£232. 5s. 5d.	8.02	£520. 15s. 6d.	5.12
Sweden	£1. 13s. 1d.	0.43	£30. 12s.	1.86	£96. 8s.	3.33	£456. 4s.	4.49
Czechoslovakia					£112. 7s.	3.88	£394. 12s. 11d.	3.89
Denmark	£3. 3s. 2d.	1.14	£28. 13s. 9d.	1.74	£150.	5.18	£233. 6s. 8d.	2.29
Switzerland	£3. 19s. 2d.	1.03	£91. 4s. 4d.	5.53	£121.	4.18	£296. 0s. 3d.	2.91
Austria	£1.	0.26	£182. 4s.	11.06			£100.	0.98
Poland					£12.	0.41	£192. 13d.	1.89
Holland	£26. 13s. 1d.	6.92	£30. 14s.	1.86	£63. 4s.	2.18	£151. 2s. 4d.	1.49
Hungary			£62. 12s.	3.80	£17. 2s. 6d.	0.59	£133.	1.31
Belgium	£3. 3s. 2d.	1.14	£31. 15s. 9d.	1.93	£47. 18s.	1.65	£98. 10s. 2d.	0.97

Bulgaria			£0. 12s.	0.04	£10. 11s.	0.36	£155. 0s. 9d.	1.52
Norway			£14. 16s.	0.90	£25. 6s.	0.87	£75. 4s. 6d.	0.74
Other Europe	£2. 11s. 3d.[b]	0.67	£40. 10s.[c]	2.46	£84. 1s.[d]	2.57	£241. 2s. 8d.[e]	2.36
Non-Europe	£8. 5s.[f]	2.11	£17. 7s.[g]	1.09	£25. 8s.[h]	0.88	£229. 9s. 11d.[i]	2.27

[a]Includes Armenia, Azerbaijan, Georgia, Ukraine, White Russia.
[b]Serbia, Spain.
[c]Cyprus, Italy, Romania, Serbia, Spain.
[d]Estonia, Georgia, Italy, Latvia, Lithuania, Romania, Yugoslavia. From 1927 Georgia was included under the USSR.
[e]Estonia, Iceland, Latvia, Lithuania, Romania, Yugoslavia.
[f]Australia, India, US.
[g]Argentina, Canada, India, Japan, US.
[h]Argentina, Canada, US.
[i]Argentina, Canada, French West Indies, India, Japan, Korea, Palestine, South Africa, US.

Note: Amounts received as subscriptions by country were reported as appendices to the ICA's triennial congress reports, in sterling (£1 = 20 shillings; 1 shilling = 12 pence (d)). Percentages have been calculated by converting the totals into pence. In 1922, with severe currency instability in many parts of Europe, it was reported that the amounts had been calculated according to the 'mean rate' of exchange. For a few years, calculated totals do not correspond to the figure given as the total subscriptions received. The figures given here may not therefore be entirely reliable and should be interpreted with care.

Sources: *Report of Proceedings at the Sixth Congress of the International Co-operative Alliance, held at Budapest, 5–8 September 1904* (London: ICA, 1905), p. 13; *Report of the Proceedings of the Tenth Congress of the International Co-operative Alliance, held at Basle, 22–25 August 1921* (London: ICA, 1921), p. 44; *Report of the Proceedings of the Eleventh International Co-operative Congress, held at Ghent, 1–4 September 1924* (London: ICA, 1925), p. 253; *Report of the Proceedings of the Fifteenth Congress of the International Co-operative Alliance, held at Paris, 6–9 September 1937* (London: ICA, 1938), p. 341.

London – an indication of the gravity of the political and economic crisis of the early 1930s.[64]

National co-operative federations were well aware of the importance of the annual congress, though its functions were changing even before the First World War. What was originally devised as a forum for debate and decision-making had, at least in the case of the established unions such as the British, become instead an annual demonstration of the strength and achievements of co-operation.[65] National congresses had also become important places for international exchange, through the practice of sending and receiving fraternal delegates from sister organisations abroad.[66] Attending the 1914 British congress in Dublin as part of a foreign delegation representing six different countries, the Swedish co-operator Anders Örne commented that the propaganda functions of the congress had replaced its role as a place of debate, but he admired the exhibition of co-operative goods organised in connection with the congress, which, he suggested, could not fail to produce 'a strong sense of the power and influence of British co-operation'.[67]

The international congresses of the ICA followed a similar evolution, where the early emphasis on debate came to be supplemented by demonstration and performance. The procedure for organising the congress was similar to that for the Second International, where the International Socialist Bureau set the agenda but other arrangements were left to the local hosts and the congress was an important opportunity for them to highlight the achievements of their own co-operative businesses.[68] The choice of host city was therefore important.[69] In 1902 the English CWS marked its commitment to the ICA by taking upon itself all the arrangements for the Manchester congress, including hosting a reception for all delegates and laying on a programme of excursions to co-operative manufacturing installations in the north of England, as well as the original Toad Lane store in Rochdale.[70] Two years later, the decision to hold the congress in Budapest was a deliberate effort to arouse interest in co-operation in the 'backward' agricultural areas of central and Eastern Europe.[71] In the uncertain atmosphere of the post-war years the congress went to a succession of small, neutral states: Switzerland (Basle) in 1921, Belgium (Ghent) in 1924 and Sweden (Stockholm) in 1927. The Stockholm congress marked the growing international prominence of Sweden: the congress was held in the magnificent setting of the newly opened Konserthus and took place just three years before the famous 1930 exhibition of architecture and design. It was also criticised for being unusually expensive.[72]

The 1924 Ghent congress was timed to coincide with the half centenary of the city's famous Vooruit co-operative society. As part of their celebrations, Belgian co-operators also organised an International Co-operative and Social Welfare Exhibition, which included displays from co-operative organisations in about thirty countries and was reported to have attracted 325,000 visitors over the three months that it was open.[73] Correspondents reviewing the exhibition in the co-operative press noted its dual function: to demonstrate the strength and prestige of the international co-operative movement to the Belgian general public, but also to increase co-operators' own awareness of the depth and reach of their movement and its achievements.[74] Danish *Andelsbladet* reported that the exhibition included displays from 'as good as all the civilised countries',[75] with the non-Europeans represented by the USA and Argentina. Pride of place was taken by the reproduction of the Rochdale Pioneers' original co-operative store, 'the Mecca to which all visitors made a pilgrimage',[76] which also displayed a letter from Robert Owen and a lock of his hair. Many national federations presented exhibits that were self-consciously modern, demonstrating the latest advances in co-operative business.[77]

The exhibition combined propaganda with overtly commercial aims. Many of the participating organisations used the exhibition to display the products of their manufacturing businesses, ranging from traditional handicrafts to the latest machine-produced goods. Visitors could enjoy the aroma of freshly-baked bread from the oven constructed by the Belgian hosts, while the French exhibit offered samples of co-operative wine.[78] For the co-operative movements of the newly independent states in central and Eastern Europe the exhibition presented a vital opportunity to assert their presence, in some cases through collaboration with state authorities. The largest exhibit was that produced by the new authoritarian government in Italy in an attempt to legitimise its efforts to incorporate co-operation into the fascist regime.[79]

The four Nordic nations were represented modestly at the exhibition. According to various accounts, they relied mainly on maps, photographs and statistical charts to illustrate the development of co-operation in their respective countries. Andelsudvalget took part, acknowledging the need to 'fly the flag' for Danish co-operation, but for some reason they were unable to finish their exhibit in time for the opening.[80] One Danish reviewer felt that this was a missed opportunity with potentially serious commercial implications, given that the British World Empire Exhibition, taking place the same summer in Wembley, had demonstrated the insecure position of Danish agricultural exports in the British markets and the need to secure new ones among the co-operative purchasing organisations of Europe.[81] Moreover, the poor showing of the Danish agricultural co-operatives handed a propaganda triumph to their urban rivals, DkF. The centrepiece of their exhibit was a model co-operative house constructed by several Copenhagen trade unions, which was reported to have drawn considerable interest among the Belgian visitors and was eventually sold locally.[82]

The 1924 co-operative exhibition was an acknowledgement that the formal business taking place on the floor of the international congress chamber mattered only partially. Meetings of other groups were arranged either side of the formal congress programme. In Ghent these included a women's congress, conferences on co-operative banking, insurance and the international wholesale, and meetings of the Centre Committee both before and after the congress.[83] Equally important were the entertainments and excursions organised as part of the programme. The social programme for the Basle delegates, for example, included the opportunity to visit the Swiss garden city of Freidorf, reflecting the interests of Bernhard Jaeggi, chair of the conference committee.[84] In Ghent, cars were laid on each morning to take delegates to local sites of co-operative interest before the start of formal congress business.[85]

Congress programmes also had to be designed to appeal to the wide range of delegates attending. A proposal to include a paper on 'The Juridical Position of Co-operation' in the programme of the 1927 Congress was rejected by the Executive, who felt, perhaps realistically, that 'the gardens of Stockholm are very beautiful [so] more delegates would be there than in the Congress hall'.[86] Instead, the Stockholm congress included an exhibition and separate conference on co-operative press and propaganda, organised by the Finnish co-operative union KK, and also an International Co-operative Summer School. This idea had been pioneered by the British Co-operative Union, but became an integral and regular part of ICA activities from 1927.[87]

By the late 1920s the congress had thus evolved from being primarily a forum for debate to a carefully managed expression of co-operative strength and unity. However, some practical difficulties remained: in common with all international organisations, the international co-operative congresses faced what could be described as the 'Babel problem'. The ICA operated in three official languages: French, English and German. German dominated communications with central and Eastern Europe, while the importance of English was guaranteed by the strength of British co-operation and the location of the Alliance's secretarial bureau in London.[88] In reflection of the ethno-nationalist thinking that dominated the era, French was associated with a 'Latin' bloc including France, Belgium, parts of Switzerland and southern Europe. After the war, the established procedure for ICA meetings was that participants would use one of the official languages with consecutive interpretation into the other two. This was of course cumbersome, time-consuming and expensive, but it was recognised as a necessary evil of participation in international meetings.[89]

The language question became more controversial during the 1920s, largely because it was connected to broader disagreements over the status of the Soviet Union in the Alliance.[90] During the preparations for the 1927 congress the Soviet delegates proposed that Russian should be given the status of official language, on the grounds that many of their members could speak nothing else. They offered to meet the extra costs of interpretation and translation, but the proposal was rejected on the grounds that it would cause practical difficulties.[91] Opposition to the idea seems also to have reflected fears that admitting Russian as an official language would further strengthen the efforts of the Soviet delegates to use the Alliance to propagandise for communism. The compromise was that all speakers at Alliance meetings were to be entitled to seek official credentials for their own interpreter, but that there would be no interpretation of the rest of the proceedings into Russian.[92] Moreover, although official ICA publications were distributed only in three languages, national federations were allowed translation rights.[93]

The Soviet delegates exercised their rights to use other languages at the 1930 congress, and in doing so demonstrated the problems of the policy and the ways in which it could be exploited to disrupt congress proceedings. Kevin Callahan describes how observers of the Second International, which had a similar three-language policy, reported that congress delegates were often restless sitting through the long translations and tended to become noisy and disruptive.[94] A Swedish delegate to the 1930 congress felt that the situation was exacerbated by the poor acoustics in the congress hall, which made the proceedings very difficult to follow. However, the language problem was most clearly demonstrated when a delegate from the Soviet Union made a long speech in Mongolian. Only when it was translated did it become clear that the contents had no relevance to the debate, which might have provoked an intervention from the chair, but there was little that could be done during the course of the speech.[95]

Some co-operators took seriously the idea of Esperanto, which chimed with the co-operative emphasis on education and self-improvement as well as the aspiration to generate international tolerance and understanding. Local retail societies in Britain offered Esperanto classes for their members, for example.[96] One advocate of Esperanto pointed out that the growth of nationalist self-determination since the Treaty of Versailles had only made the problem worse.[97] In the end, the loss of first German and then Austrian membership in the 1930s did much to establish the dominance of English as the main operating language of the Alliance, even before global expansion had become a reality.

There is some evidence that some of the representatives of the smaller countries felt disadvantaged by speaking other than the ICA's official languages.[98] But the language policy could also be used to the advantage of the Alliance. When the Soviet delegates complained that their speeches had been misrepresented in the official report of the 1927 congress, the General Secretary could counter that they had been independently transcribed by three different stenographers and the translations compared, thus removing any doubts of accuracy.[99] And it is possible that these sensitivities also influenced the unanticipated election, as president, of a man who spoke none of the official languages as his mother tongue, but was comfortable operating in all three.[100] In his nomination of Väinö Tanner, Heinrich Kaufmann mentioned the former's linguistic abilities – he spoke Finnish, Swedish and Russian as well as the three official languages – as a powerful recommendation of his merits for the post.[101]

Partly because of the language difficulties, the experience of congress for most of those attending was shaped by their participation in national delegations. Often, the national federations organised study trips in conjunction with the journey to the congress, so that their delegates could combine educational visits with tourism. For example, 13 Norwegian co-operators took part in a study trip in connection with the Glasgow congress in 1913, visiting Denmark, Germany, the Netherlands, England and Scotland. A similar trip was announced in connection with the Basle congress, to include Germany, Switzerland and possibly Belgium. A third of the costs were borne by NKL; the rest by the individuals concerned or their societies.[102] In return, the delegates were expected to report on the congress for the domestic co-operative press, sometimes filing brief reports by telegram during the congress itself and later writing longer articles summarising their experiences of the co-operative societies they had visited during their travels. Although the educational impacts were regarded as important, it should not be forgotten that they were also about sociability and pleasure. The itemised expenses for the three-man Danish delegation travelling to the Basle congress included tickets to a Swiss Alpine resort and a sailing trip on Lake Lucerne.[103]

Geography of international co-operation: committees and congresses

Despite the advances in transport that made it possible for organisations to hold regular meetings and congresses, travelling to take part in them was still confined to relatively small groups. As Rupp has commented with regard to the international women's movement, even during the interwar period participation in international meetings was largely confined to 'predominantly elite, Christian, older women of European origin'.[104] The same was true for the ICA. From the early 1920s there were regular annual meetings for the Alliance's Central Committee, while the Executive and other committees such as that of the ICWS met up to three times annually. For ease of access, many of these meetings were held in the cities of northern Germany, the Low Countries, Strasbourg or Geneva, but those attending them nonetheless often had to endure long and arduous journeys. Few denied the importance of these meetings, however. It was reported that the ICA's president Sir William Maxwell had made an extra special effort to travel to Geneva in April 1920, despite his advancing years and poor health, motivated by the significance of the first Central Committee meeting to be held since the war.[105]

By the late 1920s the ICA was arranging international meetings twice or three times each year. These gatherings included not only the official business, but also an extensive social programme. For the host city's co-operative societies, the ICA meetings were an opportunity to show off co-operative achievements and compete with one another in their hospitality. Visits to local co-operative factories were combined with entertainment and dining, which were doubtless equally important opportunities for transnational contact and exchange. The programme laid on by the British co-operative movement in 1929 (see table 2.2) includes occasions for what would now be called networking over dinner, non-co-operative entertainments including theatre and football, and also an opportunity for practical co-operative business through the factory visits.

Table 2.2 The social programme for the ICA meetings in London, October 1929

Day	Event
Tuesday	Dinner for the Executive Committee at the Hotel Russell, Russell Square (the hotel where the meetings were held)
Wednesday	Dinner for all delegates, at the invitation of the British Co-operative Union
Thursday	Theatre visit for all delegates as guests of Co-operative Wholesale Society
Friday	Dinner for all delegates, at invitation of Co-operative Wholesale Society
Saturday	Motor coach visit to the English and Scottish Co-operative Wholesale Societies' chocolate works at Luton, and the cabinet factory at Ponders End (Optional) Tickets for an English Football League match as guests of Co-operative Union
Every day	Lunch provided for all delegates at the CWS Board Dining Room

Source: TA: 334.5 KOL, Box 0.5: Papers for meetings in London, October 1929.

The location of the ICA meetings also reveals something of the changing geography of European co-operation. Geneva was an attractive venue for the ICA, as it was for many other international organisations, especially for the initial post-war meetings, but there were also efforts to spread the burdens of travel and hosting equally among the different members of the Alliance. There were also pragmatic considerations. Italy was no longer an option after the mid-1920s nor Germany after 1933, and in 1933 a special conference planned originally for Prague was re-located to Basle for a variety of reasons, among them the likelihood that the Czechoslovak government would refuse visas to the Russian delegation and the extra time needed to travel via Vienna in order to avoid crossing Nazi Germany.[106] In January 1933 the Executive ventured onto new territory by holding its meeting in Barcelona, but attendance was so depleted that a follow-up had to be arranged in Brussels a few months later and the experiment was not repeated, despite its reported benefits to the Spanish co-operative organisations.[107]

The Alliance's centre of gravity was shifting north and, in recognition of this fact, the Executive made two visits to Finland in 1935 and 1939. The journey to Helsinki was unusually long, requiring delegates to travel via ferry connections from Stockholm, Copenhagen, Stettin or Tallinn. 'Never before had the Executive travelled so far in the fulfilment of their ordinary duties', wrote the General Secretary in his report on the meetings.[108] As usual, the visit included a programme of extra-curricular activities, and delegates were invited to stay slightly longer than usual in order to participate in a motor tour to the cities of Hämeenlinna and Tampere. The outcome seems to have been a propaganda triumph for the Finnish co-operative organisations, at least as judged by the enthusiastic account published in the *Review of International Co-operation*. This suggested that the visitors had been 'shocked and thrilled' by the 'sight of the fine institutions which our fellow co-operators in Finland were able to show them'. The General Secretary's report also commented favourably on the 'great augmentation of understanding' displayed between the rival co-operative organisations SOK and KK, though this was later denied by SOK.[109]

For a relatively small group of individuals, participation in the Alliance's committees implied regular travelling: at least three times annually for the members of the Executive. In an unpublished memoir written towards the end of his life, Albin Johansson described the importance of the long journeys to ICA meetings for forging a close personal friendship between himself and Tanner.[110] Some co-operators were prepared to travel even further to attend the triennial congresses: the 1910 congress delegates' list included representatives from Argentina and Japan, for example, though this was unusual before the Second World War.[111] Because of the costs and time involved in an age of overland travel, the ICA was inevitably dominated by Europeans, just like the other international organisations of the period. But even within Europe journeys could be long and sometimes arduous. The Alliance's Dutch president, G. J. D. C. Goedhart, was forced to give notice of his resignation in 1925, as his age and ill health meant that he could no longer manage the travelling, and ICA meetings were arranged within easy reach of the Low Countries until he could be formally relieved of his duties at the 1927 congress.[112] His successor, Väinö Tanner, faced long overland journeys by sea and rail from Helsinki, as the schedule proposed for his travel to London in 1929 suggests (see table 2.3), though it did include a whole day in Stockholm, which presumably allowed him to undertake other business there, including meetings with his KF colleagues.

Table 2.3 Väinö Tanner's journey to the ICA meetings in London, October 1929

Date	Place	Time
Monday, 21 October	dep. Helsinki	1420
	arr. Turku	1836
	dep. Turku	1930
Tuesday, 22 October	arr. Stockholm	0900
	dep. Stockholm	2125
Wednesday, 23 October	arr. Hamburg	2010
	dep. Hamburg	2318
Thursday, 24 October	arr. Vlissingen	1233
	dep. Vlissingen	1330
	arr. London (via Harwich)	2115

Source: TA: 334.5 KOL, Box 0.5: 'Lontoon matka'.

Conclusion: the practice of co-operative internationalism

The co-operative movement fits Daniel Laqua's characterisation of internationalism as 'a movement, a process and an outlook'.[113] From the 1870s, co-operators were acutely aware of the existence of their movement across many countries and developed extensive networks for the exchange of information. Until the 1890s these were largely based on personal contacts, though the practice of sending fraternal delegates to national congresses was also common. Personal connections between individuals continued to shape the ICA during the early years of its existence, but from the turn of the century and especially after the First World War steps were taken to make its activities more formal and bureaucratic.

The institutional structures that were developed – a triennial international congress and regular meetings of smaller representative committees – had much in common with the arrangements adopted by other international organisations at this time. Just as in the international labour movement, delegates participated in ICA congresses as representatives of their national organisations. Further, as in the Second International, it is possible to trace an evolution in the role of international congresses away from a forum for debate towards a carefully managed opportunity to perform and display the strength of international co-operation in a succession of different European cities.

That said, the evolution of the ICA was also more complicated than this. Like other international organisations the ICA sometimes struggled to reconcile the demands of competing nationalisms in different parts of Europe. It also continued to allow the representation of local societies. Attempts to manage the international congress were not always successful and the Alliance was vulnerable to the deliberately disruptive tactics of the Soviet delegates in particular. Finally, the importance of individual contacts was by no means diminished after 1918, due above all to the relatively small numbers of co-operative leaders who participated regularly in international arrangements, most of whom must be assumed to have known each other very well.

This raises a wider question. There is evidence of a growth in 'co-operative tourism' in the interwar period, where national federations made efforts to organise study tours for members of their organisations. Often the emphasis here was on the practical exchange of knowledge, aimed at specific groups such as co-operative managers, though such excursions were often arranged in connection with participation at international congresses. But it is obvious that even participation at the triennial congress was possible for only a tiny minority of co-operators and the question remains whether such events meant anything at all for ordinary members shopping in their local co-operative store.

This is difficult to establish, of course, but there were several ways in which co-operative internationalism was communicated to the wider membership. First, the activities of the ICA were widely reported in all the Nordic co-operative journals studied for this period. These included not only reports of the formal business of the Alliance, as conducted at meetings of its Central and Executive committees, but also extensive coverage of the congresses and the exhibitions that were often organised in tandem with them. There are also many examples of illustrated accounts of the congresses and the journeys undertaken to reach them by individual delegates. Press coverage of national congresses was also used to underline the importance of international contacts.[114] The printed congress reports, listing all the member organisations entitled to send delegates, provided a valuable snapshot of the state of co-operation in different countries and a permanent record of its progress.

Second, from the early 1920s the Alliance attempted to establish the practice of celebrating an International Co-operative Day. The designation of the first Saturday in July as such a day was agreed unanimously by the Central Committee in 1922 and from 1925 the rainbow flag was adopted as the colours of the international co-operative movement.[115] Nicole Robertson suggests that the international day was an extension of the already established tradition of holding summer co-operative carnivals in Britain, for which local co-operative societies organised a varied programme of events including processions, concerts, fancy dress parades and competitions.[116] Support for this event elsewhere in Europe seems to have been more limited. An ICA memorandum on International Co-operative Day in 1926 noted that co-operators in 22 member countries had participated, but in 1930 it was reported that the day was still not universally observed, partly because it clashed with the normal harvest period in Russia, India and Poland, for example.[117] Reports in the Nordic co-operative press support this: the Finnish *Konsumentbladet* wrote that the timing of the festival in the summer period meant that it was not observed at all in Finland, while the Danish *Andelsbladet* also commented on the lack of enthusiasm compared to other countries, especially England.[118] The ICA's official co-operative day message was, on occasions, reprinted in the co-operative press, but it is impossible to say with any confidence that the day itself had any significance for Nordic co-operators.[119]

In 1935 the Swedish co-operator Axel Gjöres delivered a lecture to an international conference on the co-operative press, which was later reprinted in the Swedish journal *Kooperatören*. Gjöres began his lecture by attempting to define co-operative internationalism. It was, he argued, not only a logical extension of co-operation's moral commitment to working together (*samarbete*), but also a practical response to the growing possibilities for international exchange in economic life, facilitated by new technology. This had been halted by the war but despite the rise of economic nationalism there were still grounds for optimism that it would continue. In this context, and given the willingness of capitalist firms to collaborate across national boundaries and form international cartels, it had to be admitted that co-operation's achievements were more modest than they could have been. According to Gjöres, this was explained by the constraints imposed by internal democracy, which meant that co-operative managers were sometimes overly timid in taking decisions that they feared would be rejected by their members.

Nationalism had a very powerful grip over people's minds, and the task of co-operative educational institutions, including the co-operative press, was therefore to educate people to overcome their national prejudices and appreciate the material advantages that lay in international economic co-operation. Gjöres remained confident that technological developments, especially those in the mass media such as film and radio, together with new possibilities for mass tourism, would help to counter popular nationalist sentiments. He proposed increased co-operation between the editors of the co-operative press, including an international exchange scheme for co-operative journalists.[120] Gjöres' lecture offered a clear statement of the popular educational (*folkuppfostran*) aspirations that lay at the heart of Nordic co-operative organisations like KF, identified by Peder Aléx among others.[121] Co-operative members were not naturally inclined to internationalism, so it was the duty of their societies to educate them to see the benefits of international co-operation. Typically, these benefits were both moral-idealistic and economically practical, though Gjöres clearly placed more weight on the latter than the former.

This chapter has examined the practice and performance of co-operative internationalism at a more symbolic level, as realised above all through the organisation of the ICA and its institutions and practices. Lofty expressions of internationalism were not difficult to find. For example, according to a Finnish author writing in the 1920s, the 1913 Glasgow congress 'was more than all its predecessors characterised by a genuine and overwhelming enthusiasm for peace'.[122] In the next two chapters I turn to examine more closely what these internationalist aspirations actually meant in practice: first, for the politics and policy of co-operation (chapter 3); and second, for the organisation of trade and the distribution of goods (chapter 4).

Notes

1 See also: L. J. Rupp, *Worlds of Women: The Making of an International Women's Movement* (Princeton: Princeton University Press, 1997), p. 14.

2 These states dominated most international organisations; see: F. S. L. Lyons, *Internationalism in Europe 1815–1914* (Leyden: A. W. Sythoff, 1963), p. 17.

3 Lyons, *Internationalism*, p. 29.

4 For example, see: K. Callahan, 'Performing "Inter-Nationalism" in Stuttgart in 1907: French and German Socialist Nationalism and the Political Culture of an International Socialist Congress', *International Review of Social History*, 45 (2000), 51–87.

5 K. J. Callahan, *Demonstration Culture: European Socialism and the Second International, 1889–1914* (Leicester: Troubador Publishing Ltd, 2010), p. 80.

6 W. P. Watkins, *The International Co-operative Alliance* (London: ICA, 1970), p. 15.

7 Watkins, *International Co-operative Alliance*, p. 23; P. Gurney, *Co-operative Culture and the Politics of Consumption in England, 1870–1930* (Manchester: Manchester University Press, 1996), p. 166. On de Boyve's fluency in English, see: E. Furlough, *Consumer Co-operation in France: The Politics of Consumption 1834–1930* (Ithaca: Cornell University Press, 1991), p. 81.

8 Gurney, *Co-operative Culture*, p. 166.

9 For the debates on co-partnership, see: Gurney, *Co-operative Culture*, pp. 148–56.

10 Watkins, *International Co-operative Alliance*, p. 27; H. Wolff, 'Early days of the ICA', *Review of International Co-operation*, January 1930, pp. 1–3; February 1930, pp. 46–9.

11 For detailed accounts of the ICA's institutional history, see: Watkins, *International Co-operative Alliance*; R. Rhodes, *The International Co-operative Alliance during War and Peace 1910–1950* (Geneva: ICA, 1995); J. Birchall, *The International Co-operative Movement* (Manchester: Manchester University Press, 1997).

12 'Listan över vicepresidenterna upptager en lång förteckning över lorder, biskopar, statsmän, parlamentsmedlemmar och andra notabiliteter, vilkas namn, åskådningar och levnadsgärningar stodo i den bjärtaste kontrast mot de 28 fattiga flanellvävarnas i Rochdale.' K. E. Primus-Nyman, 'Internationella Kooperativa Alliansen: en återblick på dess verksamhet', *Kooperatören*, August 1924, pp. 263–71.

13 Rhodes, *International Co-operative Alliance*, p. 26; C. Gide, *The International Co-operative Alliance*, trans. H. J. May (London: ICA, n.d. [*c*.1919]), p. 1.

14 Wolff, 'Early days of the ICA', *Review of International Co-operation*, February 1930, pp. 46–9; June 1930, pp. 208–12.

15 *Report of the Proceedings of the Sixth Congress of the International Co-operative Alliance, held at Budapest, 5–8 September 1904* (hereafter *ICA Congress Proceedings 1904*) (London: ICA, 1905); M. Hilson, P. Markkola and A.-C. Östman, 'Introduction: Co-operatives and the social question', in M. Hilson, P. Markkola and A.-C. Östman (eds), *Co-operatives and the Social Question: The Co-operative Movement in Northern and Eastern Europe (1880–1950)* (Cardiff: Welsh Academic Press, 2012), pp. 1–2.
16 Wolff, 'Early days of the ICA', *Review of International Co-operation,* May 1930, pp. 161–5.
17 *Report of the Proceedings of the Eighth Congress of the International Co-operative Alliance, held at Hamburg, 5–7 September 1910* (hereafter *ICA Congress Proceedings 1910*) (London: ICA, 1911), p. 59. In its report to the congress (p. 38), the Central Committee noted that membership had increased by over 45 per cent in the three years since the previous congress.
18 The Central Committee's report to the 1904 congress noted that nearly 70 per cent of the Alliance's income came from Britain, followed by Germany, France, the Netherlands and Switzerland. *ICA Congress Proceedings 1904*, pp. 65–6.
19 A. Bonner, *British Co-operation: The History, Principles, and Organisation of the British Co-operative Movement* (Manchester: Co-operative Union, 1961), p. 428.
20 Rhodes, *International Co-operative Alliance*, p. 26; Birchall, *International Co-operative Movement*, p. 46. The Executive Committee's report for 1904–5 regretted the withdrawal of 23 societies, nearly all of which were members of Allgemeiner Verband der auf Selbshilfe beruhenden deutschen Erwerbs- und Wirtschaftsgenossenschaften in Germany and Austria. Työväen arkisto, Helsinki (hereafter TA): 334.5 Kansainvälinen Osuustoimintaliitto (KOL), Box 0.1: Report of ICA Executive for the year ending 30 June 1905.
21 Count de Rocquigny, 'The Duty of the State towards Co-operation: Should It Subsidise It or Not?', *ICA Congress Proceedings 1904*, p. 118.
22 *ICA Congress Proceedings 1904*, pp. 137–8.
23 *Report of the Proceedings of the Seventh Congress of the International Co-operative Alliance, held at Cremona, 22–25 September 1907* (London: ICA, 1907), pp. 59–60.
24 *ICA Congress Proceedings 1910*, p. 57.
25 *ICA Congress Proceedings 1910*, pp. 61, 3.
26 *ICA Congress Proceedings 1910*, pp. 66–7.
27 *ICA Congress Proceedings 1910*, p. 70.
28 Watkins, *International Co-operative Alliance*, pp. 87–8.
29 *International Co-operative Bulletin*, 4 June 1910, pp. 81–6.
30 Watkins, *International Co-operative Alliance*, p. 81.
31 Rhodes, *International Co-operative Alliance*, p. 36.
32 Notably from Charles Gide, in *International Co-operative Bulletin*, 5 November 1910, pp. 165–70.
33 Translation of article by Albert Thomas in 'The Eighth International Co-operative Congress, as reviewed by the Co-operative Press', *International Co-operative*

Bulletin, 3 December 1910, pp. 183–8: 183. There was more on the debate in *International Co-operative Bulletin*, 5 November 1910, pp. 165–70.

34 H. Stenius and H. Haggrén, 'Det nordiska samarbetets vardagspraktiker – vad vet vi om dem förutom att de är viktiga?', in L. Häggman (ed.), *Finland i Norden – Finland 50 år i Nordiska rådet* (Helsinki: Pohjola-Norden, 2005), p. 81; cited in J. Harvard and P. Stadius, 'A Communicative Perspective on the Formation of the North: Contexts, Channels and Concepts', in J. Harvard and P. Stadius (eds), *Communicating the North: Media Structures and Images in the Making of the Nordic Region* (Farnham: Ashgate, 2013), p. 3; Callahan, 'Performing "Inter-Nationalism"'.

35 Callahan, 'Performing "Inter-Nationalism"', 54; see also Rupp, *Worlds of Women*, pp. 109–11; M. Rodríguez García, 'Early views on internationalism: Marxist socialists vs liberals', *Revue Belge de Philologie et d'Histoire – Belgisch Tijdschrift voor filologie en geschiednis*, 84:4 (2006), 1049–73: 1054–5.

36 R. Boyce, *The Great Interwar Crisis and the Collapse of Globalization* (Basingstoke: Palgrave Macmillan, 2009), pp. 18–20.

37 C. Gide, *Consumers' Co-operative Societies*, trans. staff of the Co-operative Reference Library, Dublin (Manchester: Co-operative Union, 1921), p. 28. On co-operation and race, see also: C. Gide, 'A review of world co-operation', *International Co-operative Bulletin*, March 1926, pp. 65–71.

38 Gide, *International Co-operative Alliance*, p. 9.

39 T. Lorenz, 'Introduction: Cooperatives in ethnic conflicts', in T. Lorenz (ed.), *Cooperatives in Ethnic Conflicts: Eastern Europe in the 19th and Early 20th Century* (Berlin: Berliner Wissenschafts-Verlag, 2006).

40 Gide, *Consumers' Co-operative Societies*, p. 40. There were separate German- and Czech-speaking unions in Bohemia which continued in Czechoslovakia after 1918; see also: C. Albrecht, 'Nationalism in the cooperative movement in Bohemia before 1914', and A. Reich, 'Economic interests and national conflict: The relationship between Czech and German consumer cooperatives in Czechoslovakia between 1918 and 1939', both in Lorenz (ed.), *Cooperatives in Ethnic Conflicts.*

41 Gide, *Consumers' Co-operative Societies*, p. 138, n. 2.

42 'Echoes from the International Co-operative Congress at Hamburg, *International Co-operative Bulletin*, 14 January 1911, pp. 1–3. The Austrian union responded to the criticism the following month: 'The Question of Representation on the Central Committee of the International Co-operative Alliance', *International Co-operative Bulletin*, 11 February 1911, pp. 39–40.

43 'Report of the work of the International Co-operative Alliance – 1914 to 1919. Presented to the Central Committee at Geneva, April 1920', *International Co-operative Bulletin*, April-May 1919, p. 118.

44 'International Co-operative Alliance – 1914–1919', p. 119. The text of the resolution and the debate on it is in *Report of the Proceedings of the Ninth Congress of the International Co-operative Alliance, held at Glasgow, 25–28 August 1913* (London: ICA, 1913), pp. 39–48.

45 Watkins, *International Co-operative Alliance*, p. 117.

46 'International Co-operative Alliance – 1914–1919', pp. 121–2.

47 TA: 334.5 KOL, Box 0.1: Minutes of ICA Executive meeting, 30 June 1915. Goedhart was lauded for these efforts at a party arranged in conjunction with a 1920 Central Committee meeting in The Hague; see: 'Den kooperative internationale. Berammer verdenskongress august 1921', *Kooperatøren*, December 1920, pp. 115–16.

48 The German and French editions were suspended in August 1914, with the German one revived from January 1915, and the French a year later through publication in Switzerland. In 1917 the Executive also agreed to allow the Russian Co-operative Union to bear the costs of translating and publishing a Russian edition, but this plan was stymied by the introduction of new restrictions on the international transmission of periodicals. 'International Co-operative Alliance – 1914–1919', pp. 122–3. TA: 334.5 KOL, Box 0.1: Minutes of ICA Executive meetings, 18 November 1914; 30 June 1916; 22 September 1915; 10 November 1915; 23 February 1916. The ICA papers in the Finnish labour archives include the German language minutes; it is not clear whether the French or English ones have survived.

49 TA: 334.5 KOL, Box 0.1: Minutes of ICA Executive meetings, 25 July 1916; 19 September 1916.

50 'The Inter-Allied Co-operative Congress at Paris', *International Co-operative Bulletin*, October 1916, pp. 224–32; TA: 334.5 KOL, Box 0.1: Minutes of ICA Executive meeting, 20 February 1917.

51 TA: 334.5 KOL, Box 0.1: Minutes of ICA Executive meeting, 26 June 1918.

52 'Inter-Allied Co-operative Congress at Paris, February 1919', *International Co-operative Bulletin*, February-March 1919, pp. 21–31; 'International Co-operative Alliance – 1914–1919', p. 128.

53 'Den internationale kooperative alliances møte i Kjøbenhavn', *Kooperatøren*, June 1921, pp. 54–5.

54 G. J. D. C. Goedhart, 'Report on the Revision of the Rules of the International Co-operative Alliance', in *Report of the Proceedings of the Tenth Congress of the International Co-operative Alliance, held at Basle, 22–25 August 1921* (London: ICA, 1921), p. 71.

55 'The ICA Central Committee meetings at Copenhagen', *International Co-operative Bulletin*, April-May 1921, pp. 89–97; 'Internationella Alliansen. Kongressen i Gent', *Kooperatören*, October 1924, pp. 321–5, 341–5.

56 See chapter 3.

57 'de underlige stemmeregler'. 'Den internationale kooperative kongres i Basel', *Kooperatøren*, September 1921, pp. 70–5. This cannot be confirmed from the congress proceedings, which just gives the total number of votes cast for and against.

58 'Internationella alliansen: Kongressen i Gent', part III, *Kooperatören*, November 1924, p. 358.

59 Callahan, 'Performing "Inter-Nationalism"'; Callahan, *Demonstration Culture*; Rupp, *Worlds of Women*.

60 Histories of the ICA were often narrated in terms of developments between congresses; see: Watkins, *International Co-operative Alliance*; Wolff, 'Early days of the ICA', parts I–VIII, *Review of International Co-operation*, January-September

1930; 'Den internasjonale kooperative Alliance', *Kooperatøren*, 6, 1927, pp. 63–4.

61 On the significance of the 1924 Ghent congress in this respect, see: H. J. May, 'International co-operation in 1925', *International Co-operative Bulletin*, January 1926, pp. 2–5. The reports of the Central Committee and Executive meetings of the 1920s confirm this emphasis on internal matters: subscriptions and finance, new applications for membership, publications and procedural questions such as the status of different languages for the conduct of Alliance business.

62 H. J. M., 'The ICA in 1926', *International Co-operative Bulletin*, January-February 1927, p. 33.

63 Watkins, *International Co-operative Alliance*, p. 190; TA: 92 Väinö Tannerin osuustoimintaa kosk. puheita ja artikkeleita 1928–61: opening address to Thirteenth International Co-operative Congress, Vienna, August 1930.

64 On the decision to postpone the 1933 congress, see: TA: 334.5 KOL, Box 5: Report on meeting of ICA Executive at Barcelona, 12–13 February 1933; H. May to V. Tanner, 18 February 1933.

65 The function of the national congress as a forum for agreeing co-operative policy did not disappear entirely, however. The extraordinary 1917 congress in Britain holds a special place in national co-operative historiography as the location of the decision to seek political representation. See: M. Hilson, 'Consumers and politics: The co-operative movement in Plymouth, 1890–1920', *Labour History Review*, 67:1 (2002), 7–27.

66 Gurney, *Co-operative Culture*, pp. 89–91. Based on British co-operative sources, Gurney suggests that these types of exchanges were more prevalent in the co-operative movement than in the contemporary trade union movement, for example.

67 A. Örne, 'Brittiska Kooperativa förbundets kongress', *Kooperatören*, 1914, pp. 146–54.

68 Callahan, 'Performing "Inter-Nationalism"', p. 65. The Second International's 1891 congress was also an opportunity to promote the achievements of the Ghent co-operative Vooruit; see: H. Defoort, 'The Strongest Socialist Party in the World: The Influence of Belgian Social Democracy in International Socialism prior to 1914 as a Means to Study the Relations between Socialism and Co-operation', in P. Verbruggen and L. Soubry (eds), *Consumerism versus Capitalism? Co-operatives Seen from an International Comparative Perspective* (Ghent: Amsab-Institute of Social History, 2003), pp. 199–200.

69 Callahan, *Demonstration Culture*, p. 84.

70 *Report of the Proceedings of the Fifth Congress of the International Co-operative Alliance, held at Manchester, 21–25 July 1902* (London: ICA, 1902), pp. 417–33.

71 Wolff, 'Early days of the ICA', parts V–VI, *Review of International Co-operation*, May-June 1930, pp. 161–5; 208–12.

72 TA: 334.5 KOL, Box 0.3: Report on proceedings of ICA Executive meeting, The Hague, 24–25 November 1927.

73 D. Laqua, *Age of Internationalism and Belgium 1880–1930: Peace, Progress and Prestige* (Manchester: Manchester University Press, 2013), pp. 131–2. Reports in the co-operative press differ on the number of countries exhibiting, ranging from 28 to 32.

74 'Den kooperative Verdensudstilling', *Kooperationen*, October 1924, pp. 18–24.
75 'saa godt som alle civiliserede Lande'. 'Den internationale Andels-Udstilling i Gent', *Andelsbladet*, 30 May 1924, p. 535.
76 'det Mekka, hvortil alle Udstillingsbesøgender først gjorde deres Pilgrimsvandring'. 'En dansk Korrespondent om Udstillingen i Gent', *Kooperationen*, August 1924, pp. 174–9; G. R., 'Den internationale kooperative utstilling i Gent', *Kooperatøren*, 7, 1924, pp. 76–7.
77 'En dansk Korrespondent'; 'Den kooperative Verdensudstilling'.
78 'En dansk Korrespondent'; 'Den kooperative Verdensudstilling'.
79 'En dansk Korrespondent'; 'Den internationale kooperative utstilling'. Both reports noted that Italy had the biggest exhibit. Italy ceased to be a member of the ICA from 1926.
80 'Den internationale Andels-Udstilling i Gent'; 'Andels-Udstilling i Gent', *Andelsbladet* 8 August 1924, pp. 783–4.
81 'En dansk Korrespondent'. This was a reprint of an article about the exhibition by P. Schwanenflügel, which had originally appeared in *Svendborg Avis*.
82 'Det danske Hus paa Udstillingen i Gent', *Kooperationen*, July 1924, pp. 161–4; 'Gentin kansainvälisestä osuustoimintanäyttelystä', *Yhteishyvä*, 19 September 1924.
83 'Kansainväliset osuustoimintapäivät', *Kuluttajain Lehti*, 28 August 1924.
84 'ICA Central Committee meetings at Copenhagen'.
85 'Osuustoimintakongressi Gentissä', *Yhteishyvä*, 29 August 1924.
86 TA: 334.5 KOL, Box 0.2: Report on proceedings of ICA Executive meeting, The Hague, 30–31 January 1926.
87 H. J. M., 'The ICA in 1926', pp. 33–6.
88 According to Henry Wolff, the language question was first raised at the Budapest congress in 1904, as previously all ICA business had been conducted in English and French. Wolff, 'Early days of the ICA', part VI, *Review of International Co-operation*, June 1930, pp. 208–12.
89 A. D., 'Centralbestyrelsesmøde i Det internationale Andelsforbund', *Andelsbladet*, 5 November 1926, p. 1264. The report described the procedures as 'a rather weighty apparatus' ('et ret tungt virkende Apparat').
90 See chapter 3.
91 TA: 334.5 KOL, Box 0.3: Minutes of ICA Executive meeting, Brussels, 27 April 1927; minutes of ICA Central Committee meeting, Stockholm, 18 August 1927.
92 TA: 334.5 KOL, Box 0.4: Report on proceedings of ICA Executive meeting, Bremen, 28–31 March 1928; report on proceedings of ICA Executive meeting, Liège, 26–27 July 1928.
93 TA: 334.5 KOL, Box 0.2: Minutes of ICA Executive meeting, Antwerp, 1–2 May 1926.
94 Callahan, *Demonstration Culture*, pp. 11–13.
95 'Trettonde internationella kooperativa kongressen i Wien', *Kooperatören*, October-November 1930, p. 272.
96 N. Robertson, *The Co-operative Movement and Communities in Britain, 1914–1960: Minding Their Own Business* (Farnham: Ashgate, 2010), p. 41.

97 M. Starr, 'The Language of International Co-operation', *International Co-operative Bulletin*, April 1924, pp. 110–12.

98 For example, the obituary of Danish co-operator Anders Nielsen suggested: 'It was a hindrance to his direct participation in the discussions at the meetings that his native tongue was not among the official languages of the ICA.' A. Axelsen Drejer, obituary of Anders Nielsen, *Review of International Co-operation*, August 1928, pp. 284–6. The sense of disadvantage was also experienced in relation to the circulation of printed materials; see: TA: 334.5 KOL, Box 0.3: Report on proceedings of ICA Executive meeting, Strasbourg, 10–11 February 1927.

99 TA: 334.5 KOL, Box 0.4: Report on proceedings of ICA Executive meeting, Bremen, 28–31 March 1928.

100 It seems to have been widely assumed before the congress that the Frenchman Poisson would be elected as president; see, for example: 'Den internationasjonale kooperative Alliance', *Kooperatøren*, 6, 1927, pp. 63–4.

101 TA: 334.5 KOL, Box 0.3: Minutes of ICA Central Committee meeting, Stockholm, 18 August 1927.

102 Report on the Basle congress in *Kooperatøren*, March 1921, p. 20.

103 Rigsarkivet, Aarhus (now Viborg): Erhvervsarkivet: 06156 Andelsudvalget: 1910–64 Mødereferater mv vedr deltagelsen i ICA 1910 mm: 305: Regnskab over Udgifterne ved Deltagelsen i Basle.

104 Rupp, *Worlds of Women*, p. 51.

105 'The Geneva meetings', *International Co-operative Bulletin*, April-May 1920, pp. 109–13.

106 TA: 334.5 KOL, Box 6: Report on proceedings of ICA Executive meeting, Paris, 20–21 May 1933.

107 TA: 334.5 KOL, Box 5: May to Tanner, 18 February 1933.

108 H. J. M., 'The ICA Executive in Finland', *Review of International Co-operation*, July 1935, pp. 241–3.

109 H. J. M., 'ICA Executive in Finland'; SOK's objection was reported in *Samarbete*, 3 October 1935.

110 M. Hilson, 'A Consumers' International? The International Cooperative Alliance and Cooperative Internationalism, 1918–1939: A Nordic Perspective', *International Review of Social History*, 56:2 (2011), 203–33, n. 66.

111 *ICA Congress Proceedings 1910*, pp. 2, 9.

112 TA: 334.5 KOL, Box 0.2: Report on proceedings of ICA Executive meeting, The Hague, 30–31 January 1926.

113 Laqua, *Age of Internationalism*, p. 5.

114 For example, foreign guests to the 1920 YOL congress in Helsinki were welcomed with the publication of a special column in English in *Yhteishyvä*. 'Ulkolaisille vierasimme! To our foreign guests!', *Yhteishyvä*, 22 June 1920.

115 TA: 334.5 KOL, Box 0.1: Report on proceedings of ICA Central Committee meeting, Milan, 10–11 April 1922. The rainbow flag was adopted in 1925; see: TA: 334.5 KOL, Box 0.2: Minutes of ICA Executive meeting, Frankfurt, 30 January – 1 February 1925.

116 Robertson, *Co-operative Movement*, pp. 82–6.

117 TA: 334.5 KOL, Box 0.2: Papers for ICA Central Committee meeting, 12–16 October 1926: Memorandum on International Co-operative Day; Box 0.6: Papers for ICA Central Committee meeting, 27 March 1930: Draft report to Congress 1927–29.

118 'Firandet av den internationella kooperativa dagen i Tyskland', *Konsumentbladet*, July 1924; 'Den internationale Andelsdag', *Andelsbladet*, September 1926, p. 1019. The latter reported that International Co-operative Day had become a popular festival in some countries, including Argentina and Canada, but their source for this was probably the *International Co-operative Bulletin*, which of course sought to make the most it could of the events.

119 'Osuustoiminnan korkeimpana päämääränä on yhteiskunnan hyvinvointi', *Elanto*, 15 July 1930.

120 A. Gjöres, 'Internationalism i den kooperativa pressen', *Kooperatören*, 20, 1935, 461–70.

121 P. Aléx, *Den rationella konsumenten. KF som folkuppfostrare 1899–1939* (Stockholm/Stehag: Brutus Östlings Bokförlag Symposion, 1994).

122 'präglades mer än alla sina föregångare av en äkta och överväldigande fredsentusiasm.' Primus-Nyman, 'Internationella Kooperativa Alliansen'.

3

The politics of international co-operation: neutrality and crisis

Delivering his presidential address to the 1934 international co-operative congress in London, Väinö Tanner reflected on the profound economic and political changes which had buffeted the co-operative movement since the previous congress.[1] The early 1930s were difficult years for the ICA. In 1933 it had to take the unusual step of postponing its congress, and in the same year it lost one of its largest and most important members when the German co-operative movement was taken over by the Nazis. A year later there were fears that the same would happen in Austria, where leading co-operators were imprisoned during the civil war, and severe doubts emerged about the continued autonomy of the Austrian movement.[2] All over Europe, co-operative societies faced growing hostility from private traders, while at the same time struggling with rising customs duties, unstable prices and exchange rates, and dampened demand as a result of exceptionally high unemployment rates. Worst of all, each of these issues seriously threatened to split the Alliance as it struggled to respond to the crisis. The situation forced its members to engage in some profound soul-searching about the meaning of co-operation.

This chapter explores the changing meanings of co-operation during the crisis-ridden years of the 1920s and 1930s, as it was debated in the ICA and among its members. The chapter begins by considering the impact of the First World War and the attempts to adapt co-operation to a post-war world shaped by the ideological cleavages following the Bolshevik Revolution. By the late 1920s the Alliance was in a confident position. It had survived the war and avoided the splits that had fractured the international labour organisations. The Italian co-operative movement had been lost to fascism but the Alliance had expanded elsewhere. After a series of reforms the Alliance's organisational machinery seemed to be functioning smoothly, and in addition to its main committees it had also established an international co-operative wholesale society (the ICWS) and a committee on international banking.[3] The ICA even achieved external recognition through its participation in the League of Nations' World Economic Conference.

What the ICA still lacked, according to its critics, was a clear ideology and a recognisably co-operative programme. The different views about what this should be pushed the Alliance very hard during the interwar years as it struggled to respond to the profound political and economic crises of the early 1930s. Although it lacked a clear statement of co-operative policy, the movement did have a powerful founding myth, namely the story of the Rochdale Pioneers. Article 1 of the Alliance's rules referred to its activities as being 'in continuance of the work of the Rochdale Pioneers', and Rochdale was a common reference point not just in the UK but also internationally.[4] From 1931 the original Toad Lane store in Rochdale was opened as a museum, and came to act as a site of pilgrimage for co-operators from Britain and overseas.[5] The formal enquiry into the Rochdale principles, established by a decision at the Vienna Congress of 1930, was a milestone in the history of the Alliance; its findings would form the basis for a statement of co-operative identity and values that was to endure – with two major revisions – until the present.[6] The enquiry was moreover an attempt to define and establish the Rochdale legacy against rival claims, for example from the leaders of the Nazified co-operative movement in Germany.[7]

The Rochdale enquiry generated controversy, however, and the first attempt to codify the principles was rejected by the International Co-operative Congress of 1934. The problem was that opinions differed widely over how the 'original foundations' of co-operation were to be interpreted, especially what this meant for its relations with other political and social movements. This chapter asks how the ICA responded to the different economic and political crises of the interwar years, and how these responses differed between its members, considering what this also tells us about the balance of power within the ICA. Representatives of the Nordic countries played a prominent role in these debates, arguing vehemently for the co-operative principle of political neutrality against those who would align co-operation with the socialist labour movement.[8]

The debate on co-operative neutrality

Even before 1914 many socialists were confident that consumer co-operatives were gradually evolving closer ties with the labour movement. It was no secret that the European consumer co-operative societies drew much of their membership from working-class communities, and the leadership of local societies often overlapped with that of trade unions and socialist parties. In some cases, like the famous Vooruit co-operative in Ghent and the RACS in south-east London, there were formal agreements between the co-operative society and socialist parties.[9] The Austrian Social Democrats had made it 'quasi-obligatory' for their members to join consumer co-operatives and their Czech counterparts passed a resolution acknowledging the role of co-operation in 1907.[10] There were also examples of affinities between some consumer co-operatives and the labour movement in the Nordic countries.[11]

Supporters of this position were boosted by the Second International's 1910 decision to acknowledge co-operation as part of the class struggle, in a resolution urging trade unions, co-operatives and socialist parties to 'enter into relations more and more intimate with one another'. Co-operation was recognised as the 'third pillar' of the international labour movement, though the resolution added a caveat 'warning the working classes against the theory which maintains that Co-operation is in itself sufficient'.[12] Only a few weeks after the resolution was passed, members of the ICA gathered for their own congress in Hamburg. For some, the endorsement was uncontroversial and a vindication of their position, but others were uneasy.[13] The Swiss co-operator Hans Müller, editor of the *International Co-operative Bulletin*, delivered a paper to the congress, arguing that the co-operative movement could not 'entirely abstain from politics', but should defend its party political neutrality rigorously as it navigated between what he called 'the Scylla of internal dissension and the Charybdis of party-political dependence'.[14] In private correspondence with Hannes Gebhard, he wrote that his resignation from his position as ICA secretary was triggered partly by his differences with the social democrats who he felt were gaining influence within the Alliance.[15]

The experiences of the First World War sharpened the debate about the political affiliations of the co-operative movement. Co-operators were forced to reconsider their traditional stance of autonomy from the state as many societies found themselves incorporated into state schemes for rationing and the distribution of scarce essential goods. Such collaboration was often welcomed, for it boosted membership and was seen as vindication of the standing and importance of co-operation.[16] But it also generated conflict and resentment. For all the signs that co-operators were finding common cause with the labour movement, a snapshot of co-operative political affiliations in the immediate post-war years suggests a divided movement.

In many European states there were rival co-operative organisations, reflecting not only the de facto division of the movement into pro- or anti-socialist camps, but also religious and linguistic differences.[17] In France the division between the politically neutral Union Coopérative (UC) and the Bourses des Coopératives Socialistes (BCS) had been reconciled in 1912, but there were still important local variations.[18] These included, for example, the co-operative community of Saint-Claude in the Jura Mountains and the communist Bellevilloise co-operative in Paris.[19] Britain seemed to present an anomaly, as the only state in which the foundation of an independent Co-operative Party was attempted.[20] The small group of Co-operative Party MPs took the Labour whip in Parliament, but the relationship with the Labour Party quickly became rather strained. The matter was eventually settled at the 1927 Co-operative Congress, which passed a resolution allowing local co-operative parties to affiliate to their divisional Labour party on a voluntary basis.[21] In many places, however, the so-called Cheltenham Agreement was pre-dated by local arrangements, reflecting the enormous diversity within the movement.[22]

As discussed above, the co-operative movements in the Nordic countries were also affected by these divisions, albeit in different ways. The consumer co-operative unions of Sweden and Norway, KF and NKL, avoided a formal split, though opposing views on political affiliation were found here as elsewhere. In Norway a generational shift took place at NKL's 1919 congress, when the union's founder and president O. Dehli gave way to a younger man, Andreas Juell, who had strong ties with the labour movement.[23] Dehli had actually been re-elected to the post of president with 120 votes against 62 for a rival candidate, but he resigned as soon as the votes were declared because he felt the size of the majority against him was too large. In his resignation speech to the congress, Dehli warned his colleagues of the need to elect a leader who would act and think independently, not become 'a puppet' (*en nikkedukke*) for others' opinions, by which he presumably meant the socialist labour movement. Reporting on these events in the movement's journal *Kooperatøren*, the NKL's new secretary, Randolf Arnesen, who was himself sympathetic to the labour cause, was at pains to point out that Dehli's decision to leave was his alone: he had in no way been forced out, and Arnesen suggested therefore that the events at congress did not compromise NKL's political neutrality.[24] Subsequent efforts to commemorate Dehli's achievements underline the wish to promote the idea of historical continuity within the Norwegian co-operative movement.[25]

The situation was more complicated in Finland. Foreign visitors sometimes declared themselves puzzled by the co-existence of two rival consumer co-operative movements. In an account of Finnish co-operation first published in 1929, the Swedish co-operator Thorsten Odhe felt that 'quite incontrovertibly … it may be asserted that there was no serious difference in the conception of the character and objects of co-operative effort'.[26] But ideological differences were never entirely absent. Even before the formal split the designations *edistysmielinen* (progressive) and *puolueeton* (neutral) were being used to describe the rival factions.[27] Both sides used the pages of the co-operative press – from 1916 KK had its own organ, *Kuluttajain Lehti* – to insist on their commitment to the Rochdale principle of political neutrality while simultaneously undermining their rivals' claims to do the same, with references to the 'pseudo-neutral' co-operative movement and the 'so-called "progressive" socialist' co-operative movement, respectively. Reading the rival publications suggests, however, that the differences were probably less those of formal political affiliation, but more of the movement's internal culture and outlook, which in turn reflected the attitudes and social class of the majority of members.

The Finnish co-operative movement was inevitably affected by the civil war which began in January 1918. SOK's Helsinki operations were severely disrupted, first by the general strike and then by sporadic outbreaks of looting and confiscations. But the attempt by the revolutionary government to enforce a takeover of SOK by KK and its new wholesale OTK was resisted by the KK leadership, something that was later acknowledged by SOK.[28] Some societies affiliated to KK sustained material damage in the fighting and they were also badly affected by losses incurred from the receipt of invalid banknotes.[29] Overall, the impression is that more united the leadership of the co-operative movement than divided them in their attitudes to the conflict. Taking stock of the shocking events in the first half of 1918, representatives of both co-operative organisations offered broadly similar interpretations: that the attempt to instigate revolution was misguided, that the conflict was deeply regrettable and that co-operative managers had done their best, in very difficult circumstances, to continue to supply essential goods to their members.[30]

From the second half of 1918 both co-operative unions campaigned energetically to win the affiliation of local societies. The division was to some extent a geographical one, with SOK counting strong support among the small rural societies of Ostrobothnia, for example, and KK-OTK relying on the larger societies of cities such as Turku, Tampere and Vyborg. These divisions were not clear cut, however; neither side could claim to have a monopoly on any particular area. Tensions rose particularly in the struggle for control of the large Helsinki co-operative Elanto, which was frequently cited as one of the largest co-operative societies in the Nordic countries. SOK reacted with dismay to the decision of the Elanto board to affiliate to KK-OTK, suggesting that its management had been taken over by socialists.[31]

An important strategy for both SOK and KK-OTK was the publication of the Swedish-language journals *Samarbete* and *Konsumentbladet*, respectively. In launching *Konsumentbladet* in 1921, KK acknowledged that the majority of societies serving the Swedish-speaking population were affiliated to SOK, but insisted that the 'national' question of language differences had no place within the co-operative movement. The editor of the new paper was scathing of an initiative in 1921 to set up a new co-operative society for the Swedish-speaking parts of Helsinki.[32] Meanwhile, SOK was also facing the possibility that its Swedish-language societies – mainly those based in the western coastal areas – would secede to form their own union. This did indeed happen within the agricultural co-operative movement, but the minority was contained within SOK by the establishment of a Swedish-speaking section at the annual congress.[33] *Samarbete* was thus seen as an extremely important means of communicating with this section of the movement and favoured the Swedish-speaking societies in its editorial policy. The circulation of *Konsumentbladet* was much smaller, reflecting the fact that the majority of

KK's Swedish-speaking members were concentrated in the cities, especially the capital, and that many of them also got their co-operative news from the Finnish language journals.[34] Elanto published its own journal in a bilingual edition, without a separate editorial line.

As noted in chapter 1, however, the Swedish-language journals had another function, namely communication with sister organisations in the rest of the Nordic countries. Both SOK and KK-OTK used their contacts abroad in order to consolidate their legitimacy at home. For KK the challenge was to gain recognition as a legitimate representative of the Finnish co-operative movement, and in 1918 they wrote to all the Scandinavian organisations as well as those in Britain and the ICA to announce their existence.[35] This was followed up with invitations for fraternal delegates to attend the annual congress in 1919 and may also have been influential on the decision to launch *Konsumentbladet*, for in correspondence with KF it was acknowledged that the lack of a Swedish-language journal meant that KK was less well-known abroad than SOK.[36]

In the summer of 1920 the annual congresses of both co-operatives were held in close succession in order to allow foreign guests to attend. SOK issued invitations to all the major European co-operative unions, including those in Scandinavia and Estonia and also the ICA. The congress edition of the SOK journal *Yhteishyvä* carried an address to the foreign guests in English, while KK laid on guided excursions to Elanto facilities.[37] The guests included three from England, two from Sweden and Dehli from Norway, who also represented the ICA and in that capacity wrote up a scrupulously neutral report on both congresses for the *International Co-operative Bulletin*, which also included a full account of the division and the evolution of the two branches of the movement.[38] In 1923 the ICA's general secretary Henry May also attended the two Finnish congresses.[39]

Unlike the Finnish organisations KK and OTK, the new Danish co-operative union, DkF was not formed as a breakaway from the existing union (Andelsudvalget). Instead, the initiative came from the Social Democratic Party's leader Thorvald Stauning and his vision of co-operation as the 'third pillar' of a united labour movement.[40] The first issue of its journal *Kooperationen* carried translated articles by representatives of the more 'social democratic' current of consumer co-operation in Belgium and Austria.[41] Its affiliated societies also retained some contact with the wholesale FDB, though Henning Grelle has suggested that a major source of friction in this relationship was DkF's concern at the over-representation of small but numerous rural societies at FDB congresses, similar to the Finnish case.[42] When DkF applied for ICA membership this caused some confusion, with the ICA pointing out that there was already a Danish member of the Alliance, but DkF's affiliation was confirmed in 1924.[43] There is no evidence from the available ICA sources that DkF members participated actively in ICA meetings – they did not send a representative to the Central Committee, for example – though reports on the ICA were published in *Kooperationen.*

Tsentrosoiuz[44] and the Bolshevik challenge

The main challenge to co-operative political neutrality after the First World War came not from the social democratic labour movements of northern and central Europe, but from what was to become the Soviet Union. Consumer co-operatives were first established in Russia under the Tsarist regime but grew very rapidly after the revolution in February 1917.[45] Their existence challenged Bolshevik ambitions to gain a monopoly on power, but in the chaotic circumstances of 1917–18 they became a vital component in the distribution of food.[46] Following the November revolution, the Bolsheviks therefore began attempts to control the co-operatives and to centralise the distribution of food. The co-operatives fought to maintain their autonomy, but under a series of decrees in the spring and summer of 1919 they were re-organised into consumer communes with compulsory membership.[47] However, it seems reasonable to assume that there were some continuities, especially in the provinces, for as one historian has pointed out the party needed the expertise of co-operative managers.[48]

The wartime disruptions to communications made it very difficult for the ICA's leadership to obtain reliable information about the post-revolutionary situation in Russia and its impact on the co-operative movement.[49] As it prepared to resume its international activities in 1920, however, the Alliance was overtaken by the actions of the British government. In January 1920 Prime Minister David Lloyd George proposed to the Allied Supreme Council in Paris that the Allied trade blockade with Russia should be lifted. Moreover, trading relations were to be resumed through contacts with the Russian co-operative union Tsentrosoiuz, even though one historian has suggested that by then it was 'common knowledge' that it had become a Bolshevik organisation and that this was reflected in the composition of its trade delegation to London.[50] Nonetheless, 15 months of negotiations between the British government and the Russians followed, resulting in an Anglo-Soviet Trade Agreement signed in March 1921.[51]

The decision to lift the blockade was welcomed by the ICA in a resolution agreed at the first post-war meeting of the Central Committee in April 1920.[52] Almost immediately, however, doubts arose about the autonomy of the co-operative organisations in Soviet Russia. Were they truly co-operative, or had they been forcibly incorporated into the Bolshevik state apparatus? Despite these concerns, Tsentrosoiuz's membership of the ICA was confirmed at the international co-operative congress in Basle in the summer of 1921.[53] The apparently substantial majority – 733 votes for and 474 against – concealed significant divisions between the Alliance's all-British Executive and its Central Committee.[54] Only one of the five Tsentrosoiuz delegates had been able to secure a visa to travel to Basle, and she made a speech confirming that Tsentrosoiuz was a bona fide co-operative organisation.[55] Members of the Central Committee were sceptical, however, and proposed deferring the question until further information could be obtained. This was rejected by the Executive, who argued that Tsentrosoiuz should be given full membership rights on the formal constitutional grounds that they had paid their fees and that the composition of their delegation was an internal matter for Russian co-operators alone. This position was upheld by the congress, meaning that a majority of congress delegates voted against the Central Committee, which, as Rhodes notes, was highly unusual for the ICA.[56]

Doubts about the truly co-operative nature of Tsentrosoiuz remained, so in 1922 the ICA's Executive decided to accept an invitation from Tsentrosoiuz to send a delegation to Russia.[57] The Alliance was represented by General Secretary Henry May, joined by a seven-man delegation funded by national co-operative organisations: four of them from Britain, plus E. Poisson and Victor Serwy from France and Belgium, respectively. The delegation travelled to Moscow via Berlin and Riga, and spent a month touring co-operative businesses in different parts of Russia. They returned convinced that Tsentrosoiuz was operating in accordance with accepted co-operative principles. This was accepted by the Central Committee and the status of Tsentrosoiuz as a full member of the ICA was confirmed.[58]

The decision turned out to be a momentous one for the ICA. On the one hand, as Rita Rhodes has commented, it meant that, unlike the socialist and trade union movements, the international co-operative movement avoided a formal split.[59] On the other hand, the decision was to cause a great deal of difficulty; indeed, it is hard to conclude that the Soviet delegates were anything but a veritable thorn in the side of the Alliance throughout the 1920s. At its third congress in 1921 the Comintern adopted its 'Theses on the Work of Communists in the Co-operatives'.[60] This formed part of its 'united workers' front' strategy which aimed to revolutionise workers through the infiltration of trade unions and other working-class organisations, including consumer co-operatives.[61] The Soviet delegates to the ICA attempted to do this through critical interventions in the Alliance's internal debates, especially at congress, but as the 1920s progressed they also adopted obstructive tactics that caused much resentment.[62] Even Henry May, who as ICA General Secretary had defied the Central Committee to argue for the acceptance of Tsentrosoiuz's membership in 1921, later came publicly to regret his decision. Reflecting on his own summary of attacks by Tsentrosoiuz on the Alliance to the Central Committee in 1932, May commented: 'This Report is only a bubble on the surface of what we have had to endure for the past ten years since M. Poisson and I, and others, went to Russia and came back with the deluded idea that co-operation in Russia was voluntary.'[63]

This raises the questions of why the affiliation of Tsentrosoiuz to the ICA was confirmed in 1921 and why it remained a member throughout the interwar period and indeed during the Cold War as well. The matter is of interest, for it is directly concerned with debates about how co-operation was defined as an ideology and a movement. It should be acknowledged that the internal organisation of the Russian co-operative movement – and more broadly the policies of the Communist Party of the Soviet Union and the Comintern towards international organisations like the ICA – was not fixed but was constantly changing throughout the period. During the period of 'War Communism' in particular, some co-operators were prepared to keep an open mind on the changes taking place in Soviet Russia and to overlook the state's control of co-operatives as a temporary measure justified by the extreme circumstances.[64]

There were certainly powerful commercial incentives to cultivate relations with Soviet Russia. In 1923 the English CWS established the Russo-British Grain Export Company as a partnership with Tsentrosoiuz and other British and Soviet organisations. CWS trade with the Soviet Union grew steadily throughout the 1920s and in 1930 accounted for just under 1 per cent of total sales.[65] Other ICA members were also aware of the importance of this trade. 'Russia is the biggest consumer in the world,' declared the Czechoslovak delegate to an international co-operative trade meeting in 1922, arguing that no consumer co-operative federation could afford to ignore its role.[66] Nor could the Russian contribution to the ICA's finances be overlooked. From 1923 the subscriptions of the Soviet co-operative organisations were outweighed only by those from Britain, and in 1928 they were higher, accounting, in theory, for nearly 48 per cent of the Alliance's total receipts in subscriptions.[67]

As noted above, that Tsentrosoiuz paid its subscriptions was cited in 1921 as a reason why Russian delegates should be accredited. But this also presented a problem. As a result of mass collectivisation during the 1920s, the Soviet co-operative movement could claim a membership that far outweighed that of any other ICA member organisation. In 1930 it was reported to have 33.4 million out of a total of 48.2 million members of consumer co-operatives, or nearly 70 per cent of the Alliance's total membership.[68] Notwithstanding the long tradition of British dominance within the ICA, the Executive now became wary of claims for representation on the Alliance's committees in proportion to membership, for that would have given the Soviet delegation a clear majority and the opportunity to steer the Alliance.[69]

In his major study of British left-wing attitudes to Soviet Russia, Kevin Morgan writes that co-operative support was partly attributable to commercial pragmatism, especially in the powerful English CWS, which stood to gain from Soviet trade.[70] But also, he suggests, it reflected a more idealistic world view derived from a vision of co-operation as 'the embryo of a new social order', which seemed to be fulfilled in an idealisation of Soviet Russia. The willingness of the Bolsheviks to develop trade relations through co-operative channels chimed with a co-operative vision of trade as a means to promote international peace.[71] Further, with its 'eradication of all that was tawdry and exploitative in Soviet society', Morgan suggests, co-operators found in the Soviet Union a realisation of their visions of the 'new moral world' of the Co-operative Commonwealth.[72] Certainly, this is the impression gained from Henry May's enthusiastic, even lyrical, accounts of his trip published in the English *Co-operative News*. At the time he seemed to have been overwhelmed by his visit, suggesting that the delegation had returned

> with minds enlarged, sympathies extended and a conception of the possibilities of co-operation hitherto undreamt of ... There is a fellowship to-day amongst the Russian proletariat which is heaven in comparison to the hell which Czarism produced.[73]

These convictions may also attest to the skill of the Bolsheviks in entertaining foreign delegations, even though the ICA visit must be considered a very early example of this type of political tourism.[74]

Morgan writes that these ideas were particularly prevalent among those co-operators who were strongly committed to the movement's political neutrality in the British and French movements, while opposition to the membership of Tsentrosoiuz came from the more social democratic co-operative federations in the ICA.[75] Among the ICA delegates to Russia in 1922, May and Poisson came back convinced, while the Belgian Serwy remained much more sceptical. There is also some evidence to support this view from the accounts of Russian co-operation that were published in the Nordic co-operative journals in the first years after the 1917 revolutions. Several of them carried reprints of a speech by an exiled former member of Tsentrosoiuz to the Swiss co-operative congress, which was hostile to Bolshevism, but they also looked forward to the opportunities to resume trading relations with Soviet Russia.[76] An author 'S. J.' (presumably Severin Jørgensen) in *Andelsbladet*, hardly an organ that might be expected to have a natural sympathy for Bolshevism, suggested in September 1919 that reports of Bolshevik terror were probably over-exaggerated, and praised the emphasis on education as a means in the new regime's ambition to 'bring about more just and better living conditions for the general population and to reject tyranny and oppression from all forms of self-appointed rulers'.[77]

On the other hand, in the Nordic co-operative press the 1921 congress decision was attributed to an anomaly in the ICA rules which gave extra weight to the votes of British delegates.[78] The distribution of votes by delegation was not recorded in the official record, but the Swedish *Kooperatören* reported that most of the national delegations had voted against Tsentrosoiuz, with the exception of the British, the Czechoslovaks and some Italians and French. It also suggested that the Norwegian delegation was divided, though this was not reported in that movement's own journal, *Kooperatøren.*[79] An article in *Kooperatören* by the Swiss co-operator Hans Müller offered a critically pessimistic interpretation of the decision as 'a grave error', motivated partly by CWS commercial opportunism and also attributed to the absence of 'co-operative spirit' at the congress.[80]

Certainly, the co-operative movement was, as Kevin Morgan has shown, an important part of the wider British fascination with Soviet society throughout the interwar period. From 1929 groups of British co-operators undertook annual visits to the USSR, organised by the RACS secretary Joseph Reeves.[81] Even in 1944 the historian of the British movement, G. D. H. Cole, insisted that the collective farms of the Soviet Union could truly be considered co-operatives, on the grounds that the co-operative principle of voluntarism could not be expected to apply in a post-capitalist system.[82] This corresponds to similar views of co-operation as the realisation of the 'co-operative republic' that Morgan finds in the writings of Charles Gide, also a visitor to Soviet co-operation.[83] At the same time, however, the interest in the Soviet Union among British co-operators should not be overstated. Nicole Robertson points out that the radical political engagement found in societies such as RACS was a minority interest for most co-operators. Relatively few individuals were motivated to join a co-operative society for political reasons; they did so instead to purchase goods, to benefit from the dividend and to participate in social activities.[84] A possible exception was the Women's Co-operative Guild, widely recognised as the most politically active wing of the British co-operative movement.[85]

Throughout Europe, co-operative leaders were acutely aware of the threat that Tsentrosoiuz activities within the ICA posed for the unity of their own national movements. But co-operative attitudes to the Soviet Union cannot simply be understood in terms of the ideological divisions between reformists and revolutionaries. Reading between the lines of reports on ICA meetings and congresses suggests that the differences were rather cultural or even emotional. It was a clash between two very different mentalities: the gentle pragmatists in the ICA and the dogmatic revolutionaries of Soviet communism. Geoff Eley has written that the leaders of European social democratic labour parties were uncertain about how to respond to the radicalisation of workers after 1917 and even fearful of the expectations and militancy that the war situation had released.[86] For co-operators this situation was even more challenging. Even where co-operation was closely aligned with labour, it was undoubtedly identified with the respectable, orderly side of labour movement culture. The Bolsheviks' commitment to education, moral improvement and discipline held some appeal, but by the late 1920s this was waning. The ICA sources suggest a palpable exasperation, not with the ideological position of the Soviet representatives but with their tactics of disrupting meetings and their failure to behave according to the recognised ways of conducting co-operative business.[87]

The problem for co-operators was that if co-operation was not part of the revolutionary class struggle, as the Bolsheviks advocated, nor even the 'third pillar' of the social democratic labour movement as it was in Belgium, then what did it stand for? Given the diversity of the movement, especially internationally, political neutrality seemed to be the safest, indeed perhaps the only option for holding a fractious movement together. Yet this also presented a problem: what *did* hold the movement together? Neutrality, as Charles Gide pointed out in 1925, was in danger of becoming a platitude, as he put it: 'an inheritance from the founders to be eternally regarded out of respect for them!'[88] The challenge from Soviet Russia meant that the need for a clear statement of co-operative principle and ideology quickly became one of the most pressing matters on the ICA's agenda, and it was to take on a new urgency against the background of the political and economic crises of the 1930s.

The co-operative response to Nazism and the Rochdale enquiry

The thirteenth congress of the ICA, held in Vienna in the summer of 1930, was a moment of triumph for the international co-operative movement. The congress was the largest yet, its 554 delegates from 35 countries cited as evidence that co-operation was now 'co-extensive with the civilised world'.[89] If delegates wanted any further proof of the achievements of the movement, they could find it in visiting the impressive co-operative stores and housing schemes of 'new Vienna'.[90] The congress was moreover seen as a moment for calm and orderly reflection after the sometimes tumultuous debates of the 1920s. The work of stabilising the Alliance's finances and internal organisation was now considered to be more or less complete and, as a follow-up to the successful Stockholm congress of 1927, it was anticipated that the main item on the agenda would be the agreement of a co-operative programme and its implementation in practice.[91]

There was, however, some hint of the difficulties to come, when it was announced that the special committee working on the ICA's economic programme had been unable to reach agreement in time to present its report to congress.[92] Only one year later the Alliance's Executive Committee found itself working late into the night to try to draft an emergency response to the unfolding economic crisis.[93] By 1932 the problem of internal finances had resurfaced, as the British decision to leave the gold standard devalued subscriptions that were traditionally paid in sterling.[94] And in the spring of 1933 the Executive took the unprecedented decision to postpone the London congress planned for later that year, partly on account of the economic difficulties faced by many of its members.[95]

The cancellation of the congress was greeted with dismay by some members of the Alliance, so it was agreed to convene a special conference to discuss the economic crisis.[96] However, by the time this was held the economic crisis had also become a political one that engulfed the Alliance in a serious and damaging controversy and even threatened to split it permanently. Hitler's rise to power in January 1933 had immediate and devastating consequences for many aspects of social organisation in Germany, but the situation of the co-operative movement remained ambivalent during the first half of that year. Writing in the April edition of *Review of International Co-operation*, Henry May concluded that the German co-operatives were holding their own against the new regime, but his visit to Hamburg on behalf of the ICA the following month confirmed growing fears that the movement was losing its autonomy.[97] Nonetheless, when the matter was discussed at its May meeting, the Executive decided to keep an open mind in light of assurances from their German colleagues that they were doing their best to maintain co-operative principles.[98]

Matters came to a head in June 1933 when a hastily convened special conference was held in Basle. The last-minute announcement that the Germans would be sending a delegation, in spite of earlier indications to the contrary, threw the Executive into some confusion. Should the German delegates be accredited, out of loyalty 'to our German friends whom we have known for so many years and have worked with', in the words of British co-operator Thomas Allen? Or would the Alliance risk compromising its political neutrality by admitting representatives of an openly Nazi organisation? Despite vociferous opposition from some delegates, the Germans were allowed to attend. But as the special conference opened, the worst fears of those who had opposed the decision were realised when the leader of the German delegation took the opportunity to deliver a long speech on Nazism. This led to angry exchanges at a hotel the following evening, and the early departure of the Germans before the conclusion of the conference.[99]

The events in Basle convinced Henry May, at least, that the German co-operative movement was lost to the Alliance. In his closing remarks to the conference he referred to 'the most extraordinary attack' made by the German delegation, and his sense of hurt and outrage that the Germans had abused the goodwill shown towards them was expressed in print in his report of the events in the July edition of *Review of International Co-operation*.[100] Developments over the summer, followed through the pages of the German co-operative journal *Konsumgenossenschaftliche Rundschau*, confirmed for many the continued slide of the German co-operative movement towards full Nazification.[101] When the new German organisation applied formally for ICA membership the Executive was forced to consider the matter again. The compromise eventually agreed was that a committee should be established to monitor the situation further. By the time of the next meeting in January 1934, however, relations had irrevocably broken down, and it was agreed that the new German organisation would not be admitted to membership.[102]

It is safe to assume that most if not all co-operators were instinctively opposed to Nazism, but it is also striking that most of those speaking in the debates on the matter expressed their antipathy towards events in Germany in terms of sadness. These attitudes were partly shaped by the close personal connections between the relatively small group of men and one woman who made up the ICA's Executive. The initial reassurances about the integrity of the German co-operatives under the Nazi regime came from Klepzig, who had served on the Executive for several years.[103] The ambivalence of Albin Johansson and Väinö Tanner towards expelling the Germans – both visited the leaders of the German co-operatives during the summer and autumn of 1933 and Tanner in particular continued to express his hope that channels of communication could be kept open for the resumption of relations after the defeat of Nazism – can perhaps be traced to the close connections both men had with the German movement and especially with Heinrich Kaufmann. As a youth, Tanner had done a stint working in the German wholesale in Hamburg.[104] In a last attempt to help save the German movement from Nazism he stopped in that city on his way from Finland to an ICA meeting in Vienna, and his comments to the meeting of the Executive suggest his personal sadness at the loss of German co-operation.[105]

A problem for the ICA was that the absence of a clear programmatic statement of co-operation made it difficult to oppose German membership on the basis of co-operative principle. Speaking on behalf of KF, Anders Hedberg suggested that 'we should maintain our political neutrality above all, and we should avoid laying ourselves open to blame for flirting with Russia while rejecting Germany'.[106] 'We must be prudent so that we do not become an auxiliary of the Second International,' the French co-operator Poisson told the Executive, suggesting that if this did happen it would probably lead to organisations in Scandinavia, Switzerland and Hungary seceding.[107]

For others, the intolerable situation was a reminder of how urgent it was for the Alliance to agree on its fundamental principles. Taking stock of the state of the ICA in the *Review of International Co-operation* in the autumn of 1933, May reflected: 'We have rather drifted with the tide'.[108] His statements and writings during 1933 and after reveal his growing impatience with those arguing for a more cautious and pragmatic line. 'Political neutrality is not political impotence', he had argued in a lecture to the International Co-operative School in 1932, 'but the reservation of political activities to the defence of our transcending economic aims without regard to party or the vagaries of political conflict.'[109] The crises of the early 1930s seem to have convinced him beyond doubt that this could legitimately take co-operation into the realm of campaigns for peace, free trade and anti-fascism, provided that this did not imply formal affiliation with a political party.

This was then the context for the special committee on the Rochdale principles, which began its work in 1932.[110] The General Secretary produced a memorandum on the historical principles and the affiliated members were asked for their opinions on these via a questionnaire. The problem for the committee was that although Rochdale held a powerful emotional appeal it was difficult to find a definitive statement of what Rochdale co-operation actually meant. 'I do not know what you will accept as authoritative in this matter because there is no charter laid down which covers all the ground,' May warned the meeting that asked him to prepare the report.[111] Lecturing to the International Co-operative Summer School in 1932, he noted the quasi-religious appeal of the word 'Rochdale':

> You cannot more grievously offend the Co-operators of any country than by charging them with ignorance of, or disloyalty to, the Rochdale Principles. They will acknowledge the most extraordinary divergences in their practice but still claim that their title is clear to a place in the apostolic succession.[112]

Nonetheless, he did his best to produce a historically authentic account of the Rochdale Principles, citing extensively from the original Rochdale sources and also visiting the recently opened Toad Lane museum, where he interviewed both a former secretary of the society and the daughter of one of the original Pioneers.[113]

The seven principles of co-operation agreed by the special committee were presented to the London congress of the ICA in 1934.[114] The first four principles – open membership, democratic control, dividends in proportion to patronage, limited interest on capital – were thought to be uncontroversial and practised by the vast majority of co-operative societies. Problems arose over the fifth principle declaring the political neutrality of co-operation. Predictably, the Soviet Union's delegation moved to replace this with a commitment to international proletarian solidarity.[115] But the great surprise came when the British delegation also rejected two of the principles: on political neutrality and on cash trading. The debate had to be adjourned until the following day, when delegates agreed to a proposal from the Swedish delegate Axel Gjöres to refer the whole report back for further consideration.[116]

The British intervention came as a shock, generating profound disappointment and even anger among those who had worked on producing the report.[117] The ICA sources do not indicate the internal debates within the British delegation, but their position was doubtless reflective of the great controversy that political activities had generated within the British movement and it is possible therefore that it was motivated by an attempt to use the international forum as an intervention in this debate. A compromise was eventually agreed, but not before the matter had generated a bitter row at a meeting of the ICA's Executive.[118] Eventually, the Central Committee agreed to divide the seven principles into four fundamentals of co-operation, which would be inserted into the Alliance's statutes, and three 'methods of action' – political neutrality, cash trading and education – which would not be compulsory for members. The ICA itself would remain politically neutral, meaning that it would avoid alignment with any political party, but its members could do as they wished.[119] This was put to the Paris congress of 1937, where it was accepted.[120]

Political neutrality and the Nordic line

The agreement of the Rochdale principles was undoubtedly a milestone in the history of the ICA, but the debate surrounding their adoption was further evidence of the depth of the divisions within the Alliance and of its shifting internal geography. The formal fault line was the question of political neutrality, but the divisions went deeper than this. For the representatives of the 'social democratic' bloc – including Britain, Belgium, Austria and Czechoslovakia – co-operation was a working-class movement aspiring to challenge the capitalist system of trade and exchange. In central Europe this position was sharpened during the 1930s by open conflict with representatives of private trade.[121] Against this group stood the advocates of neutrality, who insisted that co-operation was a movement defined by its business principles alone. During the 1930s the representatives of the Nordic organisations became increasingly forthright in stating this position, and there is evidence that they were acting more and more openly as a bloc in doing this. According to a report in *Andelsbladet*, special meetings of Nordic delegations were held at ICA congresses from 1930 onwards.[122]

In fact, as the representatives of the Nordic organisations often pointed out, their unease with the direction taken by the ICA went back to the early post-war period. Andelsudvalget was not represented among the co-operative organisations from other neutral countries at the Paris conference of 1919, on the grounds that the French decision not to invite delegates from the central powers, while understandable, was incompatible with the neutrality of the Danish state.[123] Although representatives of Finland were present, there was some unease about the co-operative programme agreed there, and in January 1920 the leadership of Pellervo and SOK submitted a joint memorandum expressing these reservations. Although there is no evidence that the Danish and Finnish organisations co-ordinated their statements, their positions were similar. Both were wary of what SOK called 'the permeating idea' that the Alliance was becoming increasingly dominated by consumer societies, thus ignoring the interests of farmers. Both were also adamant that the ICA should avoid engaging in what they perceived as 'non-co-operative matters', namely the adoption of an official stance in response to international questions such as free trade, the occupation of the Ruhr and the reconstruction of war-torn regions.[124]

In response to these criticisms, and in the wake of the resolution affirming the ICA's neutrality agreed at the Ghent congress in 1924, which was publicly supported by the Danish delegation, the Executive agreed to convene a special meeting with representatives of the Nordic organisations.[125] The meeting, which took place in Stockholm in June 1925, was hosted by KF who also took it upon themselves to make the arrangements. They invited not only their Finnish and Danish colleagues but also representatives of Norway and the three Baltic countries.[126] Anders Örne drafted a memorandum in preparation for the meeting, as did A. Axelsen Drejer; SOK stuck by their statement from 1920. The meeting heard statements from representatives of all the organisations present (Andelsudvalget, SOK, KK and the Estonian co-operative union) and agreed that the concerns raised would be forwarded to the Central Committee for consideration.[127]

The available sources – correspondence about the arrangement of the meeting, the minutes of the meeting itself and reports afterwards in the co-operative press – give little sense of how serious this rift was and how it was eventually smoothed over. That the meeting was convened at all gives some idea of the importance of this matter, however, though one must suspect that the informal and off-the-record part of the meeting, among a relatively small group of individuals, was probably equally as important as the minuted business. Nonetheless, the 1925 meeting is interesting not only as evidence for the emergence of a north European caucus within the ICA but also for the extent to which the Swedes had assumed leadership of this. Their initiative gives some indication of the strength and confidence of KF and its leadership at this juncture, even to the extent of pledging themselves to increase their financial contributions to develop the Alliance in the direction they wished.

Conclusion: what was co-operation?

It seems likely that the growing gulf between May and 'those who wished to transform co-operation into a matter of facts and figures', as noted by Victor Serwy in an eulogy written just after May's death in 1939, referred to the Nordic countries.[128] By the mid-1930s the existence of a Nordic caucus within the ICA was an acknowledged fact, both externally and among the representatives of the countries themselves. The loss of first the German and then the Austrian consumer co-operatives, as well as the financial difficulties experienced by both the French and the Belgian federations in the 1930s, helped to produce a notable shift in the centre of gravity of the Alliance towards northern Europe.

This was reflected in the decision to hold two of the ICA's regular meetings in Helsinki during the late 1930s. Even so, the continued support of the Nordic co-operatives could not be taken for granted, and enthusiasm for membership was often lukewarm at best, especially among those parts of the movement more associated with agricultural interests, namely Andelsudvalget and the Finnish 'neutral' co-operatives. The threat of secession and further splits in the Alliance meant that Henry May went to the trouble of making a special tour of the Nordic region in the summer of 1933 to negotiate directly with these organisations.[129]

It must be acknowledged of course that this discussion of the meanings of co-operation has focused almost exclusively on the debates that took place among a relatively small group of co-operators, many of whom it can be assumed knew each other personally. These matters were also communicated, reported and debated in the pages of co-operative journals, both the ICA's own journal *International Co-operative Bulletin/Review of International Co-operation*, which was published in three languages, and in the national co-operative press. But it is still extremely difficult to ascertain what the implications of these debates were for the members who shopped in co-operative stores. Some of them doubtless read the journals and some may have also participated in regular meetings, either at their local society or, for a relatively small number, at national congresses. Ultimately, however, co-operation was about the goods that were bought in the co-operative store and it is to international co-operative trade that the next chapter turns.

Notes

1 '"Bland oss råder en beslutsam anda". Hälsningstal, som IKA:s president häradshövding Väinö Tanner höll på kooperativa världskongressen i London den 4 september', *Elanto*, 28 September 1934; also: Työväen arkisto, Helsinki (hereafter TA): 92 Väinö Tannerin osuustoimintaa kosk. puheita ja artikkeleita 1928–61: opening address to fourteenth ICA congress, September 1934.

2 J. Brazda, F. Jagschitz, S. Rom and R. Schediwy, 'The rise and fall of Austria's consumer co-operatives', in M. Hilson, S. Neunsinger and G. Patmore (eds), *A Global History of Consumer Co-operation since 1850: Movements and Businesses* (Leiden: Brill, 2017), pp. 281–4; R. Rhodes, *The International Co-operative Alliance during War and Peace 1910–1950* (Geneva: ICA, 1995), pp. 178–92.

3 On the ICWS, see chapter 4.

4 G. J. D. C. Goedhart, 'Report on the Revision of the Rules of the International Co-operative Alliance', in *Report of the Proceedings of Tenth Congress of the International Co-operative Alliance, held at Basle, 22–25 August 1921* (hereafter *ICA Congress Proceedings 1921*) (London: ICA, 1921), p. 72.

5 TA: HNA 14 Keskusosuusliike OTK: Ulkomaiset osuuskunnat: Co-operative Union to OTK, 3 March 1931. The centenary of the Rochdale Pioneers in 1944

was marked by the production of a film, *Men of Rochdale*, by the CWS film unit; see: A. Burton, *The People's Cinema: Film and the Co-operative Movement* (London: National Film Theatre, 1994), pp. 30–1.

6 International Co-operative Alliance, 'Co-operative Identity, Values and Principles', available at http://ica.coop/en/whats-co-op/co-operative-identity-values-principles, last accessed 3 February 2017.

7 TA: 334.5 Kansainvälinen Osuustoimintaliitto (KOL), Box 6: Report on proceedings of ICA Executive meeting, Basle, 8 June 1933.

8 See: M. Hilson, 'A Consumers' International? The International Cooperative Alliance and Cooperative Internationalism, 1918–1939: A Nordic Perspective', *International Review of Social History*, 56 (2011), 203–33.

9 H. Defoort, 'The Strongest Socialist Party in the World? The Influence of Belgian Social Democracy in International Socialism prior to 1914 as a Means to Study the Relations between Socialism and Co-operation', in P. Verbruggen and L. Soubry (eds), *Consumerism versus Capitalism? Co-operatives seen from an International Comparative Perspective* (Ghent: Amsab-Institute of Social History, 2003); P. Scholliers, 'The Social Democratic World of Consumption: The Path-Breaking Case of the Ghent Cooperative Vooruit Prior to 1914', *International Labor and Working-Class History*, 55 (1999), 71–91; R. Rhodes, *An Arsenal for Labour: The Royal Arsenal Co-operative Society and Politics 1896–1996* (Manchester: Holyoake Books, 1998).

10 On Austria, see: J. Brazda and R. Schediwy, 'Consumer Co-operatives on the Defensive: A Short Overview', in J. Brazda and R. Schediwy, *A Time of Crises: Consumer Co-operatives and Their Problems Around 1990* (Vienna: Fachbereichs für Genossenschaftswesen, 2011), p. 16, available at https://genos.univie.ac.at/fileadmin/user_upload/genossenschaftswesen/Genos/consum.pdf, accessed 3 February 2017. On the Czech social democrats, see: A. Reich, 'Economic Interests and National Conflict: The Relationship between Czech and German Consumer Cooperatives in Czechoslovakia between 1918 and 1939', in T. Lorenz (ed.), *Cooperatives in Ethnic Conflicts: Eastern Europe in the 19th and Early 20th Century* (Berlin: Berliner Wissenschafts-Verlag, 2006), p. 264.

11 See chapter 1.

12 'Co-operative News Items: The International Socialist Congress at Copenhagen', *International Co-operative Bulletin*, 1 October 1910, pp. 158–9.

13 'International Co-operative Alliance: The Eighth International Co-operative Congress as Reviewed by the Co-operative Press', *International Co-operative Bulletin*, 5 November 1910, pp. 165–70.

14 H. Müller, 'Development of Co-operative Distribution – Present and Future', in *Report of the Proceedings of the Eighth Congress of the International Co-operative Alliance, held at Hamburg, 5–7 September 1910* (London: ICA, 1911), pp. 87–91.

15 Müller wrote to Gebhard in November 1910, stating: 'It cannot have escaped your notice, that the social democratic tendency has also gained considerable influence over the leadership of the ICA. You will also understand that I am not exactly favoured by these gentlemen, because of the critical position I have taken towards social democracy.' ('Es kann Ihnen nicht verborgen geblieben sein, dass auch

im Vorstand des I.G.B. die sozial-demokratische Richtung bedeutend an Einfluss gewonnen hat. Sie werden auch begreifen, dass ich bei diesen Herren nicht persona grata bin wegen der kritischen Stellung, die ich der Sozial-Demokratie gegenüber einnehme.') Kansallisarkisto, Helsinki (hereafter KA): Hannes Gebhardin arkisto: saapuneet kirjasto I: 1882–1932: Hans Müller to Hannes Gebhard, 29 November 1910.

16 E. Furlough, *Consumer Co-operation in France: The Politics of Consumption 1834–1930* (Ithaca: Cornell University Press, 1991), p. 252; J. Earle, *The Italian Co-operative Movement: A Portrait of the Lega Nazionale delle Cooperative e Mutue* (London: Allen & Unwin, 1986), p. 18.

17 See, for example, on Czechoslovakia: Reich, 'Economic Interests'; on Germany: B. Fairbairn, 'The Rise and Fall of Consumer Cooperation in Germany', in E. Furlough and C. Strikwerda (eds), *Consumers against Capitalism? Consumer Cooperation in Europe, North America, and Japan, 1840–1990* (Lanham: Rowman and Littlefield, 1999), pp. 282–6; see also chapter 1 for the rival unions in Finland and Denmark.

18 Furlough, *Consumer Co-operation in France*, pp. 244–5, 250.

19 On the Bellevilloise, see: Furlough, *Consumer Co-operation in France*, pp. 288–9; on the 'École de Saint-Claude', see: S. Lambersens et al., 'History of Consumer Co-operatives in France: from the Conquest of Consumption by the Masses to the Challenge of Mass Consumption', in Hilson, Neunsinger and Patmore (eds), *Global History*, pp. 102–3.

20 For a summary of the debate on the formation of the Co-operative Party, see: M. Hilson, 'Consumers and Politics: The Co-operative Movement in Plymouth, 1890–1920', *Labour History Review*, 67:1 (2002), 7–27.

21 T. F. Carbery, *Consumers in Politics: A History and General Review of the Co-operative Party* (Manchester: Manchester University Press, 1969), pp. 26–32.

22 K. Manton, 'The Labour Party and the Co-op, 1918–58', *Historical Research*, 82 (2009), 756–78: 769–70; see also: N. Robertson, 'The Political Dividend: Co-operative Parties in the Midlands, 1917–1939', in M. Worley (ed.), *Labour's Grass Roots: Essays on the Activities of Local Labour Parties and Members, 1918–1945* (Aldershot: Ashgate, 2005); N. Robertson, *The Co-operative Movement and Communities in Britain 1914–1960: Minding Their Own Business* (Farnham: Ashgate, 2010), pp. 167–74; Hilson, 'Consumers and Politics'; M. Hilson, 'Co-operation and Consumer Politics in Comparative Perspective: Britain and Sweden during the First World War', in P. Verbruggen and L. Soubry (eds), *Consumerism versus Capitalism? Co-operatives Seen from an International Comparative Perspective* (Ghent: Amsab-Institute of Social History, 2003).

23 E. Lange (ed.), *Organisert kjøpekraft: Forbrukersamvirkets historie i Norge* (Oslo: Pax forlag, 2006), pp. 166–8.

24 'Formandsskifte i landsforeningen', *Kooperatøren*, July-August 1919, pp. 49–50.

25 'Advokat Dehlis plass', *Kooperatøren*, 24, 1934, p. 276; 'La oss reise advokat Dehli et monument på Advokat Dehlis plass', *Kooperatøren*, 3, 1936, pp. 33–4.

26 T. Odhe, *Finland: A Nation of Co-operators*, trans. J. Downie (London: Williams & Norgate, 1931), p. 47.

27 Aaltonen, *Finlands konsumenter i samarbete*, trans. S. Malmström (Helsinki: KK, 1954), p. 100.

28 'Den finske kooperation under borgerkrigen', *Kooperatøren*, August-September 1918, pp. 69–71 (reprint of interview given by SOK leader Emil Stavenhagen to *Konsumentbladet* (Sweden)).

29 'Finland', *Kooperatøren*, April-May 1919, pp. 27–9.

30 J. Sahlbom, 'Orsak och verkan. Tankar i anledning av revolutionen', *Samarbete*, 12 June 1918; 'Finska Centrallaget under inbördeskriget', *Kooperatören*, June 1918, pp. 116–23; 'Diktatuuriaika ja edistysmielinen osuuskauppaliike', *Kuluttajain Lehti*, 31 May 1918; 'Den finske kooperation under borgerkrigen', *Kooperatøren*, August-September 1918, pp. 69–71; 'Finland', *Kooperatøren*, April-May 1919, pp. 27–9; E. Linna, 'Fifteen years' progress of SOK', *International Co-operative Bulletin*, May 1919, pp. 81–3.

31 'Med anledning av Elantos höststämma', *Samarbete*, 10 November 1917.

32 'Till läsaren', *Konsumentbladet*, 29 January 1921; 'Ett nationalistiskt splittringshandelslag i Helsingfors', *Konsumentbladet*, 31 March 1921.

33 'Handelslagsrörelsen i svenska Finland', *Samarbete*, 24 January 1917; 'Några ord i frågan om grundandet av ett nytt centrallag för de svenska handelslagen', *Samarbete*, 7 February 1917; 'Till de svenska handelsandelslagen i Finland', *Samarbete*, 7 March 1917; 'Frågan om representationsmötenas avhållande i två sektioner', *Samarbete*, 11 May 1917; 'Handelslagens representantmöte', *Samarbete*, 16 June 1917. See also: B. Wallén, *Enighet ger styrka. Finlands Svenska Andelsförbund 80 år* (Helsinki: Finlands Svenska Andelsförbund, 1999).

34 'Till läsaren', *Konsumentbladet*, 29 January 1921; *Konsumentbladet*, 15 January 1926.

35 TA: HNA 14 Keskusosuusliike OTK: Ulkomaiset osuuskunnat: KK to Anders Örne (KF), 12 April 1917; KK to KF, NKL, FDB, n.d. 1918; KK to Co-operative Union, CWS, SCWS and ICA, 25 June 1918.

36 TA: HNA 14 Keskusosuusliike OTK: KK to KF, 9 May 1919.

37 'YOL:n 18:s edistajakokous', *Yhteishyvä*, 2 July 1920.

38 O. Dehli, 'The Finnish Congresses', *International Co-operative Bulletin*, September 1920, pp. 264–8.

39 H. May, 'My Visit to Finland', *International Co-operative Bulletin*, September 1923, pp. 218–22; October 1923, pp. 249–51.

40 H. Grelle, *Det kooperative alternativ: Arbejderkooperationen i Danmark 1852–2012* (Copenhagen: Arbejdermuseet/ABA, 2012), p. 129–31.

41 K. Renner, 'Kooperation og Sosialisering'; O. Pedersen, 'Klassekamp og Kooperation'; V. Serwy, 'Kooperation og Politik i Belgien', all in *Kooperationen*, September 1923, pp. 18–20, 43–6, 59–62.

42 Grelle, *Det kooperative alternativ*, pp. 148–9.

43 Arbejderbevægelsens bibliotek og arkiv, Copenhagen: Det kooperative Fællesforbund, 1129: Div. Korrespondance, modtagne breve, internationale 1922–26: ICA (May) to DKF, 28 December 1922; 8 January 1923. *Kooperationen*, March 1924, pp. 106–7.

44 In the English-language ICA sources the name of this organisation was usually spelled Centrosoyus. The spelling used here reflects Library of Congress convention for transcription from the Russian.

45 C. Salzman, 'Consumer Cooperative Societies in Russia, Goals v. Gains, 1900–1918', *Cahiers du Monde russe et soviétique*, 23:3–4 (1982), 351–69: 352; S. V. Veselov, 'The Cooperative Movement and Soviet Rule: The Period of "War Communism"', *Russian Studies in History*, 33:1 (1994), 52–71: 53; O. Figes, *A People's Tragedy: The Russian Revolution 1891–1924* (New York: Penguin Books, 1997; first published 1996), p. 612; M. Borrero, *Hungry Moscow: Scarcity and Urban Society in the Russian Civil War, 1917–1921* (New York: Peter Lang, 2003), pp. 36–9.

46 Borrero, *Hungry Moscow*, pp. 44–7.

47 Borrero, *Hungry Moscow*, pp. 46–50; Veselov, 'Cooperative Movement', 61–2.

48 D. J. Raleigh, *Experiencing Russia's Civil War: Politics, Society and Revolutionary Culture in Saratov, 1917–1922* (Princeton: Princeton University Press, 2002), pp. 300–1.

49 W. P. Watkins, *The International Co-operative Alliance 1895–1970* (London: ICA, 1970), p. 117.

50 M. V. Glenny, 'The Anglo-Soviet Trade Agreement, March 1921', *Journal of Contemporary History*, 5:2 (1970), 63–82: 65; K. Morgan, *The Webbs and Soviet Communism* (London: Lawrence & Wishart, 2006), pp. 191–2.

51 For an account of the negotiations, see: Glenny, 'Anglo-Soviet Trade Agreement'.

52 'The Geneva Meetings', *International Co-operative Bulletin*, April-May 1920, pp. 109–13; see also: Rhodes, *International Co-operative Alliance*, pp. 100–1.

53 The debate on the membership of Tsentrosoiuz is discussed in Rhodes, *International Co-operative Alliance*, pp. 100–16.

54 'Report on the Work of the International Co-operative Alliance since the Glasgow Congress', *ICA Congress Proceedings 1921*, pp. 27–55; see also: Rhodes, *International Co-operative Alliance*, p. 108. Swedish *Kooperatören* reported 733 votes for and only 269 against: 'Vår international: kongressen i Basel', *Kooperatören*, September 1921, p. 286.

55 *ICA Congress Proceedings 1921*, pp. 51ff.

56 Rhodes, *International Co-operative Alliance*, p. 108.

57 Rhodes, *International Co-operative Alliance*, pp. 114–16.

58 TA: 334.5 KOL, Box 0.1: Minutes of ICA Executive meeting, Milan, 9–10 April 1922; minutes of ICA Central Committee meeting, Milan, 10–11 April 1922; also: F. D. R., 'Det internationale Andelsforbunds Delegation til Rusland', *Andelsbladet*, 21 April 1922, pp. 402–4, which reprinted Poisson's account of the delegation's visit from the French co-operative journal *L'action cooperative.*

59 Rhodes, *International Co-operative Alliance*, p. 3.

60 J. Riddell (ed.), *To the Masses: Proceedings of the Third Congress of the Communist International, 1921* (Leiden: Brill, 2015), pp. 42; 809; 966–9; see also: Furlough, *Consumer Co-operation in France*, pp. 286–7.

61 K. McDermott and J. Agnew, *The Comintern: A History of International Communism from Lenin to Stalin* (Basingstoke: Macmillan Press, 1996), pp. 27, 47.

62 For complaints about this, see: H. J. May, 'Soviet Co-operation and the ICA', *International Co-operative Bulletin*, December 1927, pp. 369–72; 'Russerne og Det internationale Andelsforbund', *Andelsbladet*, 16 March 1928, pp. 308–12. See also chapter 2.

63 TA: 334.5 KOL, Box 2: Report on proceedings of ICA Central Committee meeting, Geneva, 30–31 October 1932.

64 For example: 'Det høie raad og kooperationen i Rusland', *Kooperatøren*, March 1920, pp. 13–14. It should be noted that the Norwegian Labour Party, to which many co-operators were also affiliated, had joined the Comintern in 1919, though the Norwegian co-operative movement remained formally neutral.

65 J. F. Wilson, A. Webster and R. Vorberg-Rugh, *Building Co-operation: A Business History of the Co-operative Group, 1863–2013* (Oxford: Oxford University Press, 2013), pp. 181–5, table 5.2.

66 Kooperativa Förbundets arkiv, Stockholm (hereafter KF): ICWS 1919–25: Minutes of meeting of ICWS, Milan, 12 April 1922.

67 Annual subscriptions by member state were recorded in appendices to the congress proceedings. Until 1926 separate contributions were listed for Russia, Armenia and Ukraine (from 1919), Georgia (from 1920), Azerbaidjan (from 1924) and White Russia (from 1926). From 1927 these were all included under the USSR (see table 2.1). The USSR subscriptions are recorded in the congress proceedings throughout the 1930s, but reports of ICA Executive meetings indicate that their payment was severely in arrears during the period 1930–33, causing financial problems for the Alliance.

68 H. J. M., 'The International Co-operative Alliance in 1930', *Review of International Co-operation*, February 1931.

69 TA: 334.5 KOL, Box 0.7: Report on proceedings of ICA Central Committee meeting, Vienna, 24 August 1930. Some members proposed that the Soviet Union's subscriptions should be capped to avoid this problem.

70 Morgan, *The Webbs*, pp. 192–3. For CWS trade with Russia and the Soviet Union, see: Wilson, Webster and Vorberg-Rugh, *Building Co-operation*, pp. 184–5.

71 Morgan, *The Webbs*, pp. 183–93. Co-operative ideas about trade and peace are discussed further in chapter 4.

72 Morgan, *The Webbs*, pp. 190–201.

73 H. J. May, 'The Return from Moscow', *Co-operative News*, 1 April 1922. May's detailed account of the delegation's visit was published in the *Co-operative News* in several instalments in April and May 1922.

74 On the interwar 'pilgrimage to Russia', see: M. David-Fox, *Showcasing the Great Experiment: Cultural Diplomacy and Western Visitors to the Soviet Union 1921–1941* (Oxford: Oxford University Press, 2012).

75 Morgan, *The Webbs*, pp. 186–7.

76 A. Gjöres, 'Kooperationen i Ryssland. En redogörelse för dess gestaltning och utveckling', *Kooperatören*, October 1918, pp. 200–11; 'Fra Udlandet: Bolschevismen og Andelsbevægelsen', *Andelsbladet*, 31 January 1919, p. 72; 'Den ryska

kooperationen under sovjetregimen', *Kooperatören*, July 1920, pp. 109–10, also reprinted in *Kooperatøren*, October 1920, pp. 103–4.

77 'Bolschevikernes Mening er dog at søge at faa tilvejebragt retfærdigere og forbedrede Livsvilkaar for den store Befolkning og afkaste al Tyranni og Undertrykkelse fra selvbestaltede Magthavere i enhver Skikkelse.' S. J., 'Bliver Brugsforeningerne i Rusland den russiske Befolknings Redning?', *Andelsbladet*, 19 September 1919, p. 761.

78 See also: Rhodes, *International Co-operative Alliance*, p. 108.

79 'Vår international: kongressen i Basel', *Kooperatören*, September 1921, pp. 284–8; 'Den internationale kooperative kongres i Basel', *Kooperatøren*, September 1921, pp. 70–5.

80 H. Müller, 'Kring Baselkongressen', *Kooperatören*, November 1921, pp. 341–7.

81 Morgan, *The Webbs*, p. 200.

82 Cole wrote that he had 'always failed to see how those who look forward to the "Co-operative Commonwealth", in which presumably Co-operation will have become universal, can regard voluntary membership as essential to true Co-operation irrespective of the character of the State system – however essential it may be to preserve its voluntary basis as long as it is growing up inside a capitalist social system'. G. D. H. Cole, *A Century of Co-operation* (Manchester: Co-operative Union, 1944), p. 354.

83 Morgan, *The Webbs*, pp. 197–8.

84 Robertson, *Co-operative Movement.*

85 On the Women's Co-operative Guild in the interwar period, see: G. Scott, *Feminism and the Politics of Working Women: The Women's Co-operative Guild 1880s to the Second World War* (London: UCL Press, 1998).

86 G. Eley, *Forging Democracy: The History of the Left in Europe, 1850–2000* (Oxford: Oxford University Press, 2002), pp. 225–9.

87 One delegate remarked at a meeting in 1932 that the absence of the Soviet delegates meant that, for once, they had been able to get through the agenda of the meeting. TA: 334.5 KOL, Box 2: Report on proceedings of ICA Central Committee meeting, Geneva, 30–31 October 1932.

88 KF: CC Protokoll och bilagor, 1920–1957: Report on proceedings of meeting of Central Committee, Paris, October 1925.

89 H. J. M., 'The Vienna Congress', *Review of International Co-operation*, August 1930, pp. 281–3; H. J. M., 'The International Co-operative Alliance in 1930', *Review of International Co-operation*, February 1931, pp. 41–7.

90 'Internasjonal kooperasjon', *Kooperatøren*, 18, 1930, pp. 205–7. These developments were noted by Dr Renner in his speech welcoming delegates to congress, reported in 'Trettonde internationella kooperativa kongressen i Wien', *Kooperatören*, October-November 1930, pp. 264–85.

91 V. Tanner, 'Into Clearer Water', *Review of International Co-operation*, August 1930, pp. 283–5; H. J. M., 'The Vienna Congress', *Review of International Co-operation*, August 1930, pp. 281–3.

92 TA: 334.5 KOL, Box 0.7: Report on proceedings of ICA Central Committee meeting, Leipzig, 27 March 1930; 'Trettonde internationella kooperativa kongressen i Wien',

Kooperatören, October-November 1930, pp. 264–85; H. J. May, 'International Co-operation and the World Crisis', *Review of International Co-operation*, January 1932, pp. 4–11.

93 TA: 334.5 KOL, Box 1: Report on proceedings of ICA Executive meeting, Paris, 27–28 September 1931.

94 H. J. May, 'International Co-operation and the World Crisis', *Review of International Co-operation*, January 1932, p. 6; TA: 334.5 KOL, Box 3: Report on proceedings of ICA Executive meeting, Prague, 29–30 June 1932.

95 TA: 334.5 KOL, Box 5: Report on proceedings of ICA Executive meeting, Barcelona, 12–13 February 1933; May to Tanner, 18 February 1933.

96 TA: 334.5 KOL, Box 5: Report on proceedings of ICA Executive meeting, Brussels, 8–9 April 1933.

97 H. J. May, 'Co-operation on the Defensive', *Review of International Co-operation*, April 1933, pp. 121–4.

98 TA: 334.5 KOL, Box 6: H. J. May, 'Mein Besuch nach Finnland, Deutschland, Schweden und Dänemark', confidential report to ICA, May 1933; report on proceedings of ICA Executive meeting, Paris, 20–21 May 1933.

99 TA: 334.5 KOL, Box 6: Report on proceedings of ICA Executive meeting, Basle, 8 June 1933; report on proceedings of Special International Conference, Basle, 9–10 June 1933.

100 TA: 334.5 KOL, Box 6: Report on proceedings of ICA Executive meeting, Basle, 8 June 1933; Special International Conference, Basle, 9–10 June 1933; H. J. May, 'The Basle Conference – and After!', *Review of International Co-operation*, July 1933, pp. 241–9.

101 May, 'The Basle Conference'; H. J. May, 'Transformation of the German Movement', *Review of International Co-operation*, September 1933, pp. 336–9.

102 TA: 334.5 KOL, Box 9: Report on proceedings of ICA Executive meeting, Cannes, 16–18 January 1934.

103 Emmy Freundlich, the Austrian delegate to the Executive, urged her colleagues to overlook their personal allegiances to Klepzig: 'There is our friend Klepzig, he has to do what they want him to do and cannot help himself. He is a broken man, but that is no reason why to save him we should sacrifice our Alliance. I would not save my own brother if by doing so, I gave strength to the Nazi system. Are we to sacrifice our International Organisation because of our former friendship for Hamburg?' TA: 334.5 KOL, Box 7: Report on proceedings of ICA Executive meeting, Vienna, 6–8 October 1933.

104 Both had forged close relationships with Heinrich Kaufmann in particular. On Tanner, see: J. Paavolainen, *Nuori Tanner menestyvä socialisti. Elämäkerta vuoteen 1911* (Helsinki: Tammi, 1977), pp. 123–34; J. Paavolainen, *Väinö Tanner sillanrakentaja. Elämäkerta vuosilta 1924–1936* (Helsinki: Tammi, 1984), pp. 135–8; on Johansson, see: H. Stolpe and S. Stolpe, *Boken om Albin Johansson I: Liv-minnen-gärning* (Stockholm: Rabén & Sjögren, 1969), pp. 130–2. For Johansson's assessment of the 'tragic fate' of the German co-operative movement, see: 'Den tyske kooperasjon nettop nu', *Kooperatøren*, 13, 1933, p. 152; for Tanner's account, see: 'The German Co-operative Situation', *Review of International*

Co-operation, November 1933, pp. 401–2; 'Saksassa taistellaan osuuskaupoista edelleen', *Elanto*, 16 October 1933.

105 TA: 334.5 KOL, Box 7: Report on proceedings of ICA Executive meeting, Vienna, 6–8 October 1933.

106 TA: 334.5 KOL, Box 7: Report on proceedings of ICA Executive meeting, Vienna, 6–8 October 1933.

107 TA: 334.5 KOL, Box 7: Report on proceedings of ICA Executive meeting, Vienna, 6–8 October 1933.

108 H. J. May, 'Whither the ICA?' *Review of International Co-operation*, September 1933, pp. 321–3.

109 TA: 334.5 KOL, Box 4: H. J. May, 'The Rochdale Principles of Cooperation', lecture to Twelfth International Cooperative School, 1932.

110 H. J. May, 'International Co-operation and the World Crisis', *Review of International Co-operation*, January 1932, pp. 4–11. The following also draws on Hilson, 'Consumers' International?', 210–14.

111 TA: 334.5 KOL, Box 4: Report on the Special Committee meeting on the Rochdale Principles, Strasbourg, 4 February 1932.

112 TA: 334.5 KOL, Box 4: May, 'The Rochdale Principles of Cooperation'.

113 TA: 334.5 KOL, Box 3: Memorandum on the principles of the Rochdale Pioneers, presented to the special committee on the Rochdale Principles, 28 June 1932.

114 *Report of the Proceedings of the Fourteenth Congress of the ICA, held at London, 4–7 September 1934* (hereafter *ICA Congress proceedings 1934*) (London: ICA, 1934), pp. 131ff.

115 *ICA Congress proceedings 1934*, pp. 162–4.

116 *ICA Congress proceedings 1934*, pp. 173–4.

117 H. J. May, 'The Orientation of the International Co-operative Movement', *Review of International Co-operation*, July 1935, pp. 244–51.

118 TA: 334.5 KOL, Box 10: Report on proceedings of ICA Executive meeting, Vienna, 25 June 1936.

119 TA: 334.5 KOL, Box 11: Report on proceedings of ICA Central Committee meeting, Warsaw, 24–25 September 1936; 'Report: The Present Application of the Rochdale Principles', in *Report of the Proceedings of the Fifteenth Congress of the International Co-operative Alliance, held at Paris, 6–9 September 1937* (hereafter *ICA Congress Proceedings 1937*) (London: ICA, 1938), pp. 145–67.

120 'Debate on the Report', *ICA Congress Proceedings 1937*, pp. 168–73.

121 TA: 334.5 KOL, Box 7: Report on proceedings of ICA Executive meeting, Vienna, 6–8 October 1933.

122 'Den 14. internationale Andelskongres i London', *Andelsbladet*, 14 September 1934, pp. 1421–4.

123 S. Jørgensen, 'Det internationale Andelsforbunds Virksomhed', *Andelsbladet*, 21 November 1919, pp. 939–41.

124 TA: 334.5 KOL, Box 7: Papers for meeting of ICA Special Committee on Economic Policy, 7 October 1933: Pellervo/SOK, 'To the Central Committee of the International Co-operative Alliance', 22 January 1920; 'YOL:n 18:s edustajakokous: Kansainvälinen osuustoiminta', *Yhteishyvä*, 11 June; Rigsarkivet,

Aarhus (now in Viborg): Erhvervsarkivet: 06156 Andelsudvalget: 1921–1962 Korrespondance mv med ICA: A. Nielsen to J. Haslam, 27 July 1922; A. Axelsen Drejer, 'Andelsbevægelsens Neutralitet', *Andelsbladet*, 4 September 1925, pp. 891–6.

125 *Report of the Proceedings of the Eleventh International Co-operative Congress, held at Ghent, 1–4 September 1924* (London: ICA, 1925), pp. 219–26; 'Kansainvälinen Osuustoimintaliitto keskustelua sen puolueettomuudesta', *Yhteishyvä*, 7 August 1925; KF: Exekutivkommittén 1920–1963 (documents relating to the Nordic neutrality meeting); 'ICA meetings at Stockholm', *International Co-operative Bulletin*, August 1925, pp. 232–3.

126 NKL declined because the date clashed with their own national congress. KF: Exekutivkommittén 1920–1963: A. Juell to A. Örne, 6 March 1925.

127 'ICA meetings at Stockholm', *International Co-operative Bulletin*, August 1925, pp. 232–3.

128 KF: ICA Centralstyrelsen VU 1940 5.19: V. Serwy, 'The Man of Peace Through Co-operation and Co-operation Through Peace', unpublished MS, written 1940 for ICA Executive meeting.

129 TA: 334.5 KOL, Box 6: H. J. May, 'Mein Besuch nach Finnland, Deutschland, Schweden und Dänemark', confidential report to ICA, May 1933.

4

Nordisk Andelsforbund (NAF), co-operative trade and Nordic co-operation during the interwar period

For the vast majority of men and women who joined co-operative societies and used their services, co-operation was essentially about goods. Whether it was the farmer delivering his milk to the co-operative dairy, or the 'woman with the basket' shopping at the stores, no amount of peace resolutions could conceal the fact that co-operation was above all concerned with the material world: the practical organisation of the production and distribution of food and other everyday commodities.

In the historiography this has sometimes been regarded as a failing, symptomatic of the limits to co-operative ambitions. Sidney Pollard argued that the English co-operative movement had been deradicalised in the mid-nineteenth century, as it abandoned its heroic Owenite past for 'shapeless yearnings' based on 'the firm ground of profitable shopkeeping'.[1] During the twentieth century the pursuit of 'profitable shopkeeping' continued to motivate the consumer co-operative movement, caught between the need to remain competitive in a changing economic environment, and to retain its distinctive co-operative identity.[2] Questions of trade were a central concern for co-operators in the period covered by this book, and were frequently debated both within the ICA and within the national federations. Such matters were never purely technical or commercial, however; instead, they lay at the heart of debates about the meaning of co-operation and its distinctiveness as an economic system.

The commercial strategies of co-operation have been widely explored – the significance and meaning of the dividend, in particular – but historians have paid less attention to the international dimensions of this debate.[3] International trade was certainly a very important aspect of co-operative activity. Soon after its foundation in 1863 the English CWS started to buy goods overseas. By the turn of the century it had built up a dense network of overseas supply chains and depots, and, like all European consumer co-operatives, was increasingly dependent on overseas trade to secure supplies of essential goods such as tea, coffee, sugar and grain.[4]

As Frank Trentmann has shown, the iconic 'cheap loaf' was crucial in generating popular support for free trade in Britain before the First World War.[5] Co-operators were also profoundly aware of the meanings carried by the goods that they traded. By the early twentieth century exhibitions of co-operative manufactured goods had become a regular feature of international and national congresses, and co-operative societies in different countries were beginning to debate the merits of advertising.[6] The war itself produced a 'sharpened awareness of the interdependence between consumers and producers' in Trentmann's words, and gave further impetus to the view that international trade should be organised co-operatively.[7] But that aspiration proved harder to achieve in practice, and efforts to organise an international co-operative wholesale society (the ICWS) under the auspices of the ICA during the 1920s and 1930s ended largely in frustration.

There was one conspicuous success, however: Nordisk Andelsforbund (NAF). This was founded in 1918 by three Scandinavian co-operative wholesales (FDB, KF and NKL) and by the late 1930s had become a very significant commercial actor, especially in the markets for coffee and dried fruit.[8] The activities of NAF are of interest not only for what they reveal about co-operative trade but also as a successful example of practical Nordic co-operation during the interwar period.

This chapter examines co-operative debates on international trade, within the ICA and more widely. The first part considers debates about co-operative trade in the ICA. Many co-operators were instinctively wedded to free trade and economic liberalism, but were forced to acknowledge that the changed economic circumstances of the post-war period brought new challenges. In the second part, the focus is on efforts to put theory into practice through the establishment of NAF and the ICWS. The third part continues this discussion by examining the reasons for the success of NAF, compared to the relative failure of the ICWS. The chapter also explores the thinking behind these organisations. Was NAF above all a pragmatic business strategy for small states, or was it also the expression of a more idealistic view of the role of international co-operative trade? For some of its founders, it was rooted in the belief that Nordic co-operation presented an opportunity to secure peace in the region, but this vision faded to be replaced by interest in the potential for co-operation to tackle the problems of international trusts and cartels on the one hand, and to overcome the conflict of interest between consumers and producers on the other.

Debates on co-operative trade

In 1817 economist David Ricardo wrote that free trade 'binds together, by one common tie of interest and intercourse, the universal society of nations throughout the civilised world'. Peace was a precondition for successful trade, he argued, but free trade would itself help to promote international prosperity, peace and co-operation between nations.[9] This was a principle that many within the co-operative movement subscribed to. Trentmann has described free trade as 'central to the identity and memory of the co-operative movement' in Britain, shaped by memories of the 'hungry forties' of the Corn Laws and high bread prices as the context for the emergence of the Rochdale Pioneers.[10] Co-operators departed from liberals, however, in arguing that only trade organised on co-operative, rather than competitive, principles would truly promote peace between nations.[11] This aim was formalised in Article 1 of the ICA's rules agreed at the Basle congress of 1921: 'to substitute for the present competitive regime of private interest a co-operative system in the interests of the whole community and based upon mutual self-help.'[12]

Assumptions about the superiority of free trade were shaken by the outbreak of the First World War. As Robert Boyce has shown, globalisation did not come to an abrupt end in 1914. Many wartime measures intended to regulate the supply and demand of food and other commodities were abolished after 1918, as part of wider efforts to restore pre-war conditions in the international economy.[13] At the same time, however, there were also signs of fundamental changes. Alexander Nützenadel and Frank Trentmann have pointed out how the war made Europeans 'painfully aware' of their dependence on exports for the most basic and essential foodstuffs, and generated a new enthusiasm for 'international mechanisms of co-ordinating food, of eliminating cycles and stabilising markets'.[14]

In 1916 the French co-operator and economist Charles Gide had argued that the greatest post-war challenge facing co-operators would be to defeat protection and restore international trade. By 1919, however, he was ready to acknowledge that although free trade had brought many benefits for consumers, ultimately it was no better than protection, for it stimulated 'competition and war in all its forms'.[15] The war had demonstrated the need for a more regulated system of international trade, and for co-operators to support the work of the League of Nations in taking practical steps towards this end.[16]

As the work of the ICA was resumed after the war, it became clear that co-operators were not united on this position, however. The continued adherence of the British co-operative movement to free trade after 1918, even while other working-class organisations were moving towards endorsing a more regulated system, is well-documented.[17] The most eager defence of the policy in the international sphere was to come not from Britain, however, but from Sweden. The debate was led by Anders Örne, and presented in his paper to the international co-operative congress in 1921.[18] Writing on behalf of KF in the *International Co-operative Bulletin*, Örne argued that 'protection and reaction are synonymous. Everywhere the advocates of Protection are among the most zealous defenders of militarism.' He suggested that only free trade could guarantee peace and encourage the spread of political freedom. Co-operation knew no limits – 'we co-operators have reached a stage when we need the whole world for the sphere of our activity' – and in the name of economic efficiency wholesale societies could be expected to relocate their productive activities overseas, if necessary. KF urged that the question of the ICA's official position on free trade be deferred until the League of Nations had begun its activities and the economic situation had stabilised.[19]

The position taken by Örne and KF demonstrates a striking confidence in free trade as the best guarantee of prosperity and stability. During the 1920s this developed into a more coherent theory of co-operation as the guarantor of economic freedom, competition and efficiency, all in the name of protecting the interests of the consumer. In KF's own programme from 1922 it was stated that 'the right to the freest possible commerce is a fundamental premise for healthy economic life'.[20] Similar ideas were also expressed in Anders Örne's 1924 book *Kooperativa idéer och spörsmål*, which appeared in an English translation in 1926.[21] In practice, as the 1920s progressed, this increasingly came to be associated with KF's attempts to tackle the problem of monopoly capitalism, outlined in Albin Johansson's address to the 1927 congress.[22] But, typically of co-operation, this was never purely a theoretical question. One of the most pressing issues for co-operative societies after the war was practical: how were they to overcome the difficulties they were facing in securing goods, and what measures could be taken to co-ordinate international trade between them?

International co-operative trade in practice: ICWS and NAF

Discussions about the desirability of an international co-operative wholesale society began before the First World War. A resolution was passed at the ICA's 1907 congress establishing a committee of the representatives of national wholesale societies to study schemes for international joint purchasing.[23] This committee met several times and even went so far as to agree draft rules for a new international trading organisation, but these proposals were rejected at a special meeting convened in connection with the 1910 congress. The matter was debated in the pages of the *International Co-operative Bulletin*, with the Norwegian co-operator O. Dehli accusing the larger wholesales of overlooking the interests of the smaller organisations who stood to gain most from an international agreement.[24]

Discussion of the matter was revived at the wartime conferences and a meeting of representatives of the national wholesale societies was convened in London in September 1919, hosted by the English CWS. This meeting agreed in principle to establish an international committee of wholesale societies as the first step towards the establishment of a fully independent organisation promoting international trade and exchange within the co-operative movement.[25] The new ICWS was conceived as a natural extension of the activities of the national wholesales, and as a first step each society was encouraged to establish a specialist export department. This would be the precursor to the exchange of commercial information, aided by a central bureau to collect statistics.[26]

From the outset, it was clear that the English CWS would play a leading role in the efforts to establish international co-operative trade, reflecting British dominance of the ICA and the relative strength of the British co-operative organisations, especially the CWS, at the end of the Great War. Charles Gide, writing in the early 1920s, cited the CWS as an example of the all-powerful wholesale, possessing 'an indefinite degree of power' and the potential to 'reign almost despotically over all English co-operators'.[27] The CWS dominated international co-operation, even though the rapid growth of the German and Austrian wholesales had started to challenge this before 1914.[28] Sidney and Beatrice Webb suggested that other European countries 'less intimately associated with overseas dependencies and the mercantile marine [than Britain]' had made little progress in developing their international trade before the war.[29]

Evidence for the dominance of the English CWS is also provided by the trade comparisons produced by the ICWS (see table 4.1). Between them, the English and Scottish wholesale societies accounted for over 80 per cent of the total value of imports to all European co-operative societies in 1922, and this share fell only slightly as trading conditions stabilised across the continent during the 1920s. The English CWS alone imported goods to the value of over £34.7 million in 1930, which utterly dwarfed the imports of the other ICWS members. Scotland and Germany between them accounted for approximately £8 million of imports, while Finland and Sweden were the only other countries where the total value of imports was more than £1 million.

There were early signs that the English co-operators were prepared to support the ICWS following a favourable resolution passed at the national congress in 1919.[30] From the perspective of the CWS, however, one important controversy had to be resolved if they were to give the ICWS their full support. The German co-operator Heinrich Kaufmann proposed, in a paper presented to the 1921 congress, that the new ICWS should be formally part of the ICA, based on the close and organic relationships found between central co-operative unions and national wholesales in most of Europe.[31] The CWS representatives rejected this and remained adamant that the two organisations should remain entirely separate and independent from one another, mirroring the autonomy of the CWS within the British Co-operative Union.[32] A compromise was agreed, by which the ICWS was established under a Memorandum of Agreement rather than being registered as a co-operative society under English law, and the matter of its relations with the ICA was left open until it had developed

Table 4.1 Purchases from abroad by ICWS members, as percentage of total imports by co-operative societies, 1922, 1929 and 1930

	Imports as % of total			Total value of imports (GBP)
	1922	**1929**	**1930**	**1930**
England	79.5	70.8	70.7	34,729,538
Scotland	5.7	6.3	8.6	4,224,422
Germany	3.0	8.5	7.7	3,765,696
Finland	2.2	3.3	3.1	1,512,216
Sweden	1.3	3.3	3.0	1,464,530
Switzerland	3.8	2.0	2.0	991,630
Czechoslovakia	2.0	1.0	1.0	513,951
Austria	n/a	0.9	0.9	453,699
France	1.0	1.0	0.7	346,442
Estonia	n/a	1.1	0.7	353,832
Norway	0.5	0.5	0.4	208,437
Latvia	0.3	0.6	0.4	210,779
Belgium	0.4	0.3	0.2	118,276
Poland	0.1	0.2	0.2	118,020
Holland	0.3	0.2	0.2	81,232
Bulgaria	n/a	0.2	0.01	6,017
Total				49,098,717

Note: Value of trade expressed in GBP as given in the original, calculated according to contemporary exchange rates. Only one figure is given for Finland in the sources, so presumably this includes both OTK and SOK.
Source: Työväen arkisto, Helsinki: HNA 14 Keskusosuusliike OTK: ICWS Annual Report, 1922–23; 1930–31.

further.[33] But the debate, which sparked some strong criticism of the CWS from the ICA's general secretary, illustrated a fundamental difference of outlook between the English representatives and their European counterparts. This difference was to shape the debates on international co-operative trade throughout the next two decades.[34]

The formal objective of the ICWS was to collect and distribute commercial information, which would then be used to develop and promote trade between co-operative organisations within Europe and beyond.[35] This aim was guided by two principles: firstly, the desire to promote international trade within the co-operative movement, by enabling wholesale societies to find a co-operative market for their surplus products overseas. This was seen as a logical continuation of co-operative progress from local retail society to national wholesale. In the words of the Webbs, it offered 'a vision of the whole of the international transmission of commodities being managed as imports by interlocked communities of consumers, without any toll of profit to the capitalist trader or banker'.[36] Secondly, international co-operative exchange was conceived as part of a wider ambition to integrate the different sections of the co-operative movement, connecting agricultural and industrial producer co-operatives with distributive societies. The theoretical background to this position had been presented in some detail by Heinrich Kaufmann in a paper to the ICA congress in 1913. Kaufmann identified four stages of inter-co-operative trade, of which international exchange between wholesales in different countries remained insignificant, with the exception of goods to the value of £3.2 million bought by the CWS in Denmark.[37]

The ambition to develop international co-operative trade proved more difficult to realise than expected. One of the first actions of the ICWS was to circulate lists of commodities that could be supplied or were desired by different national members, in an effort to match supply with demand. This was not successful and the minutes of the early 1920s listed many examples of why inter-co-operative trade was not functioning as planned. Wines and spirits produced by the French and Estonian wholesales, respectively, could not be sold in English co-operative stores, for example; Norwegian goats' cheese was found not to be suitable for the English market; and so on.[38] The German wholesale's offer to supply hardware to Danish co-operators was rejected by FDB on the grounds that it would introduce an unnecessary middleman into existing trading relationships, since the Danes already had their own travelling buyers negotiating directly with manufacturers in Germany.[39] Moreover, trade was severely hampered by the difficult international situation. Co-operative societies in the war-damaged parts of Europe were facing instability in international exchange rates and considerable difficulties securing credit. As the ICWS secretary put it in his first annual report, 'the conditions of Europe have been against business being transacted during the past year'.[40]

Writing in the *International Co-operative Bulletin* in 1922, Henry May criticised the slow progress of the ICWS, and made little effort to conceal his view that the excessive caution of the ICWS' English leaders was to blame for the 'spectacle of such futility, lack of vision or even appreciation of the advance which co-operation has made in nearly every country during the war'.[41] His comments were later echoed by the Belgian Victor Serwy, who also criticised what he saw as the excessively cautious attitudes of the English CWS that had hindered further developments. Serwy, writing in 1923, stated: 'Our British comrades … have not displayed all the activity that could be desired

… [They show] a prudence and reserve which appear to be excessive.' As so often happened in co-operative debates, the example of the Rochdale Pioneers was cited as an exhortation to pursue progress in the face of adversity.[42]

Enthusiasts for international wholesale could point to an important precedent: NAF, or the Scandinavian Co-operative Wholesale Society as it was usually referred to in English-language sources. Commercial links between the Nordic co-operative organisations had been established at the beginning of the century, with the Swedish, Norwegian and Finnish societies making some of their purchases through the Danish wholesale FDB.[43] In 1911 representatives of all four Nordic countries met to consider a proposal to formalise this collaboration, through the establishment of a central office in Copenhagen for joint purchasing.[44] The scheme proved impossible to realise, largely because FDB's director felt unable to take on the extra work, but the NKL chairman Dehli returned to the idea in the autumn of 1917 while visiting his Swedish colleagues in Stockholm.[45] KF now took up the initiative and a committee was established to prepare for the formal constitution of a new organisation at a further meeting in Kristiania, held on 26 July 1918. NAF was registered as a co-operative society under Danish law, with its main office in Copenhagen. It raised its working capital through the issue of shares to its member organisations, in proportion to their annual turnover, and its trading surplus was distributed to members in proportion to purchases.[46]

The immediate rationale behind the establishment of NAF, as Keijo Hummelin has suggested, was the disruption to trade during the war.[47] Indeed, assessing the NAF's development in 1931, its director Frederik Nielsen suggested that it might not have been founded but for the wartime trade difficulties.[48] Acting jointly would give the Nordic wholesales much greater clout in the international markets, and NAF would thus be concerned above all with imports of so-called 'colonial' goods such as coffee, tea, sugar and dried fruit.[49] Unlike ICWS, NAF would not be concerned with *inter*-Nordic co-operative trade, even though this had increased during the war.[50] Instead, the main focus of activity was the establishment of commercial relations with export companies and to this end advertisements were placed in international trade directories as trading relations were resumed.[51] NAF's role was to acquire information about markets and suppliers, to receive samples of goods where appropriate and to negotiate offers. Members were then informed of these offers, and invited, though not obliged, to place orders for goods that were shipped directly to the purchaser. The most important market for these transactions was London and only a year after NAF's foundation its board took steps to establish a branch office there; this began its work in 1921.[52]

By 1924, after nearly five years of trading, NAF was thus well-established, with offices in both Copenhagen and London. Its most important commodity was coffee, for which it employed a specialist buyer, but it had also become a significant purchaser and importer of dried fruit from the Californian markets.[53] This raised the possibility of whether the example of NAF was relevant to the development of international co-operative trade more broadly. Certainly there were signs that the leaders of KF in particular were prepared to take an active part in shaping international co-operative debates. Nonetheless, the founders of NAF were initially reluctant to put their organisation forward as a model for the ICWS. In a draft letter to the ICA in 1919, the KF board suggested that NAF was 'recommendable also for groups of nations of similar economical type', but in a separate memorandum they also warned against the concentration of co-operative purchasing power within an international wholesale, for fear that it would give the impression of excessive demand and thus drive up prices.[54] Instead, they proposed the establishment of a central co-operative clearing house, based in London, to handle all international transactions between co-operative societies. This would help to improve the exchange of information between co-operative wholesales, and would also help ease the problems in international currency transactions that were severely hindering trade.[55]

The KF proposal was not taken up, but the example of NAF returned to the international agenda in the early 1920s, as the rules of the new ICWS were debated.[56] In 1922 the NAF rules were translated for circulation among members of the international wholesale committee. Albin Johansson explained that this was intended not as a formal proposal, but as an example 'to show what forms do actually exist in other parts of the world for this purpose'.[57] The rules were duly discussed, but it was agreed that it would be premature to adopt them as the basis for the embryonic ICWS.[58]

In 1924 KF proposed a new international scheme for the joint purchase of coffee. NAF had the sole agency for the import of Brazilian coffee to Scandinavia, and the ICWS secretary agreed that 'an International Agency would be a business-like and profitable investment', provided that the details could be worked out satisfactorily.[59] A special meeting of co-operative coffee experts indicated general approval for buying coffee through NAF, even though the German and French representatives noted that they could probably purchase more cheaply in local markets, where they could take advantage of exchange rate fluctuations.[60] KF representatives Albin Johansson and Anders Hedberg even went so far as to commit their organisation to bearing any losses incurred as the result of a trial scheme, but they had run ahead of themselves as far as NAF was concerned. When the ICWS Executive discussed the scheme again in Stockholm in June 1925, NAF director Frederik Nielsen stated that it was impossible for his organisation to admit new members. The ICWS had no option but to establish its own agency and since there was no support for this, the matter was allowed to drop.[61]

The failure of the coffee scheme was the precursor to further attempts to develop the ICWS as an agency, none of which was successful. In 1928 another proposal from Albin Johansson was agreed in principle but had to be abandoned when it became clear that the largest ICWS member, the English CWS, would not support it.[62] Instead, from 1931, the ICWS began a tentative scheme for the joint purchase of dried fruit, using the CWS's established networks of supply.[63] These efforts persisted for a few years but were never entirely satisfactory. Some members complained that the CWS prices were too high; others that the quality of the goods did not suit their particular needs.[64]

By the 1930s many co-operators were becoming openly frustrated with the slow progress of the ICWS. Writing in the *Review of International Co-operation* in 1930, the Czechoslovak representative Emil Lustig referred to 'wearying negotiations' that had been 'dragging on for a number of years', and complained that 'fully ten years have passed and yet there is not the slightest sign that a positive stone has been laid in the foundation of the future ICWS'.[65] Even the ICWS's own officers were prepared to admit that the joint purchasing scheme had met with only limited success, and although it might be 'unjust to say that this action has been useless', in the words of the president A. J. Cleuet, 'it must be frankly stated that it has been inadequate'.[66]

Meanwhile NAF seemed to go from strength to strength. The accession of the two Finnish wholesales in 1928 was a significant boost to trade, and although the financial crisis of 1929 meant that turnover fell in 1930/1, the volume of goods handled actually increased.[67] NAF's most important commodities were coffee (by 1936 it was handling a quarter of a million sacks annually), dried fruit, sugar, rice and spices, but imports of raw materials also increased, particularly of soya beans and copra destined for KF's edible oil factory opened in 1932.[68] The success of NAF in contrast to the ICWS was not lost on Nordic co-operators. 'After 20 years Nordisk Andelsforbund now stands as a model for international collaboration,' declared the Norwegian journal *Kooperatøren* in 1938. These successes were attributed by the journal 'not least to wise and skilful leadership' but also to its foundation on sound co-operative principles.[69]

At the meetings of the ICWS during the late 1920s and 1930s, Albin Johansson became more and more critical of ICWS's aim to develop trade between co-operative wholesales. This, he argued, 'was not in the real sense international trade. It was rather the development of National trade.'[70] The only satisfactory way to promote international co-operative trade was through the foundation of an international agency, like NAF. In 1935, after a long discussion on the future of the ICWS, it was decided to invite NAF director Nielsen to make a detailed presentation on the operations of NAF to an ICWS meeting.[71] As with the proposed coffee scheme some ten years previously, some ICWS members felt that the best way to proceed would be for NAF to admit new members, but once again a request to this effect was refused.[72] Instead, in September 1936 the establishment of an international agency was formally agreed for a trial period of two or three years in the first instance.[73] A sub-committee began work on the practicalities, and received a significant boost a year later when the previously hostile English CWS announced that it would agree to join the new agency, on the condition that they would not necessarily be required to give it their business.[74]

The international co-operative trading agency now became a reality. Known by the acronym INCALIM (to avoid confusion with the ICA), the International Co-operative Agency was registered as a co-operative society under English law in October 1937, and the experienced Dutch co-operator M. W. Dijkstra was recruited to run its office in the Port of London.[75] There were still difficulties to be overcome. In his first report Dijkstra insisted that for many commodities the Agency was able to offer prices similar to or better than those quoted by private agents, and urged members to show loyalty by placing their orders with it, but the representatives of some wholesales continued to express doubts that London was the best market for their purchases.[76] Soon, though, the Agency was overtaken by events. The fall of democratic regimes in central European in 1938 meant that trade was lower than anticipated for that year, and the outbreak of hostilities a year later stifled all schemes for the promotion of international trade.[77]

NAF and ICWS: explaining success and failure

The question as to why NAF succeeded and the ICWS was a relative failure reveals quite a lot about international co-operative relations in the interwar period. Contemporaries sometimes attributed NAF's success to the cultural similarities of the Nordic countries, which shared 'a more or less common basic language and national life'.[78] As Robert Boyce has observed, racism was 'ubiquitous' in interwar Europe, where not only confirmed Nazis but also 'publicists, academics, politicians and statesmen in the democratic powers … frequently employed racial categories in their discourse and allowed them to influence their thinking on international affairs'.[79] There is nothing to suggest that co-operators were any different in thinking in this deterministic way. The cultural similarities of the Nordic countries were assumed to produce 'a commonness of demand', which made joint purchasing viable.

Although some were sceptical about NAF as a model for an international agency, it was hoped it might inspire the establishment of similar regional organisations elsewhere in Europe.[80] When the agency question was discussed in 1936, two such proposals were put forward: one for Belgium, France and Switzerland, 'having the same language and buying the same products', and one for the four central European wholesales (Austria, Hungary and the two Czechoslovak organisations).[81] This revived an idea that had pre-dated the foundation of the ICWS, when the Belgian co-operator Victor Serwy proposed in 1919 that the wholesales should group themselves on 'racial' lines: Anglo-Saxon, Latin, Slavonic and Teutonic. A similar proposal for five regional trading groups was made in 1930.[82]

The similarities between the Nordic co-operative organisations could not be taken for granted, however. NAF was not merely the expression of a pre-determined Nordic solidarity; it played its own role in the creation of both a regional identity and a common market. For example, it was reported that on joining NAF in 1928 the two Finnish wholesales had been obliged to make changes to their coffee-buying policies in order to fall in with the joint demands of the other members.[83] By the 1930s all five national wholesales were actively trying to co-ordinate their participation in the ICWS, for example by sending common representatives to meetings.[84] In some cases the business relations between the four countries were strengthened by individual contacts, with the close relationship between KF's Albin Johansson and NAF's Frederik Nielsen acting as a central pivot.[85] Nordic co-operators were also keen to convey the impression of regional solidarity to other ICWS members. 'It would be fortunate', suggested Nielsen, corresponding with the other Nordic wholesales before an ICWS meeting in 1932, 'if the office in Manchester again got the impression that we are united on this matter.'[86]

This outward show of unity nonetheless concealed some differences of opinion among the Nordic federations about the scope of NAF. For Albin Johansson, NAF seems to have been envisaged as a first stage in the more ambitious aim of establishing an international co-operative wholesale society. The Danish representatives, Frederik Nielsen in particular, were much more cautious about the possibility of extending NAF. Denmark was one of the three ICWS members to vote outright against the establishment of an international agency in 1936, preferring instead the regional model.[87] As director of NAF, Nielsen turned down the formal request that his organisation should change its constitution to allow the accession of new members, and refused to allow NAF's London manager to take on the extra work of supporting an ICWS agency office.[88] Johansson seems to have thought that Nielsen could have been persuaded to change his mind, but he was wrong.[89] ICWS officials wrote to Johansson, following a meeting with Nielsen in London, that he (Nielsen) 'was invulnerable to all our powers of persuasion', and it was 'evident' that he shared the view of some other NAF members that any extension 'would be but "the thin end of the wedge" to an ultimate internationalisation of Nordisk Andelsforbund'.[90] The ICWS secretary R. Lancaster, 'reading between the lines', as he put it, concluded that the opposition to the proposal came from the Danish federation, and that Nielsen wished to avoid splitting NAF's own board by putting the matter to a vote.[91]

These differences seem to have been managed more or less amicably, aided perhaps by the close personal relationship between Johansson and Nielsen, but they are illustrative of the wider dynamics of inter-Nordic relationships in this period. Historians have pointed out the asymmetrical nature of Nordic co-operation with regard to other organisations.[92] Monika Janfelt has, for example, shown the importance of the Danish–Swedish axis to the activities of the Nordic associations founded after the First World War, while Norwegian attitudes were shaped by reluctance to be drawn into anything resembling the former union with Sweden. Finland remained relatively peripheral, at least during the 1920s.[93] The deep splits within the Norwegian labour movement presented a hindrance to Norway's full participation in other international organisations, such as the ILO, while Finnish involvement was sometimes hindered by language difficulties.[94]

These imbalances were also reproduced in NAF. The Danish wholesale FDB was by far the largest organisation, accounting for almost two thirds of NAF's total turnover during the years 1919–27, while the trade of FDB and KF combined dwarfed that from Norway, which accounted for just under 4.5 per cent (see table 4.2). This was attributed by Norwegian co-operators to 'our country's situation and particular circumstances'.[95] The two Finnish organisations between them accounted for around a fifth of the total after they joined in 1928. From the late 1920s the balance was shifting in favour of KF, which coincided with its emergence as one of the most visible and influential co-operative unions internationally (see table 4.3).

However, KF's emerging dominance in NAF was nowhere near as one-sided as that of the English co-operative movement within the ICWS (see table 4.1). There was thus a fundamental difference between NAF and the ICWS in this respect. Asked about KF's position within NAF in 1936, Frederik Nielsen

Table 4.2 Percentage shares of NAF annual turnover, by member, 1919–27

	Share of NAF annual turnover (%)								
Member	**1919**	**1920**	**1921**	**1922**	**1923**	**1924**	**1925**	**1926**	**1927**
Norges Kooperative Landsforening (NKL)	3.0	2.9	3.0	4.2	3.7	4.3	5.8	3.1	8.1
Kooperativa Förbundet (KF)	23.2	26.0	21.0	32.8	35.6	38.4	41.9	33.2	32.1
Fællesforeningen for Danmarks Brugsforeninger (FDB)	73.8	71.0	75.9	62.0	60.7	57.3	52.3	63.6	59.8

Source: Hummelin, *Nordisk Andelsforbund*, pp. 50–1.

Table 4.3 NAF annual trade as percentage of total, by member, 1928–40

	Share of NAF total annual trade (%)												
Member	**1928**	**1929**	**1930**	**1931**	**1932**	**1933**	**1934**	**1935**	**1936**	**1937**	**1938**	**1939**	**1940**
SOK	0.8	9.2	14.6	10.8	13.7	13.6	10.7	12.1	9.1	9.4	7.7	7.2	0.6
OTK	0.4	9.3	13.1	9.7	10.2	8.7	9.3	8.3	9.8	10.0	10.8	6.2	4.7
NKL	3.4	4.3	3.7	2.8	5.4	4.2	4.3	5.0	2.9	3.0	2.7	2.5	1.8
KF	45.2	40.0	33.1	43.6	41.2	51.6	56.6	58.2	62.0	65.0	59.6	66.2	71.1
FDB	50.2	37.2	35.5	33.0	29.5	21.8	19.2	16.4	16.1	12.5	19.2	18.0	21.7

Note: FDB figures for 1938 and 1939 include a small amount of goods purchased by Vejle Steam Mill, which were listed separately in the reports.
Source: Työväen kirjasto, Helsinki: Nordisk Andelsforbund aarsberetninger, 1928–40.

told ICWS members that he could see no reason why NAF would not be able to function without KF, even though by this time it accounted for the lion's share of the trade.[96] An international agency without the English CWS was unthinkable, however.

Even after the question of the relationship between the ICA and the ICWS had been settled, the English representatives continued to treat all proposals for the further development of international co-operative trade with extreme circumspection. But they did not oppose the ICWS outright, for it also represented a business opportunity to exploit their global network of trading contacts in order to supply European partners.[97] The ICWS annual report for 1922/3 noted that over 70 per cent of co-operative trade was with non-European countries, and that 67 per cent of this was accounted for by just six commodities, namely wheat, bacon and lard, butter, sugar, coffee and rice.[98] The CWS made offers to supply these and other goods to other ICWS members, and when the possibility of a scheme for the joint purchase of tea was discussed in 1923, their representatives were swift to point out that they effectively controlled the London market, meaning that they could 'execute any orders on the best possible terms, providing the money is forthcoming when required'.[99]

In 1931 the CWS proposed a new scheme for the joint purchasing of dried fruit. Under the arrangement, ICWS members were invited to place their fruit orders with the English buyers who travelled annually to the eastern Mediterranean to negotiate directly with producers. Californian dried fruits were also supplied through the CWS office in New York.[100] The scheme immediately ran into problems. Many wholesales were critical of the prices offered, stating that they were able to buy more cheaply elsewhere.[101] The NAF representative pointed out that his organisation negotiated directly with the growers in California, thus avoiding the delays incurred by communicating with New York, and that NAF members purchased more fruit from this source than the CWS did.[102] The likely result of the scheme for NAF, he explained, was that the member organisations would have to pay commission on goods received at less favourable prices.[103] A Swiss delegate to a fruit buyers' meeting in 1931 was also critical, stating that no one organisation should profit from a joint-purchase scheme. The Swiss wholesale felt no animosity to the 'great nations', he said, but added that 'the smaller nations would feel much happier by purchasing through their own international organisation'.[104] For their part, the CWS insisted that they placed their buyers at the disposal of the ICWS 'only for the purpose of service', but the scheme had faltered because ICWS members were reluctant to commit themselves to placing orders.[105] Nonetheless, the arrangement continued until the mid-1930s, with the English representatives insisting that the only hindrances to further progress were beyond their control, arising from the severe disruptions to international trade.[106]

The attitudes of the English CWS drew criticisms from representatives of other organisations in the ICWS, especially KF. Writing to a Danish colleague in 1921, Anders Örne complained that a KF proposal for an international co-operative bank had won support from the French and German wholesales but 'had been totally misunderstood by the English',[107] who were interested only in making sure they kept control of ICWS. Part of the problem with the ICWS, according to Albin Johansson, was that it relied on the CWS for its funding.[108] Accordingly, in 1928 KF made a new proposal for the establishment of an international co-operative agency on the NAF model.[109] In private correspondence with Väinö Tanner, the ICA president, Johansson expressed his hope that the imminent retirement of ICWS chairman Golightly, of the English CWS, would remove one of the obstacles to developing the agency.[110] In the event, however, not even KF's offer of £1,000 to meet the initial running expenses could save the scheme in the face of the English view that the Agency would become 'a mere middleman and so in effect a taxing agency', and thus detrimental to CWS interests.[111]

Johansson became increasingly outspoken in his criticism of what he clearly saw as English efforts to maintain control of the ICWS and hinder its development. 'Again and again admirable proposals had been made', he said, speaking in response to the rejection by the ICWS of a new KF proposal to investigate the possibilities for the joint production of margarine in 1931, 'but at the moment of putting them into effect the Committee allowed themselves to be influenced by some new consideration … and, consequently, nothing was done'.[112]

Idealism and pragmatism

Seen in this light, the efforts to organise international co-operative trade during the interwar period could certainly be interpreted as an example of the limitations to the realisation of international co-operative visions. 'Why is it that a sort of stage fright seizes us when it is suggested that we should … take our stand beside [the world's] capitalist exponents, and compel the recognition of our co-operative system as an integral part of the economic life to-day?' asked Henry May, commenting in 1932 on the failure to achieve progress in international co-operative banking or trading. Copious information had been collected on both activities, he noted, and reports had been produced, but 'something is lacking in fervency and zeal for the great achievement which awaits enlightened advance'.[113]

Part of the problem was, of course, the need for national co-operative businesses to protect their commercial interests, which tended to override questions of international co-operative principle. By the early 1930s within the ICWS this seemed to have crystallised into conflict between the larger members, especially the CWS, which sought to protect their established channels of supply, and the co-operative wholesale businesses in the smaller nations, for whom an international agency seemed to be a sensible and pragmatic response to an uncertain commercial world. At a meeting in Warsaw in 1936 the Austrian delegate Korp stated bluntly that he represented a poor organisation and added that 'he wished to see some reward for time and money spent in attending meetings. He would be failing in his duty if he returned home without reporting some decision regarding the agency.'[114]

The example of NAF fits with this interpretation that support for international co-operative trading was a pragmatic strategy for the co-operative unions of small states, motivated above all by the practical difficulties of securing scarce commodities in disrupted markets. Although NAF was widely discussed as an example of international co-operative success, that success was often attributed to the sound business acumen of its directors rather than to the coherence of its ideological programme. But it is not quite accurate to regard NAF as being exclusively motivated by commercial interests. For an older generation of co-operators who had first mooted the idea before 1914, NAF was an example of 'practical Scandinavianism'.[115] It was at least partly motivated by the belief that co-operation between the Nordic countries would help to promote peace and soothe tensions in the region after the end of the Swedish-Norwegian union in 1905. For G. H. von Koch, collaboration between the Nordic co-operative movements was part of the Scandinavianism 'which we desire so much, so that we can eventually be in a position to maintain our independence in the face of powerful external enemies'.[116] At its inaugural meeting in 1918 NAF was described as 'an attempt at practical collaboration between the countries which will also be very significant for peace', and its roots in an established tradition of regional collaboration and mutual assistance were also emphasised by Frederik Nielsen in his presentation of NAF to the ICWS in 1936.[117]

The establishment of NAF also reveals much about the relationship between Finland and the Scandinavian countries. Neither of the Finnish wholesales joined NAF until 1928, and the minutes from the founding meeting make no mention of Finland. The official explanation for this, circulated in the co-operative press, was that this was due to the 'difficult and uncertain conditions the country was facing' in the aftermath of the 1918 civil war, meaning that the Finnish co-operatives had decided to stay out of the negotiations.[118] Correspondence between NKL and the different organisations in the run up to the meeting suggests, however, that delegates from both OTK and SOK had every intention of taking part, with NKL officials taking steps to help them secure their visas.[119]

A few days before the July 1918 conference, OTK telegraphed the other Nordic organisations to inform them that their delegate Väinö Tanner had not been granted a visa and would therefore not be attending. They also expressed their dismay at the provision in the rules that new members would only be accepted unanimously, a clause which they feared might make it difficult for them to join in the future, presumably due to a veto from SOK, which at this point was still expecting to be represented. The long telegram conveys the animosity existing at that time between the two Finnish organisations.[120] It was followed up with a letter to the Swede Anders Örne, in the erroneous belief that he had been appointed as the new NAF secretary, which emphasised OTK's political neutrality and confirmed its desire to join NAF.[121] Representatives of SOK, meanwhile, stated publicly that they had been forced to withdraw from NAF's founding meeting at the eleventh hour, due to fears that Finnish membership would compromise perceptions of Scandinavian neutrality and thus place the other members at risk of trade sanctions from the entente states, led by Britain.[122]

Inter-Nordic tensions receded during the 1920s, but the peace-building aspiration was replaced by newer, and distinctly co-operative, ideological concerns. One of the original aims of NAF was to try to replace private suppliers with co-operative ones; as Nielsen put it in his statement to the ICWS, 'to carry the co-operative line beyond the oceans, making the goods pass through the consumers' organisation from place of production until delivered to the consumer'.[123] The early meetings therefore discussed proposals for the development of jointly owned shipping lines and even overseas plantations, to guard against the danger that 'emerging forces' in capitalist business would seek to strengthen control of imports.[124] In the summer of 1918 Nielsen was already making enquiries, through his contact with a Danish emigrant resident in California, about the purchase of an orchard, though this idea had to be abandoned due to the rapidly rising land prices and NAF turned instead to seeking direct negotiations with local growers and packers.[125] But the aspiration remained, that NAF would help establish the 'most direct contacts possible … between consumers and producers'.[126] According to Nielsen, the successes of NAF made possible the establishment of more ambitious schemes for Nordic co-operation, such as that for the joint production of lightbulbs during the 1930s.[127]

Conclusion

The authors of a recent business history of the English CWS have argued that it was a pioneer of 'supply chain management' in the UK. As part of its efforts to supply the needs of millions of co-operative customers, the CWS rapidly developed extensive overseas operations after its foundation in 1863, establishing a network of warehouses, depots, factories and plantations in Europe, the Americas, West Africa and Australasia.[128] From the turn of the century other European co-operatives developed similar operations, in parallel with the expansion of international trade in the period 1870–1914. The potential for re-organising international trade along co-operative lines was therefore frequently debated within the movement long before 1914, shaped also by the liberal internationalist belief that trade between nations was also a force for peace.

The First World War was seen as a watershed, offering an opportunity for co-operators to realise their ambition to reshape international trade. Immediately following the cessation of hostilities, efforts were made to convene an international co-operative wholesale society operating independently of the ICA. The ICWS met regularly throughout the interwar period and experimented with various schemes for the joint purchase of certain commodities, but it was never able to realise the more ambitious hopes invested in it and was regarded by many in the ICA as a disappointment, if not an outright failure.

In a lecture delivered to the ICA's 1946 congress, Anders Örne left his audience in no doubt about why the ICWS had not achieved more during the interwar period:

> The wish to establish international co-operative collaboration has foundered on the strength of British co-operation, which meant that it could establish an international purchasing organisation on its own. [The ICWS has been] no more than a discussion club, a meeting place for the representatives of the affiliated wholesales.[129]

Örne's assessment, that the disproportionate dominance of the English CWS allowed them to dominate the international debate and steer the ICWS according to their own interests, echoed the criticisms of his KF colleagues. At the same time, co-operators in Sweden and the other Nordic countries could also point to an example of success in international co-operative trading in NAF, which functioned as a joint import agency for the five Nordic co-operative wholesales. For many observers both within and outside the Nordic region, NAF stood as an example of the pragmatic, non-ideological nature of Nordic co-operation: of what could be achieved through sound business management based on the practical application of co-operative principles. But it was not entirely devoid of idealism. For an older generation of co-operators in particular, who had experienced the period of regional tension after 1905, NAF was an example of 'practical Scandinavianism' and the ability of co-operation to promote international brotherhood. According to its director, Frederik Nielsen, it had also made possible more ambitious schemes for international co-operation, in particular the joint venture in the manufacture of lightbulbs, which is considered in the next chapter.

Notes

1 S. Pollard, 'Nineteenth-Century Co-operation: From Community Building to Shopkeeping', in A. Briggs and J. Saville (eds), *Essays in Labour History, 1886–1923* (London: Macmillan, 1960), p. 102.
2 E. Furlough and C. Strikwerda, 'Economics, Consumer Culture and Gender: An Introduction to the Politics of Consumer Co-operation', in E. Furlough and C. Strikwerda (eds), *Consumers against Capitalism? Consumer Co-operation in Europe, North America and Japan, 1840–1990* (Lanham: Rowman and Littlefield, 1999).
3 See, however: K. Friberg, 'A Co-operative Take on Free Trade: International Ambitions and Regional Initiatives in International Co-operative Trade', in M. Hilson, S. Neunsinger and G. Patmore (eds), *A Global History of Consumer Co-operation since 1850: Movements and Businesses* (Leiden: Brill, 2017).
4 J. F. Wilson, A. Webster and R. Vorberg-Rugh, *Building Co-operation: A Business History of the Co-operative Group, 1863–2013* (Oxford: Oxford University Press, 2013), pp. 126–33.
5 F. Trentmann, *Free Trade Nation: Commerce, Consumption and Civil Society in Modern Britain* (Oxford: Oxford University Press, 2008), p. 88.
6 P. Jonsson, 'From Commercial Trickery to Social Responsibility: Marketing in the Swedish Co-operative Movement in the Early Twentieth Century', in Hilson, Neunsinger and Patmore (eds), *Global History*.
7 F. Trentmann, 'Before Fair Trade: Empire, Free Trade and the Moral Economies of Food in the Modern World', in A. Nützenadel and F. Trentmann (eds), *Food and Globalization: Consumption, Markets and Politics in the Modern World* (Oxford: Berg, 2008), p. 261.
8 K. Hummelin, *Nordisk Andelsforbund NAF 1918–1993: Konsumentkooperativt samarbete i Norden*, trans. J. and N. Degerman (Copenhagen: NAF, 1998); T. Odhe, *Scandinavian Co-operative Wholesale Society 1918–1958* (Copenhagen: NAF/Det danske forlag, 1960). The Finnish organisations SOK and OTK joined in 1928; Icelandic SÍS in 1949. Also: S. O. Hansen, 'Nordisk kooperativt samarbeid. Et lite kjenr felleskals.' Unpublished manuscript, 2005. I am grateful to Espen Ekberg for bringing this to my attention.
9 D. Ricardo, *The Principles of Political Economy and Taxation* (London: G Bell, 1911; first published 1817), p. 114; cited in M. W. Zacher and R. A. Matthew, 'Liberal International Theory: Common Threads, Divergent Strands', in C. W. Kegley, Jr. (ed.), *Controversies in International Relations Theory: Realism and the Neoliberal Challenge* (New York: St Martin's Press, 1995), pp. 105–50: 114.
10 Trentmann, *Free Trade Nation*, pp. 45–9.

11 P. Gurney, *Co-operative Culture and the Politics of Consumption in England, 1870–1930* (Manchester: Manchester University Press, 1996), pp. 100–1.

12 G. J. D. C. Goedhart, 'Report on the Revision of the Rules of the International Co-operative Alliance', in *Report of the Proceedings of the Tenth Congress of the International Co-operative Alliance, held at Basle, 22–25 August 1921* (hereafter *ICA Congress Proceedings 1921*) (London: ICA, 1921), p. 72.

13 R. Boyce, *The Great Interwar Crisis and the Collapse of Globalization* (Basingstoke: Palgrave Macmillan, 2009), pp. 3–4.

14 A. Nützenadel and F. Trentmann, 'Introduction: Mapping Food and Globalization', in A. Nützenadel and F. Trentmann (eds), *Food and Globalization: Consumption, Markets and Politics in the Modern World* (Oxford: Berg, 2008), p. 11.

15 'The International Co-operative Congress at Paris', *International Co-operative Bulletin*, October 1916, pp. 224–32; 'Inter-Allied Co-operative Congress at Paris', *International Co-operative Bulletin*, February-March 1919, pp. 21–31.

16 'Inter-Allied Co-operative Congress at Paris'; 'The Revival of International Co-operation: The Paris Conference and After', *International Co-operative Bulletin*, August-September 1919, pp. 153–7.

17 M. Hilton, *Consumerism in Twentieth-Century Britain* (Cambridge: Cambridge University Press, 2003), p. 106; Trentmann, *Free Trade Nation*, pp. 209–11.

18 See: P. Aléx, *Den rationella konsumenten. KF som folkuppfostrare 1899–1939* (Stockholm/Stehag: Brutus Östlings Bokförlag Symposion, 1994), pp. 103–4; A. Örne, 'The Policy of International Co-operation', *ICA Congress Proceedings 1921*, pp. 101–20. Örne's contribution is also discussed in: Friberg, 'Co-operative Take'.

19 A. Örne, 'Notes on Commercial Policy', *International Co-operative Bulletin*, August-September 1919, pp. 160–1.

20 'Vi anse rätten till möjligast fri företagsverksamhet vara ett fundamentalt villkor för ett sunt ekonomiskt liv.' A. Gjöres, *Konsumentkooperation i Sverige* (Stockholm: Tidens förlag, 1925), pp. 108–9.

21 A. Örne, *Kooperativa idéer och spörsmål* (Stockholm: Kooperativa Förbundets bokförlag, 1924); A. Örne, *Co-operative Ideals and Problems*, trans. J. Downie (Manchester: Co-operative Union, 1926).

22 A. Johansson, *Aktuella kooperativa problem* (Stockholm: Kooperativa Förbundets bokförlag, 1927). See also chapter 5.

23 *Report of the Proceedings of the Seventh Congress of the International Co-operative Alliance, held at Cremona, 22–25 September 1907* (London: ICA, 1907), p. 138.

24 'The International Co-operative Wholesale Federation' (reprint of article in *Kooperatøren* by O. Delhi), *International Co-operative Bulletin*, 11 February 1911, pp. 36–9; 'International Co-operative Wholesale Federation' (response to Dehli from Union of Swiss Distributive Societies), *International Co-operative Bulletin*, April 1911, pp. 104–10; 'International Co-operative Wholesale Federation' (response from O. Dehli), *International Co-operative Bulletin*, 10 June 1911, pp. 159–61.

25 'The Inter-Allied Co-operative Congress at Paris', *International Co-operative Bulletin*, October 1916, pp. 225–32; 'Inter-Allied and Neutral Conference, 26–28

June', *International Co-operative Bulletin*, June-July 1919, pp. 102–6; 'International Trading Relations: The Conference of Wholesale Societies in London', *International Co-operative Bulletin*, August-September 1919, pp. 162–9.

26 Kooperativa Förbundets arkiv, Stockholm (hereafter KF): ICWS 1919–25: First annual report of ICWS to ICA, 1921.

27 C. Gide, *Consumers' Co-operative Societies*, trans. staff of the Co-operative Reference Library, Dublin (Manchester: Co-operative Union, 1921), pp. 131, 133–4.

28 Gide, *Consumers' Co-operative Societies*, p. 139.

29 S. Webb and B. Webb, *The Consumers' Co-operative Movement* (published by authors, 1921), pp. 284, 288 n. 1.

30 'International Trading Relations', *International Co-operative Bulletin*, August-September 1919, pp. 162–9.

31 H. Kaufmann, 'The Relations to be Established between the ICA and an International CWS', *ICA Congress Proceedings 1921*, pp. 144–58.

32 'International Trading Relations'; KF: ICWS 1919–25: Minutes of meeting of ICWS, Basle, 23 August 1921.

33 KF: ICWS 1919–25: Minutes of meeting of ICWS sub-committee, London, 2 November 1921; Työväen arkisto, Helsinki (hereafter TA): HNA 14 Keskusosuusliike OTK: Ulkomaiset osuuskunnat: Memorandum of Agreement for ICWS; notive of meeting of ICWS in Prague, 24 March 1924.

34 'Notes and Comments', *International Co-operative Bulletin*, October 1921, pp. 252–6.

35 TA: HNA 14: Memorandum of agreement for ICWS, 1924; Notice of meeting of ICWS in Prague, 24 March 1924.

36 Webb and Webb, *Consumers' Co-operative Movement*, p. 289.

37 H. Kaufmann, 'The Direct Exchange of Goods between Distributive Societies, Agricultural and other Productive Societies, also between the Wholesale Societies in the Different Countries', *Report of the Proceedings of the Ninth Congress of the International Co-operative Alliance, held at Glasgow, 25–28 August 1913* (London: ICA, 1913), pp. 48–76.

38 KF: ICWS 1919–25: ICWS sub-committee minutes, 2 November 1921; 30 January 1922.

39 KF: ICWS 1919–25: ICWS sub-committee minutes, 12 January 1921.

40 KF: ICWS 1919–25: ICWS first annual report, 1921.

41 'Notes and Comments', *International Co-operative Bulletin*, October 1921, p. 255. May's comments were refuted: 'The English CWS and the Basle Resolutions: A reply to H. J. May', *International Co-operative Bulletin*, January 1922, pp. 19–21; KF: ICWS 1919–25: Minutes of ICWS sub-committee, Brussels, 30 January 1922.

42 V. Serwy, 'Towards an International Co-operative Wholesale Society', *International Co-operative Bulletin*, April 1923, pp. 73–5.

43 A. Hedberg, *Samköp i Norden. Konsumentkooperation i fem länder* (Stockholm: Kooperativa Förbundets bokförlag, 1956), p. 266; 'Nordisk Andelsforbund', *Kooperatøren*, 7, 1928, pp. 78–80.

44 S. Jørgensen, 'Bidrag til "Nordisk Andelsforbund"s tilblivelseshistorie', *Kooperatøren*, October-November 1918, p. 78.
45 Jørgensen, 'Bidrag til "Nordisk Andelsforbund"'; 'Økonomisk samarbeide mellem Nordens kooperarører', *Kooperatøren*, April 1918, pp. 25–6.
46 'Nordiska Andelsförbundets tillkomst och organisation', *Kooperatören*, November 1918, pp. 236–40; Riksarkivet, Oslo (hereafter NRA): PA 1394 Coop/NKL BA: Serie K Nordisk og internasjonalt samarbeid L0011 Nordisk Andelsförbund 0004 Korrespondance mm 1916–43: Grundregler for 'Nordisk Andelscentral' eller De nordeuropæiske Brugsforeningers Centralforening for fælles Vareindkøb.
47 Hummelin, *Nordisk Andelsforbund*, pp. 38–40, 43–4; Odhe, *Scandinavian Co-operative Wholesale Society*, p. 21.
48 Frederik Nielsen, 'Nordisk Andelsforbund', *Kooperatøren*, 10, 1931, pp. 130–1.
49 NRA: PA 1394 Coop/NKL BA: Grundregler for 'Nordisk Andelscentral'.
50 F. Wendt, *Cooperation in the Nordic Countries: Achievements and Obstacles* (Stockholm: Nordic Council, 1981), p. 22.
51 Rigsarkivet, Aarhus (now in Viborg) (hereafter DRA): Erhvervsarkivet: 02042 Nordisk Andelsforbund: 1918–76 Korrespondance, almindelig.
52 NRA: PA 1394 Coop NKL BA: NAF to NKL, 6 October 1919; Hummelin, *Nordisk Andelsforbund*, p. 48.
53 Hummelin, *Nordisk Andelsforbund*, p. 49.
54 KF: ICWS 1919–25: KF Board to Henry May, n.d. (1919), draft; ICWS handlingar 1919–22, 42.1: Memorandum respecting the economic connections between the co-operative wholesale societies in different countries issued by the Co-operative Union and Wholesale Society of Sweden, 25 September 1919. The memorandum was also reprinted in *International Co-operative Bulletin*, November-December 1921, pp. 299–302.
55 KF: ICWS handlingar 1919–22, 42.1: Memorandum.
56 KF: ICWS 1919–25: International Wholesale Society Sub-Committee minutes, 2 November 1921.
57 TA: HNA 14: Memorandum of agreement for ICWS, 1924. Johansson made the same point in a letter to his German colleague Heinrich Kaufmann: KF: ICWS 1919–25: Albin Johansson to Heinrich Kaufmann, 25 January 1923; also Broderick (ICWS) to Johansson 10 February 1923; also ICWS secretary's report on the NAF rules, produced for ICWS meeting in Hamburg, May 1923.
58 TA: HNA 14: Replies of committee members on proposed statutes, 1923.
59 KF claimed to be the largest European co-operative importer of coffee, after France. KF: ICWS 1919–25: Memorandum on coffee in Scandinavian co-operation, n.d. 1924; ICWS Secretary's report on coffee, January 1925.
60 KF: ICWS 1926–46: Minutes of special meeting of ICWS Executive and coffee buyers, 2 February 1925; report of the special sub-committee on coffee buying; KF: ICWS 1919–25: Correspondence on coffee scheme: Hedberg to Lancaster, 28 March 1925; Lancaster to Johansson, 21 April 1925.
61 KF: ICWS 1926–46: Report of the special sub-committee on combined coffee buying; minutes of ICWS Executive meeting, 25 June 1925.

62 TA: HNA 14: Minutes of ICWS Executive meeting, 22 August 1930; minutes of full meeting of ICWS, 23 August 1930; ICWS circular to members, 30 September 1930.
63 TA: HNA 14: ICWS circular 4 July 1931.
64 TA: HNA 15: Minutes of ICWS Executive meeting, 29 September 1931; minutes of full meeting of ICWS, 2 October 1931.
65 E. Lustig, 'The Question of the International ICWS', *Review of International Co-operation*, January 1930, pp. 6–7.
66 A. J. Cleuet, 'International Co-operative Trade', *Review of International Co-operation*, August 1934, pp. 274–5; A. J. Cleuet, 'The Immediate Tasks of the International Co-operative Wholesale Society', *Review of International Co-operation*, April 1935, pp. 121–2.
67 Työväen kirjasto, Helsinki (hereafter TK): NAF aarsberetning 1930, 1931.
68 TK: NAF aarsberetning 1932. Copra was derived from coconuts and used in the manufacture of margarine.
69 'NAF står nu efter 20 års virke som et mønster for internasjonalt samarbeide'. 'Nordisk Andelsforbund', *Kooperatøren*, 15 March 1938, p. 85; also: 'Nordisk Andelsforbund', *Kooperatøren*, 7, 1928, pp. 78–80.
70 TA: HNA 14: Minutes of ICWS Executive meeting, 23 November 1927.
71 TA: HNA 15: Minutes of ICWS Executive meetings, 28 June 1935; 13 October 1935.
72 TA: HNA 15: Minutes of full meeting of ICWS, 26 September 1936; KF: ICWS 1926–46: NAF (Nielsen) to ICWS, 4 November 1936.
73 TA: HNA 15: Minutes of full meeting of ICWS, 26 September 1936.
74 TA: HNA 16: Minutes of ICWS Executive meeting, 3 September 1937.
75 TA: HNA 16: International Co-operative Agency to OTK, 6 September 1938: Explanatory Schedules for the General Meeting of Members to be held 27 September 1938.
76 TA: HNA 16: International Co-operative Agency to OTK, 6 September 1938: manager's report; memorandum from Mr Cleuet on the position of the French CWS, 6 July 1938.
77 W. Dijkstra, 'International Co-operative Trade', *Review of International Co-operation*, April 1939, pp. 184–7.
78 TA: HNA 15: Minutes of meeting of ICWS Executive and commercial managers, London, 30 January 1936; ICWS circular to all members regarding the proposed agency, 8 May 1936; 'Co-operative International Trading: Interesting Conference in London', *Review of International Co-operation*, March 1936, pp. 87–9.
79 Boyce, *Great Interwar Crisis*, p. 18.
80 TA: HNA 15: Minutes of meeting of ICWS Executive and dried fruit buyers, Brussels, 25 April 1932.
81 TA: HNA 15: Minutes of meeting of ICWS Executive and commercial managers, London, 30 January 1936.
82 'International Trading Relations', *International Co-operative Bulletin*, August-September 1919, pp. 165–6; E. Lustig, 'The Question of the ICWS', *Review of International Co-operation*, January 1930, pp. 6–7.

83 TK: NAF aarsberetning, 1930.
84 KF: ICWS 1926–46: Margarinfabrikken 'Norge' to Albin Johansson, 7 January 1931; Frederik Nielsen to Albin Johansson, 10 January 1931; Albin Johansson to Ivan Vaksdal, 21 January 1931.
85 KF: Albin Johanssons personarkiv: Albin Johansson's unpublished memoir of Frederik Nielsen; H. Stolpe and S. Stolpe, *Boken om Albin Johansson I* (Stockholm: Rabén & Sjögren, 1969), pp. 224–5.
86 'jeg synes, det vilde være heldigt, at Kontoret i Manchester paany faar Indtrykket af, at vi i det foreliggende Spørgsmaal er en Enhed.' TA: HNA 14: NAF to OTK, 23 May 1932.
87 TA: HNA 15: Minutes of ICWS Executive meeting, Edinburgh, 11 July 1936; ICWS circular to all members, 26 September 1936.
88 KF: ICWS 1926–46: ICWS to Nielsen, 6 October 1936; NAF to ICWS, 5 November 1936.
89 KF: ICWS 1926–46: Johansson to Lancaster, 4 March 1937.
90 KF: ICWS 1926–46: ICWS to Johansson, 20 March 1937.
91 KF: ICWS 1926–46: Lancaster to Cleuet, 2 March 1937.
92 J. Strang, 'Introduction: The Nordic Model of Transnational Cooperation?', p. 9, and N. Götz, H. Haggrén and M. Hilson, 'Nordic Cooperation in the Voluntary Sector', p. 57; both in J. Strang (ed.), *Nordic Cooperation: A European Region in Transition* (London: Routledge, 2016).
93 M. Janfelt, *Att leva i den bästa av världar. Föreningen Nordens syn på Norden 1919–1933* (Stockholm: Carlssons bokförlag, 2005), pp. 24, 126, 149ff.
94 H. Heldal, 'Norway in the International Labour Organisation 1919–1939', *Scandinavian Journal of History*, 21:4 (1996), 255–83; Janfelt, *Att leva*, p. 150; L. Kaukiainen, 'From Reluctancy to Activity: Finland's Way to the Nordic Family during 1920s and 1930s', *Scandinavian Journal of History*, 9:2–3 (1984), 201–19.
95 'Vårt lands beliggenhet og særegne forhold.' 'Nordisk Andelsforbund', *Kooperatøren*, 7, 1928, pp. 78–80.
96 TA: HNA 15: Minutes of meeting of ICWS Executive and commercial managers, 30 January 1936.
97 Thus in 1922 CWS representatives reported on a new agreement with the New Zealand Farmers' Association for the supply of butter, cheese and frozen meat, which they were prepared to extend to other wholesales. TA: HNA 14: Minutes of ICWS meeting, Essen, 2 October 1922.
98 TN: HNA 14: Third annual report of ICWS 1922–23.
99 TA: HNA 14: Minutes of ICWS meeting, 23 April 1923; KF: ICWS 1919–25: Minutes of ICWS sub-committee meeting, 13 October 1920, 12 January 1921.
100 TA: HNA 14: Minutes of meeting of ICWS dried and canned fruit buyers at Brussels, 15 April 1931.
101 TA: HNA 15: Minutes of ICWS Executive meeting, 29 September 1931; Minutes of meeting of ICWS Executive and dried fruit buyers, 25 April 1932.
102 TA: HNA 15: Minutes of meeting of ICWS Executive and dried fruit buyers, 25 April 1932.

103 TA: HNA 14: Nielsen to Alanen (OTK), 12 April 1932.
104 TA: HNA 14: Minutes of meeting of ICWS dried and canned fruit buyers, 15 April 1931.
105 TA: 334.5 KOL: Minutes of meeting of ICWS Executive and dried fruit buyers, 10 April 1933; minutes of full meeting of ICWS, 3 September 1934; minutes of meeting of ICWS dried fruit buyers, 12 April 1935.
106 TA: HNA 15: Minutes of ICWS Executive meeting, 1 September 1934; minutes of full meeting of ICWS, 3 September 1934; ICWS annual report to ICA 1934–35.
107 '[Förslaget] missuppfattades fullständigt av engelsmännen, som överhuvud ej vilja höra talas om annat än att verksamheten skall börja med varuomsättning och tydligen mena, att det engelska Cooperative Wholesale Society bör bli kooperationens Faellesforening eller åtminstone ledaren därför.' DRA: Erhvervsarkivet: 02042 NAF: 1918–76 Korrespondance almindelig: Örne (KF) to Nielsen (Den Danske Andelsbank), 15 July 1921.
108 KF: Albin Johanssons personarkiv: Diverse XIII: 'Utdrag ur International Co-operative Wholesale Societys handlingar, sammanställd av Keler på uppdrag av Albin Johansson', pp. 7–8.
109 KF: ICWS 1926–46: Albin Johansson to Golightly, 12 July 1928; TA: HNA 14: Minutes of ICWS Executive meeting, Liège, 28 July 1928; report on proceedings of ICWS sub-committee meeting, Hamburg, 9 October 1928; TA: 334.5 KOL, Box 0.5: Minutes of ICWS Executive meeting, Geneva, 6 November 1928; minutes of full meeting of ICWS, 6 November 1928.
110 KF: ICWS 1926–46: Albin Johansson to Väinö Tanner, 17 October 1928; 16 November 1928.
111 TA: 334.5 KOL, Box 0.5: Minutes of ICWS Executive meeting, 2 May 1929.
112 TA: HNA 14: Minutes of joint meeting of ICWS and ICA executives, 14 April 1931.
113 H. J. May, 'International Co-operation and the World Crisis', *Review of International Co-operation*, January 1932, pp. 4–11.
114 TA: HNA 15: Minutes of ICWS Executive meeting, 24 September 1936.
115 'Nordisk Andelsforbund', *Kooperatøren*, 7, 1928, pp. 78–80.
116 'som vi saa meget attraar, for at vi til slutning kan være i stand til at opretholde vor selvstændighet overfor ydre mægtige fiender'. Correspondence between Severin Jørgensen and G. H. von Koch, reprinted to mark the founding of NAF; see: Jørgensen, 'Bidrag til "Nordisk Andelsforbund"', pp. 76–9.
117 'et forsøk paa praktisk samarbeide landene imellem som ogsaa vil faa sin store betydning som fredsfaktor'. 'Nordisk Andelsforbund konstitueret', *Kooperatøren*, August-September 1918, p. 6; KF: ICWS handlingar 1936: F. Nielsen, 'Nordisk Andelsforbund – Organisation and Work', presented to ICWS January 1936.
118 'de vanskelige og usikre forhold landet befinder sig i'. 'Nordisk Andelsforbund konstitueret', *Kooperatøren*, August-September 1918, p. 6.
119 NRA: L0011 NAF 0004 Korrespondance mm 1916–43: NKL to SOK, 10 July 1918; SOK to NKL, 15 July 7 1918.
120 NRA: L0011 NAF 0004 Korrespondance mm 1916–43: telegram Finska andelspartiaffären (OTK) to NKL, 22 July 1918. The telegram was also published in

the Finnish co-operative press: 'Pohjoismaiden Osuustoimintaliitto perustettu', *Kuluttajain Lehti*, 5 August 1918.

121 TA: HNA 14: KK to Anders Örne, KF, 10 August 1918.

122 The statement was made in an article in *Samarbete*, 8 August 1918; copy included in NRA: L0011 NAF 0004 Korrespondance mm 1916–43: Correspondence NKL (Juell) to FDB, 27 September 1918. This explanation was also confirmed by Anders Örne: 'Miksi SOK jätettiin Pohjoismaiden osuustoimintaliiton ulkopuoluelle?', *Kuluttajain Lehti*, 3 September 1918.

123 KF: ICWS handlingar 1936 42.7: Frederik Nielsen, 'The Nordisk Andelsforbund – organization and work'; paper presented to meeting of International Co-operative Wholesale Society (ICWS), January 1936.

124 'de krafter som er i bevægelse'. 'Økonomisk samarbeide mellem Nordens kooperatører', *Kooperatøren*, April 1918, pp. 25–6.

125 NRA: L0011 Nordisk Andelsforbund Korrespondance mm 1916–43: FDB (Frederik Nielsen) to NKL, 1 August 1918; NAF to H Chr Jacobsen, Los Altos, 7 August 1918; 3 September 1918; NAF to NKL, 1 December 1918.

126 'Det vil søke mest mulig direkte forbindelse etableret mellem forbrukerne og producenterne.' 'Nordisk Andelsforbund konstitueret', *Kooperatøren*, August-September 1918, pp. 63–71.

127 F. Nielsen, 'Nordisk Andelsforbund', *Kooperatøren*, 10, 1931, pp. 130–1.

128 A. Webster, J. F. Wilson and R. Vorberg-Rugh, 'Going Global. The Rise of CWS as an International Commercial and Political Actor, 1863–1950: Scoping an Agenda for Future Research', in Hilson, Neunsinger and Patmore (eds), *Global History*, pp. 560–2; Wilson, Webster and Vorberg-Rugh, *Building Co-operation*.

129 'Önskningarna att åstadkomma ett internationellt kooperativt samarbete ha strandat på att den brittiska kooperationen … haft sådan storlek, att den ensam förmått bygga upp en egen internationell inköpsorganisation. [ICWS var] icke annat än en diskussionsklubb, en träffpunkt för representanter från de anslutna partihandelsföreningarna.' A. Örne, '*Det internationella varuutbytet från konsumentsynpunkt'. Föredrag vid IKA:s sextonde kongress i Zürich den 10 oktober 1946* (Stockholm: Kooperativa Förbundets bokförlag, 1946), pp. 5–6.

5

Co-operation and the emergence of the Nordic 'middle way'

In 1931 the Norwegian journal *Kooperatøren* published an article by NAF director Frederik Nielsen, assessing the development of his organisation. Nielsen concluded that economic collaboration through NAF had now become taken for granted (*en selvfølge*) by the Nordic consumer co-operative unions, and, moreover, that NAF had contributed to raising awareness of Nordic 'brotherhood' (*broderskapet*) in co-operative circles worldwide.[1] The efforts of the Nordic co-operative unions to adopt a common position on matters such as neutrality likewise helped to raise the profile of the region within the ICA.[2] During the 1930s this perception spread more widely, as Nordic co-operation attracted the interest of foreign journalists. The best-known of these was the American Marquis Childs, whose bestselling book *Sweden – the Middle Way* (1936) dealt extensively with co-operation. Following Childs, President Roosevelt's 1936 Inquiry on Co-operative Enterprise in Europe also devoted much of its attention to the Nordic countries, and the documents that it generated provide an important snapshot of the status of the movement and its significance for ordinary consumers in the mid-1930s.[3]

This final chapter returns to the question of the distinctiveness of the co-operative movements in the Nordic countries, while at the same time considering the significance of co-operation for the emergence of the idea of the Nordic 'middle way' in the 1930s. It is argued that there were three main reasons for the attractiveness of Nordic co-operation. First, co-operation had a reputation for promoting social harmony and reconciling the divisions between producers and consumers, farmers and workers. Second, it attracted interest as an example of modernisation in both agriculture and retailing. Third, co-operation came to be associated with economic efficiency and the smooth functioning of capitalism, particularly in its battles against trusts and monopolies. The co-operative movement was thus a significant influence on emerging perceptions of Scandinavia as a model region, a positive example of democracy and stability in the turbulent international context of the 1930s.[4] This was a mutually reinforcing process where co-operation contributed to ideas of the Nordic 'middle way', while interest in the region also led many observers to discover co-operation as an idea.[5] The focus here is on international perceptions of the Nordic co-operative movements, but the chapter also asks what international interest in co-operatives in particular can reveal about the image of the Nordic region and emerging ideas of the Scandinavian or Nordic middle way.

Co-operation and social harmony: Denmark as model

In his study of the international image of Scandinavia, Kazimierz Musiał noted the importance of what he refers to as 'Danish, agriculture-based progressiveness' in the 1920s, which he argues 'prepared the ground for the increasing interest in the Scandinavian solutions in the decades to come', and eventually the idea of a Scandinavian or Nordic model.[6] The Danish co-operative dairies were exhibited at the world's fair in Paris in 1900,[7] and widely cited as a model for reformers in other agricultural countries such as Ireland, though here interest in co-operation was stimulated partly by a fear of losing out to Danish competition in the British butter market.[8] As Musiał notes, international interest in Denmark really took off during and after the First World War. Denmark's neutrality and successful adaptation to international markets meant that it came to be seen as 'an exemplary country capable of providing patterns of socially engineered development' by writers in the UK and the USA.[9] The dynamism of its agricultural sector and rural life in general was contrasted with the stagnation of farming elsewhere and that dynamism was attributed to the twin influences of the co-operative movement and the folk high schools.[10]

Sometimes these accounts were quite hyperbolic. In his 1921 book on Danish co-operation American lawyer Frederic C. Howe described Denmark as 'quite the most valuable political exhibit in the modern world' and worthy of study by statesmen.[11] According to Howe, the co-operative movement was all-pervading and had transformed the lives of farmers, creating a new political and social order where 'men work and govern as a single undertaking'.[12] Moreover, co-operation also offered an inoculation against state socialism, allowing the Danish farmer to become 'his own capitalist'. It was thus 'the great cohesive element in the democracy of Denmark … an experiment station in freedom'.[13] Howe was criticised by his reviewers for his 'extravagance of statement' and the superficial nature of his coverage.[14] But he returned to the theme in the mid-1930s and his book was reissued in an enlarged edition in 1936, though its impact was not as extensive as that achieved by Childs' book on Sweden published in the same year.[15]

Danish co-operators were certainly aware of the esteem in which their movement was held abroad.[16] In a 1922 letter to the editor of the British co-operative journal *The People's Year Book*, Anders Nielsen referred to 'the incense which now from abroad – not from Denmark – is burned to the so-called exemplary Danish co-operative undertakings'. He was writing to refuse a request for an article on a matter he regarded as non-co-operative, fearing that he risked undermining his movement's international reputation if he were to compromise its political neutrality.[17] It is also possible that commercial interests played a part, given the business links between Danish agricultural producers and the powerful English CWS. Danish-British trade grew sharply during the 1880s as the CWS established commercial contacts with Danish co-operative dairies and export societies.[18] The CWS opened its own branch in Copenhagen in 1881 to negotiate directly with its Danish suppliers and this was followed by depots in Aarhus (1891), Odense (1895) and Esbjerg (1905).[19]

The authors of the most recent business history of the CWS argue that the organisation's contacts with the Danish co-operative movement 'came to exemplify the possibilities of international collaboration between quite different co-operative movements', and that 'ideological conviction' was one of the reasons why 'the CWS was a most welcome actor in the Danish market'.[20] Further research is needed on the nature of this relationship from the Danish side, including for example why the CWS decided to open its own abattoir and bacon factory in the Jutland town of Herning in 1899.[21] After all, the CWS's influence in Ireland, which was also an important supplier of dairy produce, was not supportive of local attempts to establish independent co-operative creameries, though the CWS historians make no suggestion of similar tensions in Denmark.[22] For the CWS buyers, it was perhaps not so much co-operative ideology as the quality of the Danish goods that was paramount, guaranteed through the famous 'Lur' mark adopted by the co-operative dairies in 1900 and applied to bacon from 1906.[23] But like any brand, co-operative trademarks could also carry other meanings. According to Frederic C. Howe, it was the Lur mark on the shell of his breakfast egg in a London hotel that first sparked his interest in Danish co-operation.[24]

The commercial interests of co-operative businesses were thus important in shaping their international relationships, but this is not to say that ideological interests were absent. For the ICA, the Danish co-operative movement provided a valuable example of the prospects for an integrated co-operative system, which had the potential to reconcile the opposing interests of producers and consumers, workers and farmers. In his address to the ICA congress in 1913 on the direct exchange of goods between distributive societies, the German co-operator Heinrich Kaufmann called for closer relations between producer and consumer co-operatives. It was in the interests of the urban working class to support agricultural producers, he argued, for better standards of living in the countryside would stem migration to the cities and the downward pressure on wages that this provoked.[25] At the same congress, a written communication from Severin Jørgensen cited the harmonious relations prevailing between consumer and producer societies in Denmark, and their shared aims in opposing 'the system which has hitherto prevailed in all commercial activity – in trade and in production – according to which the greater part of the profits go to individual peasants'.[26]

Not all representatives of consumer co-operation were prepared to accept that they shared common interests with agricultural producer co-operatives. The matter was discussed in some detail in response to a paper by the Swiss co-operator Bernhard Jaeggi that was commissioned for the ICA's 1927 congress. Jaeggi concluded that consumer societies were unable to undertake agricultural production on a large scale and that some form of collaboration with agricultural co-operatives was therefore inevitable.[27] But when Jaeggi's draft paper was discussed at the Central Committee before the congress, the Czechoslovak representative suggested that agricultural co-operatives in his country had 'understandings with private capitalists', while the Finnish KK delegate referred directly to the clash of interests between town and countryside over the price of agricultural commodities.[28] Further objections were raised when the ICA's General Secretary proposed the admission of the Canadian Wheat Pools for membership of the Alliance, following his visit to them in 1928. Delegates from Germany and Austria again expressed concerns that these organisations were 'really based on capitalist principles' and Albin Johansson argued that to admit them would be 'bringing together people with opposing interests to our own'.[29]

The matter went to the heart of the question of what co-operation meant and what it hoped to achieve. Were co-operatives fundamentally anti-capitalist or was their aim to operate as commercially successful businesses in a capitalist economy? Did the word 'co-operation' suggest an aspiration to achieve social harmony between farmers and workers with ostensibly opposing interests, or was the ICA primarily an organisation of *consumers*? The question gained a new urgency in 1929 when the Alliance's Executive got wind of a proposal, emanating from a Czechoslovak agriculturalist called Klindera, to set up a new International Federation of Agricultural Co-operation. The staunchest advocates of consumer co-operation urged the ICA to take little notice of this initiative, which they felt was likely to be short-lived. Others were more cautious, however, arguing that the existence of a rival co-operative organisation would risk stamping the ICA as a socialist organisation of consumers.[30] It was not stated openly, but the implication was that to allow this to happen would be to play into the hands of the USSR and their attempts to co-opt the ICA into the international class struggle. The Executive decided to respond by asking the ILO's Albert Thomas to convene an international committee on consumer-agricultural relations, but the question was also addressed directly in the Central Committee's report to the 1930 congress. This stated explicitly that membership of the ICA was open to all types of co-operative organisation, but it added that

> the broad basis of the consumers' organisation should govern their constitution on the grounds that the only economic unit which guarantees the realisation of co-operative principles is the consumer. The consumer as the basis of our Movement is not a fetish, but an irresistible economic proposition.[31]

This triggered the question of what the principles of consumer co-operation actually were, which was to be settled by the decision to establish an enquiry on the Rochdale principles at the same time.[32]

The need for compromise was also supported by evidence of the continued expansion of the ICA. Taking stock of the events of 1930 in the *Review of International Co-operation*, Henry May reported that of the 70 million individuals estimated to be members of an ICA-affiliated co-operative society in 1930, the majority (48.2 million) were members of consumer co-operatives, but a substantial minority (22.4 million) were members of agricultural producer societies. There were a further 15 million members of credit societies. Moreover, the growth in membership of agricultural societies marked an extension of the Alliance beyond its European origins. The new members who joined the Alliance in 1930 included societies in Canada, Argentina, India, Tannu-Tuva, Mongolia and Persia.[33] The membership of some of these societies was short-lived and their influence was limited, for the Alliance remained an exclusively European organisation in terms of those who attended its meetings.

There is also some evidence that this expansion triggered unease. In 1929 a delegate objected to the proposed admission of new members in Turkey, Mongolia, Korea, 'and places the names of which we have never heard', asking: 'Are we not essentially a Consumers' Organisation and should we not endeavour to remain true to that character of our Organisation?'[34] For others, however, the presence of such organisations was vital proof of the ICA's claim to stand as the sole representative of the international co-operative movement, in its broadest definition.

The results of the special committee established to discuss inter-co-operative relations were inconclusive, not least because its convenor Albert Thomas died suddenly and prematurely in 1932.[35] However, the emerging economic crisis gave a new impetus to those advocating closer relations between producers' and consumers' organisations. The emergency resolution adopted by the Central Committee in 1931 declared that co-operation offered a solution to the crisis because it 'puts to an end the inequalities between the resources of the consumer and producer'.[36] This was a theme that was to return frequently during subsequent years. In his paper to the special ICA conference on the crisis in 1933 – which, as noted, was rather overshadowed by the controversies over German co-operation – the French co-operator Poisson referred to 'the disequilibrium between the forces of consumption and production', and suggested that a truly co-operative system had the potential to deliver a 'just price' for both consumers and producers, though it was not clear how this would be achieved.[37]

In the context of this emphasis on the harmony of co-operation as a system, the Nordic co-operative organisations took on a special importance for the Alliance. In particular, the Central Committee for the Danish co-operatives – Andelsudvalget – could stand as a model of an integrated co-operative movement, which combined the interests of consumer and producer co-operatives under one umbrella. Relations between the ICA and the Danish co-operative movement soured during the early 1920s, unsettled by concerns that the Alliance was becoming exclusively an organisation of consumer co-operatives, making its rhetoric and actions appear increasingly socialist as a result. As discussed, this eventually resulted in a special meeting with the Nordic and Baltic organisations to reassure them about the Alliance's neutrality, but it also gave rise to some doubts within Andelsudvalget about the utility of continued Danish membership in the ICA. In an internal briefing produced for Andelsudvalget, A. Axelsen Drejer recommended that the Danish co-operatives retain their membership, partly in order to avoid handing the initiative to the rival organisation of Danish working-class co-operatives, DkF. But he also wrote that Danish co-operation had a special role within the ICA, for there was 'scarcely anywhere else that one can see people from different social classes united in co-operative societies as here in this country'. He concluded that 'the Danish co-operative movement has more significance for the ICA than the other way round'.[38]

Danish co-operators thus had a duty – it was implied – to remain within the Alliance and guide the international co-operative movement on the preferred path.[39] Drejer was invited to lecture on inter-co-operative relations to the International Co-operative Summer School in 1928, on the grounds that the Danish system offered 'an entirely different plan and system' from that put forward by Jaeggi to the 1927 congress.[40] The point was echoed in several contributions to *Review of International Co-operation* written by Drejer during the 1930s.[41]

KF and theories of consumer co-operation

Despite these discussions of the role of agricultural producer co-operatives, in practice the ICA remained dominated by the representatives of consumer co-operatives until after the Second World War.[42] As Frank Trentmann has observed, the consumer remains rather an elusive category in historical research. Explicit attempts to theorise the economic role of consumption and consumers did not emerge until the late nineteenth century and even then were debated largely outside the mainstream of liberal economic thought.[43]

One important contributor to this debate was the French economist and co-operator Charles Gide, who argued that consumers were essential in stabilising capitalist society and redressing the imbalances between consumption and production that caused periodic crises.[44] In Gide's vision, consumer co-operatives would play a central role in the creation of a new economic and social order, for, as he put it, 'we are all consumers, we will henceforth be our own sellers, bankers, entrepreneurs'.[45] He also noted that all consumer societies aspired ultimately to undertake their own production, and consumer co-operation was thus capable of meeting all human needs, intellectual and moral as well as material.[46]

Gide's concept of a Co-operative Republic, where production and consumption were organised in harmony through consumer co-operative societies, was influential on the 'Nîmes school' of French co-operation, but by extension also on the ICA.[47] Gide's insistence on the universality of the consumer found echoes elsewhere, for example in the works of American social theorist Horace Kallen.[48] Paradoxically, the most strongly consumerist of the Alliance's members were often those for whom the consumer interest remained subordinated to the concept of co-operation as the 'third pillar' of the socialist labour movement. As the ICA resumed its activities after the First World War, the leaders of Sweden's KF began signalling their ambitions to shape international co-operative debates. The most important individual here was KF's Anders Örne, who by the mid-1920s had established an international reputation as one of the foremost theorists of co-operation.

In 1921 Örne presented a paper to the ICA congress where he summarised the co-operative programme in seven principles.[49] This statement, described by ICA historian W. P. Watkins as the first distinctively Scandinavian contribution to international co-operative thought, drew on a pamphlet 'De sju grundsatserna' ('The Seven Principles') in 1919, which was also adopted as KF's programme.[50] Örne's book on co-operation was translated into English and published by the CWS in 1926, and his seven principles were also re-stated by his KF colleague Albin Johansson in a paper presented to the ICA's 1927 congress.[51] Örne's principles were presented as being derived from the Rochdale tradition, but they differed to those eventually included in the ICA's co-operative principles of 1937. The Rochdale practice of distributing the surplus in the form of a dividend on purchase was included, as were the commitments to democratic organisation (one member one vote) and to education, but in his other points Örne was more practical, for example specifying the need for co-operative societies to deliver unadulterated goods, to use fair measures and to sell at market prices. The insistence that societies raise their own capital was, Peder

Aléx suggests, derived more from the Schulze-Delitzsch credit co-operatives than from Rochdale.[52]

What is striking about Örne's principles is their prosaic nature. This was no grand vision of the future co-operative commonwealth, but rather a practical guide to how to organise a co-operative business. The ways and means were specified but the eventual outcome was missing. Örne himself acknowledged the 'meagreness' (*torftighet*) of his seven principles; as he put it: 'They include not a single word of revolutionary incitement, not the slightest hint of sociological depth.'[53] Nonetheless, he was convinced that, 'such apparently simple rules, applied consistently, would lead directly to a society completely different to the current one'.[54]

The fundamental difference between co-operation and capitalism was implicit in the arrangements for the redistribution of the surplus through the dividend, the provision for democratic control on the basis of one member one vote, and the strictly limited interest paid on the share capital held by individual members. Through these mechanisms co-operation would transcend the divisions of class and avoid the 'antagonism of interests' prevailing in the established economic system.[55]

These views were largely shared by Örne's Nordic colleagues, as indicated by the expressions of unity at the 1925 special conference, which united even the representatives of the two Finnish organisations. Where the Swedes differed from their counterparts in Denmark and Finland, however, was in their insistence on the primacy of the consumer societies as the form of co-operation with the greatest potential for development.[56] As Katarina Friberg has pointed out, there was nothing inevitable about the dominance of consumer co-operatives in KF; at its foundation in 1899 the new organisation was intended to be open to all types of co-operation.[57] But the Swedish co-operative union never became truly mixed along the lines of Andelsudvalget in Denmark or the Finnish organisations. During the 1920s KF made concerted efforts to win the support of farmers, recognising their status as consumers who needed to be supplied not only with household items but also with agricultural requisites such as feed, seed and fertiliser through local co-operative stores. This was partly triggered by the perception of some signs of hostility among farmers towards KF, which carried the threat that they would form a rival organisation similar to the Finnish Pellervo.[58] In this respect, the situation in KF in the 1920s seemed to mirror that within the ICA: overtures to farming interests were stimulated by the need to forestall attempts to establish rival organisations, but were also driven by the growing theoretical interest in the promotion of direct links between consumers and producers.

A problem for KF in trying to develop a working relationship with agricultural co-operatives was that, unlike Denmark and Finland, Sweden lacked strong central agricultural organisations. Agricultural purchase societies were affiliated to Svenska Lantmännens Riksförbund (SLR, Swedish farmers' national union) founded in 1905, but the producer societies were relatively slow to develop central organisations. During the 1920s SLR began to assert the interests of farmers more strongly and this brought it into conflict with KF's efforts to supply farmers through its network of co-operative stores.[59] In January 1929 this rivalry became open conflict following KF's acquisition of a fertiliser factory at Gäddviken near Stockholm. The original intention was that KF would itself manufacture fertiliser for supply to farmers, but after prolonged negotiations with SLR it was forced to retreat and lease the factory to a consortium of companies.[60] In the co-operative press this was represented as an example of KF's successful collaboration with its agricultural partners as part of its strategy to break the fertiliser trust and reduce prices for farmers (see below), but this portrayal concealed the conflict behind these negotiations.[61]

Indeed, when the question of relations between consumer and producer organisations was discussed in the ICA, the representatives of KF and in particular Albin Johansson frequently took a strongly consumerist line. Nonetheless, this did not undermine the perception of Nordic co-operation as a force for social harmony in a world of conflict. In his address to the 1927 congress Johansson insisted on the need for the co-operative movement to remain politically non-aligned, 'for Swedish co-operation is comprised of consumers from all social classes and all political parties'.[62] Nordic co-operation thus offered two models of social harmony: the Swedish one – inherited from the Nîmes school – of the universality of the consumer, transgressing the boundaries of class and politics, and the Danish one of an integrated system harmonising the interests of producers and consumers, town and countryside. As interest in the theory of disequilibrium and the role of the co-operative movement as a means to tackle this gained ground in the wake of the Great Depression, so too did interest in the Nordic co-operative movements as an example of a model response to these problems. But KF in particular also attracted attention for another reason: its campaign against the trusts.

Efficiency and modernity: KF and the trusts

The First World War is often understood to mark a watershed in the development of the international economy, ending the pre-1914 era of liberal globalisation and ushering in a new period of economic nationalism and planning. After the war, governments took steps to try to restore the conditions of pre-war liberalism, but this proved much more difficult than expected and, as is well known, failed to prevent the catastrophe of the Great Depression a decade later.[63] At the same time, as contemporaries contemplated their shattered world in 1918, it was quite clear that other longer term economic changes were underway, especially relating to the organisation of business. For, in response to the more challenging economic conditions of the 1870s and after, capitalist businesses had turned to new strategies of concentration, combination and rationalisation.[64] These trends were already apparent before the war, but were to become much more pronounced in the two decades following it.

How were co-operators to respond to this new era of capitalism? They were certainly well aware of it. In their 1921 book on the British consumer co-operative movement, Sidney and Beatrice Webb noted the 'steadily growing revolt and resentment of the [co-operative] members against the aggression of the Trusts, Combinations, and Amalgamations now dominating the markets of the world'. The trend had been greatly stimulated by government interventions during the war, which had forced the English and Scottish wholesales to take action to secure supplies of raw materials and manufactured goods.[65] Awareness of these changing circumstances also led many co-operators to question their traditional support for free trade, as discussed in chapter 4.

In their programmatic statement from 1921, KF leaders attempted to bridge the gap between a self-understanding of co-operation as the antidote to free and unregulated competition on the one hand, and co-operation in opposition to monopoly on the other. They stated: 'The antithesis of co-operation is profit-seeking economy, organized in the form of undertakings whose proprietors regard the production and the distribution of profits merely as the means whereby to procure gain to themselves.'[66] Anders Örne noted how co-operation had emerged in the context of the conditions of free competition of the nineteenth century, but was now facing a new challenge in the rise of private monopolies.[67]

During the 1920s the leaders of KF made increasingly strenuous and prominent efforts to realise these visions through measures to tackle the problem of monopoly. In doing so they could draw on experiences of several important conflicts in the years immediately before the war, which had attracted wide attention in Sweden and were influential in shaping KF's development. The establishment of KF's wholesaling business in 1908 provoked the Swedish retailers' association (Sveriges Minuthandlares Riksförbund) to ask wholesale merchants to boycott co-operative retailers, and in 1908 the margarine cartel Pellerin agreed to cease supplying KF.[68] KF responded by co-ordinating a national boycott of Pellerin and its sister company Zenith, with the support of trade unions and the labour movement, but it also took the more drastic step of buying its own factory. The action worked and the cartel immediately agreed to resume supplies to the co-operative societies and also to reduce its prices. As Ingrid Millbourn has noted, the outcome was significant in that it demonstrated that cartels could be defeated through investments in co-operative production.[69]

After the war the idea of developing co-operative production as a means to tackle the problem of monopoly became well-established in KF, especially under the leadership of Albin Johansson. This was a period when the phenomenon of trust capitalism was widely debated in Sweden and indeed the other Nordic countries. A state enquiry on trusts and cartels had been established in 1911 and in 1920 there were proposals to introduce state controls on monopolies, followed by new legislation in 1925 providing for investigation of businesses suspected of monopolistic tendencies.[70] Johansson and his KF colleagues remained sceptical about the adequacy of legislation as a response to the problem, however, arguing instead that co-operation needed to develop its own production to protect itself and its consumer-members from the risk of boycotts and price fixing. Johansson insisted that co-operative production should never become an end in itself; rather it should only be undertaken when there was enough capital and when there was a risk of restrictions to the supply of goods.[71] By the late 1920s KF could boast several examples of successful action in this way that were reported in the international press. Its purchase of the Tre Kronor mill in 1922 was reported to have drastically reduced the price of flour and it had been equally successful in breaking a cartel in the manufacture of galoshes.[72]

Albin Johansson was a professional co-operator who had begun his career managing a co-operative store in a Stockholm suburb before joining KF in 1907. According to his biographer, Herman Stolpe, Johansson's belief in the ability of consumer co-operation to hold its own under conditions of free competition was shaped partly by his tutors at the Stockholm business school – including economic historian Eli F. Heckscher – and by his first-hand experience of the German co-operative movement.[73] As Johann Brazda and Robert Schediwy have commented, Johansson was in some respects the epitome of the new, business-minded, pragmatic co-operative leader that was emerging in Europe after 1918, advocating the need to concentrate on practical matters rather than engaging in wider political struggles.[74] But Johansson's pragmatism should not necessarily be read as being devoid of idealism. Throughout the 1920s and 1930s he insisted, sometimes with an enthusiasm that seemed to border on obsession, on the need for the co-operative movement to tackle the problem of monopolies if it were to protect the interests of co-operative consumers. In an article for the *Review of International Co-operation* in 1928, he argued that capitalism had advanced through international collaboration; if co-operation were to combat the negative influence of the trusts then it would have to do the same. The only way to do this was through practical work to promote international co-operative trade.[75]

Johansson proposed a succession of different schemes to the ICWS, all aimed explicitly at tackling what he saw as the growing threat to consumer interests from international monopoly capitalism. He proposed joint action to start the international manufacture of linoleum, and circulated a paper to the ICWS proposing the establishment of a co-operative bureau to monitor information on trusts and cartels. The bureau would be located in Stockholm and KF would meet its costs, provided other members appointed and supported their own representatives.[76] Both of these proposals were rejected, and a meeting of margarine experts convened by the ICA in 1931 concluded that the prominent Jurgens–van den Bergh trust presented no significant threat to the supply of either raw materials or the finished product.[77] Matters were changing fast though, and a new report in 1936 noted that margarine had become a controversial and 'political' commodity, especially in the years 1930–35. The capital-intensive nature of its production meant that the industry was prone to concentration; by 1934 the giant Dutch-English combine Unilever was reported to control about 74 per cent of the world production of margarine. The company was also a major consumer of the global production of edible oils.[78] The report acknowledged that the operation of the combine was an example of 'the great organizational and economic potentialities of capitalist enterprises', not least in its contribution to the rational organisation of production. It was also concerned that the extent of Unilever's control had contributed to raising artificially the price of a commodity considered essential by most working-class households.[79]

Margarine was an old battlefield for KF, but also one of its conspicuous successes. In 1932 it also began to manufacture its own edible oils, and the imports of commodities needed for this grew to form a significant part of the goods handled by NAF during the 1930s.[80] By the late 1930s KF had factories for the production of a wide range of commodities, including vegetable oils, coffee, shoes, superphosphates (fertiliser), leather goods, galoshes, tyres and other rubber goods, confectionary, cash registers and porcelain, as well as margarine, flour and other milled grain products.[81] Although KF leaders liked to emphasise the pragmatism of their business decisions, the symbolic value of these commodities should not be overlooked.

Margarine can be seen, in Harriet Friedmann's words, as 'a microcosm of industrial food as a whole', typical of the new types of industrial food commodities that emerged in the late nineteenth century and the transnational chains associated with their production and distribution.[82] Invented in France in 1870 and first commercially produced in the Netherlands, margarine was attractive as a cheap alternative to butter, but it also raised fears about the possibilities of adulteration, which governments attempted to address through regulation. Nonetheless, margarine quickly became established as a staple of working-class diets across Europe.[83] An investigation carried out by the ICA in 1936 found that margarine was popular everywhere except France, where it was very tightly controlled, and that it had played a significant role in helping to address deficiencies in fats for Europe's growing urban population.[84]

If margarine demonstrated co-operation's capacity to take on the manufacture of an essential modern commodity, then the production of electric lightbulbs carried an even greater symbolic potential. The crowning achievement of KF's battle against the trusts was widely acknowledged to be its breaking of an international lightbulb cartel, which became one of the most visible Nordic successes in co-operative manufacturing during the interwar period. The Luma factory was founded in Stockholm in 1928, intended as a direct challenge to the powerful 'Phoebus' trust. According to KF, the trust controlled much of the production of lightbulbs in interwar Europe, and this had contributed to a marked rise in the price of what was becoming an increasingly important consumer item in Sweden. KF's decision to begin work constructing its own factory in 1928 was enough to trigger a significant fall in the trust's prices, from 1.35 kronor per bulb to 1.10.[85] It was described by the Norwegian co-operative journal as 'a milestone in co-operation's struggle against the trusts'.[86]

By 1931 KF's factory was in full operation and already exceeding its planned production of 8,000 bulbs per day.[87] Its significance lay not only in its effects on domestic prices but also in the aspiration to make the Luma venture an international one, involving the other Nordic co-operative federations in their struggle against international monopoly. After several years of operating Luma as a purely KF venture, a new federation, Kooperativa Lumaförbundet, was established in Copenhagen in May 1931. Like NAF, it was run as a consumer co-operative society with the Nordic co-operative wholesale federations as its members.[88]

In 1934 Norges Kooperative Landsforening (NKL) bought its own lamp factory, which was modernised under the guidance of Luma, and in 1939 Luma was extended to Scotland, where a factory was opened as a partnership between KF and the Scottish CWS.[89] The project was hailed as an instant success, which contributed to significant reductions in the prices of lightbulbs throughout the Nordic countries, and it was praised not only by its Swedish founders but also by Henry May, the secretary of the ICA.[90] As the 'first international co-operative factory', Luma was a challenge to 'the masterly inactivity of International Co-operation ... in the fields either of combating the Trusts or of rationalising the production and supplies in general', wrote May. It deserved to be widely emulated,

> in order that we may establish the claim of Co-operation as the only bulwark of the consumer, the only remedy for the present topsy-turvy economic system, and the only effective means of removing the present world depression.[91]

Like margarine, electric lightbulb production was capital intensive and required considerable technical expertise. Reports on the original Luma factory in the co-operative press praised its 'hypermodern' control of raw materials and production methods, supported by an in-house laboratory for scientific testing.[92]

The result was a product that was not only cheaper than the lightbulbs produced by the cartel but also longer lasting.[93] Not only that, but the laboratory was also designed to generate its own propaganda. The lightbulbs were tested by burning them continuously in a giant glass tower, so that, as Danish *Andelsbladet* reported, 'the Luma light streams out through the glass walls over Stockholm and proclaims to everyone with eyes in his head the consumers' struggle against the international lamp monopoly'.[94] Co-operative Luma lightbulbs stood as a metaphor for the ways in which co-operation could enlighten the world, while at the same time they helped ease the dark northern winters for co-operative consumers.[95]

Rational modernity: co-operation and the Nordic 'middle way'

As the Luma example illustrates, Nordic co-operators were well aware of the potential importance of the goods that they supplied to convey the meanings of co-operation, above all its modernity. The same also applied to their buildings.[96] The central federations such as KF and Finland's SOK, and the large urban consumer societies such as Elanto, took great pride in the modernity of their operations. Modern buildings and factories were presented as metaphors for the efficiency and rationality of consumer co-operation, replacing the traditional hand-to-mouth strategies of small private retailers.[97] 'The present spacious and handsome shops … contrast violently with the mean dilapidated premises of the remaining private traders,' wrote the Swedish co-operator Thorsten Odhe of the Helsinki co-operative Elanto.[98] The opening of a new co-operative department store or production facility – Elanto claimed to have the largest bakery in northern Europe – or the celebration of a jubilee was an excellent opportunity to assert the achievements of co-operation.[99] Such events were doubtless intended partly as an outward demonstration of the movement's strength, but an important target was also the co-operative's own members. In 1935, for example, Elanto members were invited to participate in a week-long series of festivities and an exhibition of co-operative goods, arranged to commemorate the co-operative's thirtieth anniversary.[100]

While the set pieces of congresses, anniversaries or the inauguration of major new buildings offered opportunities to stage large events directed at co-operative audiences at home and abroad, attention was also paid to the more everyday questions of the branding, advertising and display of goods. Pernilla Jonsson has shown how KF was a pioneer of such retailing innovations as shop design and branding in the early twentieth century, and topics such as the arrangement and presentation of stock were discussed in detail in the pages of *Kooperatören*.[101] Some of the traditional co-operative ambivalence to advertising, as a capitalist trick to mislead consumers and create false desires, remained. As Peder Aléx has argued, however, KF came to re-interpret advertising as a form of consumer education, aimed at stimulating rational consumption.[102] In his address to the ICA's 1927 congress in Stockholm, Albin Johansson stated the KF position that the main task of consumer co-operation was to further the rational organisation of distribution, and, notably, he was prepared to argue that this should be pursued even if it came at the expense of member democracy.[103]

The rational modernity of the consumer co-operative movement also had an outward significance, chiming as it did with broader contemporary ideas of Sweden and the Nordic countries as being at the vanguard of modernity. It is widely acknowledged that the Stockholm Exhibition of 1930 was influential in generating international interest in Swedish architecture, design and industry.[104] Peter Stadius has written that the interwar period was a time when the international image of the Nordic countries was transformed. In contrast to the earlier focus on nature and climate, there now emerged, especially in the 1930s, an idea of the region as 'a future-oriented and functioning mass democratic society'.[105] This has to be seen, of course, in the context of the problems of the era: in Europe, the Nordic region became a source of hope in the struggle against fascism and communism, while in the USA Sweden in particular attracted interest for its rapid recovery from the Great Depression.[106]

The co-operative movement had its own role to play in the establishment of this narrative, starting as discussed with interest in Danish agricultural co-operatives from the turn of the century. From the 1930s, however, as the Danish agricultural model faltered with the abandonment of free trade, the focus of attention shifted towards Sweden and KF as an example of the role of consumer co-operation in modern industrial society. One of the best-known texts on Sweden in this era – Marquis Childs' bestseller *Sweden – the Middle Way* (1936) – was not exclusively about co-operation, nor was it the only text on the Scandinavian co-operative movements to appear during the 1930s, but it was certainly very significant.[107] Piebe Teeboom writes that the book went through nine printings and 25,000 copies were sold in 1936 alone, and it was also widely debated.[108]

American interest in Scandinavian co-operatives reached its peak in the summer of 1936 following the publication of Childs' book. Childs devoted the first four chapters to co-operatives, including KF, NAF and housing co-operatives. He also included a chapter on agricultural co-operatives in Denmark.[109] He was particularly interested in the co-operative campaigns to break monopolies and devoted several pages to describing the Luma initiative.[110] Co-operation in Sweden was not symptomatic of a drift towards collectivism, wrote Childs; rather, it was 'a brake to halt the excesses of capitalism; to prevent monopoly and the narrow concentration of wealth; in short to check the very tendencies by which capitalism tends to destroy itself'.[111] His analysis echoed Frederic C. Howe's insistence that co-operation in Denmark was reforming capitalism rather than replacing it.[112] Co-operation had become 'the very texture of everyday life in Denmark', wrote Howe, but it had also contributed to ending the gulf between economic and political life, where the privileged few governed the many engaged in economic activities.[113]

In June 1936 Childs' book was cited by President Roosevelt as the inspiration for his decision to establish the Inquiry on Co-operative Enterprise in Europe.[114] A committee of six spent two and a half months in Europe in the summer of 1936, visiting co-operative societies and interviewing their leaders together with prominent individuals from business and politics in Britain, Czechoslovakia, France, Ireland and Switzerland. The bulk of their time and attention was directed towards Scandinavia, especially Sweden, and the Nordic co-operatives took a prominent position in the Inquiry's report.[115] By the time the report was published early in 1937 the President's interest in co-operatives had waned and the report had relatively little impact on the New Deal debates of the late 1930s.[116] But Nordic co-operation continued to attract the interest of foreign authors. It was reported in the *Review of International Co-operation* that the publication of Childs' book had 'resulted in a crowd of American visitors to study co-operative enterprise on the spot', and Albin Johansson told the ICA's Executive that he had received several offers of expenses-paid lecture tours in America.[117]

Indeed, co-operative societies featured prominently in many of the travelogues and social reports published on the Nordic region during the late 1930s. J. Hampden Jackson cited Finland as an example of a 'middle way between private enterprise and the State', which had achieved a capitalist system 'shorn of its nineteenth-century ruthlessness and trimmed to the egalitarian ideals of the twentieth century'.[118] One of the keys to this success was the agricultural co-operative movement.[119] O. Grimley, who had joined a group of American writers to tour agricultural co-operatives was impressed with the scientific and rational approach of the co-operatives he found in Norway, and commented how they helped Norwegians to 'learn to co-operate in a larger sense – working together, instead of fighting each other to the detriment of both themselves and the nation as a whole'.[120] This point was also made by the members of the Roosevelt commission, when KF laid on a dinner for them that was attended by representatives of Swedish business and politics. So impressed were they by the social harmony and sense of shared responsibility that this conveyed, that they sent a copy of the seating plan to the President as part of their preliminary report on co-operation in the Scandinavian countries.[121]

Inevitably, these accounts conveyed an idealised picture of co-operation in the Nordic countries. Although Childs in particular was criticised for this by his reviewers, it is rare – in the English-language accounts at least – to find any overtly hostile or critical accounts of Nordic co-operation.[122] This was probably due to the overwhelming emphasis on the pragmatic, non-ideological nature of Nordic co-operation and its success in mitigating the worst excesses of capitalism and thus stabilising it. In his description of KF, Childs noted the emphasis on practical problems: a 'curious resistance to abstract arguments' and 'little consideration for the ultimate aim of rebuilding society'.[123] Indeed, he argued that co-operation could barely be considered a movement at all because it was so 'free of proselytism'.[124] This chimed with co-operators' own insistence on the political neutrality of their movement and helps explain why, in an era of ideological extremes, pragmatism came to be strongly associated with the idea of the Swedish and Nordic 'middle way'.[125]

Conclusion

Peder Aléx has analysed the development of co-operative thought in detail, in his study of the leading thinkers in KF during the first four decades of the twentieth century. He rightly notes the diversity of co-operative ideology, but suggests that the conception of co-operation's role coalesced around moral improvement: resolving class conflict, guaranteeing freedom, democracy and peace, and promoting rationalisation. This last point referred not just to the rational organisation of retailing and distribution, but also in the home, where co-operation was intended to educate consumers to be aware of their true needs.[126]

Although there are continuities in these ideas running throughout the period, co-operative ideology was never fixed. Aléx analyses how one of KF's leading thinkers, Anders Örne, moved away from his earlier support of Charles Gide's co-operative republic, where competition would cease to exist, towards advocacy of co-operation as the best guarantee of free trade and free competition. This position was supported by other leading figures in KF.[127] 'We consider the right to as much freedom as possible in business activities to be a fundamental condition for a sound economic life', wrote Axel Gjöres in 1925.[128] The principle of free competition was applied within the movement, moreover, with each society free to choose its own supplier. In 1945 Albin Johansson published a book insisting more strongly than ever on co-operation as a movement for freedom that would prevent the need for state intervention.[129]

This was not just a purely theoretical debate, however; it was also to be realised through practical action. KF's successful actions to break monopolies in the different industries discussed above were widely referred to, especially within the other Nordic countries. Addressing the Danish workers' co-operatives, Frederik Nielsen of the FDB referred to KF's successful actions against the galoshes monopoly as an example of what could be achieved when 'the consumers understand what a defensive weapon they have in the co-operative stores'.[130] In Norway the struggle was conceived in terms of the national interest: the takeovers of factories manufacturing tobacco and linoleum demonstrated the vulnerability of a small country to international capital, while NKL's factories, by contrast, were 'Norwegian through and through'.[131] NKL also criticised the revised Norwegian law on trusts, on the grounds that it compromised economic freedom and 'in reality opened the door for economic dictatorship' through its provisions for forced cartellisation in certain industries.[132]

The struggle against monopolies, for example in the electric lightbulb industry, certainly came to form an important part of co-operation's self-image during the 1930s in particular.[133] The struggle was not always as straightforward as it first seems. Norwegian historians have noted that the NKL leadership actually entered into a secret agreement in 1936 for the sharing of patent information with the Phoebus trust, a decision which brought them into conflict with their own organisation and with KF.[134] Co-operation was, as always, shaped here by the need to balance principles with business pragmatism. But the self-image was undoubtedly cemented by the international interest in Swedish and Nordic co-operation during the 1930s, which continued into the post-war era.

Co-operation continued to be cited as an essential feature of the Nordic democracies and their successful management of capitalism during the 1950s, and it was reported that in 1955 alone KF received more than 2,000 visits from foreigners keen to understand 'how Sweden does it'.[135] This interest was not just confined to Sweden.[136] Rather, the successful collaborations between the Nordic co-operative organisations contributed to shaping international perceptions of *Norden* as a coherent region.[137]

Notes

1 F. Nielsen, 'Nordisk Andelsforbund', *Kooperatøren*, 10, 1931, p. 131.

2 On the similar importance of Nordic co-operation in the contemporary League of Nations, see: N. Götz, 'Blue-Eyed Angels at the League of Nations: The Genevese Construction of Norden', in N. Götz and H. Haggrén (eds), *Regional Cooperation and International Organizations: The Nordic Model in Transnational Alignment* (London: Routledge, 2009).

3 See: M. Hilson, 'Consumer Co-operation and Economic Crisis: The 1936 Roosevelt Inquiry on Co-operative Enterprise and the Emergence of the Nordic "Middle Way"', *Contemporary European History*, 22:2 (2013), 181–98.

4 On the international interest in the Nordic region during the 1930s, see: K. Musiał, *Roots of the Scandinavian Model: Images of Progress in the Era of Modernisation* (Baden-Baden: Nomos Verlagsgesellschaft, 2002); P. Stadius, 'Happy Countries: Appraisals of Interwar Nordic Societies', in J. Harvard and P. Stadius (eds), *Communicating the North: Media Structures and Images in the Making of the Nordic Region* (Farnham: Ashgate, 2013); J. Kurunmäki and J. Strang, 'Nordic Democracy in a World of Tensions', in J. Kurunmäki and J. Strang (eds), *Rhetorics of Nordic Democracy* (Helsinki: Finnish Literature Society, 2010).

5 On the co-operative 'third way', see also: K. Miklóssy, 'The Nordic Ideal of a Central European Third Way: The Finnish Model of Hungarian Modernisation in the 1930s', in M. Hilson, P. Markkola and A.-C. Östman (eds), *Co-operatives and the Social Question: The Co-operative Movement in Northern and Eastern Europe (1880–1950)* (Cardiff: Welsh Academic Press, 2012).
6 Musiał, *Scandinavian Model*, pp. 43, 50.
7 C. Bjørn, *Fortid med fremtid: Danske Andelsselskaber 100 år 1899–1999* (Copenhagen: Danske Andelsselskaber, 1999), p. 15.
8 K. H. O'Rourke, 'Property Rights, Politics and Innovation: Creamery Diffusion in pre-1914 Ireland', *European Review of Economic History*, 11 (2007), 359–417: 397.
9 Musiał, *Scandinavian Model*, pp. 42–4.
10 Musiał, *Scandinavian Model*, pp. 42–54.
11 F. C. Howe, *Denmark: A Cooperative Commonwealth* (New York: Harcourt, Brace and Company, 1921), p. iii.
12 Howe, *Cooperative Commonwealth*, p. vii.
13 Howe, *Cooperative Commonwealth*, pp. 30, 59, 198.
14 Reviews by A. Cance in *American Economic Review*, 11:3 (1921), 503–4; V. E. Helleberg in *American Journal of Sociology*, 27:2 (1921), 259; F. A. Ogg in *Political Science Quarterly*, 36:4 (1921), 688–9.
15 F. C. Howe, *Denmark: The Coöperative Way* (New York: Coward-McCann, 1936); also: F. C. Howe, 'The Most Complete Agricultural Recovery in History', *Annals of the American Academy of Political and Social Science*, 172 (March 1934), 123–9.
16 Musiał, *Scandinavian Model*, p. 50.
17 Rigsarkivet, Aarhus (now Viborg) (hereafter DRA): Erhvervsarkivet: 06156 Andelsudvalget: Artikler mm til *The People's Year Book* 1922, Anders Nielsen to James Haslam, 27 July 1922.
18 J. F. Wilson, A. Webster and R. Vorberg-Rugh, *Building Co-operation: A Business History of the Co-operative Group, 1863–2013* (Oxford: Oxford University Press, 2013), pp. 90–2.
19 Wilson Webster and Vorberg-Rugh, *Building Co-operation*, pp. 91, 126.
20 Wilson Webster and Vorberg-Rugh, *Building Co-operation*, p. 90.
21 Wilson Webster and Vorberg-Rugh, *Building Co-operation*, p. 129.
22 P. Doyle, '"Better Farming, Better Business, Better Living": The Irish Co-operative Movement and the Construction of the Irish Nation-State, 1894–1932' (PhD thesis, University of Manchester, 2013), pp. 80–7.
23 C. Bjørn (ed.), *Dansk mejeribrug 1882–2000* (n.p.: De danske Mejeriers Fællesorganisation, 1982), pp. 147–9; E. H. Pedersen et al., *De første hundrede år: Danske slagterier 1887–1987* (Copenhagen: Danske Slagterier, 1987), pp. 48–53; D. M. Higgins and M. Mordhorst, 'Reputation and Export Performance: Danish Butter Exports and the British Market, c.1880–c.1914', *Business History*, 50:2 (2008), 185–204.
24 Howe, *Coöperative Way*, p. 1; Musiał, *Scandinavian Model*, pp. 46, 51.
25 H. Kaufmann, 'The Direct Exchange of Goods between Distributive Societies, Agricultural and Other Productive Societies, also between the Wholesale Societies

in the Different Countries,' *Report of the Proceedings of the Ninth Congress of the ICA, held at Glasgow, 25–28 August 1913* (hereafter *ICA Congress Proceedings 1913*) (London: ICA, 1913), pp. 48–76.

26 *ICA Congress Proceedings 1913*, pp. 100–2.

27 B. Jaeggi, 'Relations between Consumers' and Agricultural Co-operative Societies', *Report of the Proceedings of the Twelfth Congress of the ICA, held at Stockholm, 15–18 August 1927* (hereafter *ICA Congress Proceedings 1927*), pp. 149–63.

28 Työväen arkisto, Helsinki (hereafter TA): 334.5 Kansainvälinen Osuustoimintaliito (KOL), Box 0.3: Report on proceedings of special meeting of ICA Central Committee, Brussels, 28 April 1927.

29 TA: 334.5 KOL, Box 0.4: Report on proceedings of ICA Executive meeting, Liège, 26–27 July 1928; TA: 334.5 KOL, Box 0.5: Report on proceedings of ICA Executive meeting, London, 1 October 1929.

30 TA: 334.5 KOL, Box 0.5: Report on proceedings of ICA Executive meeting, London, 1 October 1929.

31 TA: 334.5 KOL, Box 0.7: Report on proceedings of ICA Central Committee meeting, Leipzig, 27 March 1930; 'Report of the Central Committee on the Work of the International Co-operative Alliance, 1927–1929', Agenda of the Thirteenth International Co operative Congress, Vienna, 25–28 August 1930, p. 23. There were some objections to the word 'fetish'. This was left to stand in the English version of the published report, but the Central Committee agreed to change the French version.

32 See chapter 3.

33 H. J. May, 'The International Co-operative Alliance in 1930', *Review of International Co-operation*, February 1931, pp. 41–7.

34 TA: 334.5 KOL, Box 0.5: Report on proceedings of ICA Central Committee meeting, London, 3–4 October 1929.

35 TA: 334.5 KOL, Box 3: Report on proceedings of ICA Executive meeting, Prague, 29–30 June 1932.

36 TA: 334.5 KOL, Box 1: Minutes of ICA Central Committee meeting, Paris, 30 September – 1 October 1931.

37 E. Poisson, 'The International Co-operative Movement and the World Economic Conference', paper to Special Conference of the ICA in Basel, June 1933. Included in TA: 334.5 KOL, Box 6: H. May to V. Tanner, 27 May 1933.

38 'Næppe noget andet Sted ser man Folk af de forskellige Samfundsklasser saaledes samlet i Andelsselskaberne som her i Landet … den danske Andelsbevægelse snarere har Betydning for ICA en omvendt.' DRA: Erhvervsarkivet: 06156 Andelsudvalget 1921–1962 korrespondance mv med ICA 322: A. Axelsen Drejer, 'Den danske Andelsbevægelses Deltagelse i det internationale Samarbejde' (n.d. 1926).

39 A. D., 'Centralbestyrelsesmøde i Det internationale Andelsforbund', *Andelsbladet*, 5 November 1926, pp. 1263–7.

40 TA: 334.5 KOL, Box 0.4: Report on proceedings of ICA Executive meeting, Bremen, 28–31 March 1928.

41 A. Axelsen Drejer, 'Relations between Consumers' and Agricultural Co-operative Societies', *Review of International Co-operation*, May 1929, pp. 180–91;

A. Axelsen Drejer, 'The Structure and Organisation of the Co-operative Movement in Denmark', *Review of International Co-operation*, September 1930, pp. 358–65; A. Axelsen Drejer, 'The Co-operative Movement in Denmark: Its Position, Importance and Spirit', *Review of International Co-operation*, March 1935, pp. 81–5; also: A. Hedberg, 'Farmers' Co-operation in Denmark', *Review of International Co-operation*, February 1930, pp. 53–6.

42 R. Rhodes, *The International Co-operative Alliance during War and Peace 1910–1950* (Geneva: ICA, 1995), pp. 26–7; S. Webb and B. Webb, *The Consumers' Co-operative Movement* (published by authors, 1921), p. 282, which argues that the ICA had definitely become an association of consumers as early as 1901.

43 F. Trentmann, 'The Modern Genealogy of the Consumer: Meanings, Identities and Political Synapses', in J. Brewer and F. Trentmann (eds), *Consuming Cultures, Global Perspectives: Historical Trajectories, Transnational Exchanges* (Oxford: Berg, 2006).

44 For a discussion of Gide's co-operative thought, see: E. Furlough, *Consumer Cooperation in France: The Politics of Consumption 1834–1930* (Ithaca: Cornell University Press, 1991), pp. 83–97.

45 C. Gide, *Congrès international* (1889), pp. 6–7; cited and translated in Furlough, *Consumer Cooperation in France*, p. 86.

46 C. Gide, *Consumers' Co-operative Societies*, trans. staff of the Co-operative Reference Library, Dublin (Manchester: Co-operative Union, 1921), pp. 1, 3.

47 On Gide and the Nîmes School, see: Furlough, *Consumer Co-operation in France*, pp. 83–97.

48 H. M. Kallen, *The Decline and Rise of the Consumer: A Philosophy of Consumer Co-operation* (New York: D. Appleton-Century, 1936), pp. ix–xi; H. M. Kallen, 'Philosophical and Ethical Aspects of Consumer Co-operation', *Annals of American Academy of Political and Social Science*, 191 (May 1937), 1–6.

49 This is also discussed in M. Hilson, 'A Consumers' International? The International Cooperative Alliance and Cooperative Internationalism, 1918–1939: A Nordic Perspective', *International Review of Social History*, 56:2 (2011), 203–33.

50 P. Aléx, *Den rationella konsumenten. KF som folkuppfostrare 1899–1939* (Stockholm/Stehag: Brutus Östlings Bokförlag Symposion, 1994), pp. 103–4; W. P. Watkins, *The International Co-operative Alliance 1895–1970* (London: ICA, 1970), p. 129.

51 A. Örne, *Co-operative Ideals and Problems*, trans. John Downie (Manchester: Co-operative Union, 1926); A. Johansson, *Aktuella kooperativa problem* (Stockholm: Kooperativa Förbundets bokförlag, 1927).

52 Aléx, *Den rationella konsumenten*, pp. 104–8.

53 'Det innehålla icke ett enda ord med eggande revolutionär klang, icke den minsta antydan om sociologiskt djupsinne.' A. Örne, *De sju grundsatserna. Kooperationens program i kort sammanfattning* (Stockholm: Kooperativa Förbundets bokförlag, 1934; first published 1919), p. 6.

54 'dessa till synes så anspråkslösa regler, konsekvent tillämpade, måste leda direkt fram till ett samhälle av helt annan typ än det nuvarande.' Örne, *De sju grundsatserna*, p. 6.

55 Örne, *Co-operative Ideals*, p. 2.
56 A. Örne, 'Till kooperationens teori. Spridda randanateckningar till två artiklar i *Kooperatören*', *Kooperatören*, 23, December 1922, pp. 397–403.
57 K. Friberg, 'Visions and Organisation: Kooperativa Förbundet and the Social Question in Sweden', in Hilson, Markkola and Östman (eds), *Co-operatives and the Social Question*.
58 O. Ruin, *Kooperativa Förbundet 1899–1929: En organisationsstudie* (Lund: Rabén & Sjögren, 1960), p. 203.
59 Ruin, *Kooperativa Förbundet*, pp. 196–208.
60 Ruin, *Kooperativa Förbundet*, pp. 208–12.
61 T. Dehli Laurantzon, 'Sveriges kooperasjon og jordbruket', *Kooperatøren*, 21, 1932, p. 263; 'Swedish Agricultural and Consumers' Co-operation', *Review of International Co-operation*, May 1932, pp. 203–5; 'Agreement between the Swedish Consumers' and Agricultural Organisations', *Review of International Co-operation*, November 1936, pp. 426–8.
62 'ty den svenska kooperationen är f.n. sammansatt av konsumenter ur alla samhällsklasser och alla politiska partier.' Johansson, *Aktuella kooperativa problem*, p. 40.
63 E. Hobsbawm, *Age of Extremes: The Short Twentieth Century 1914–1994* (London: Michael Joseph, 1994), pp. 85–97. For another view, see: R. Boyce, *The Great Interwar Crisis and the Collapse of Globalization* (Basingstoke: Palgrave Macmillan, 2009), who suggests that business as usual was successfully resumed after the war and halted only after 1929 by the Slump.
64 For an overview of this development, see: Hobsbawm, *Age of Extremes*, pp. 42–5.
65 Webb and Webb, *Consumers' Co-operative Movement*, pp. 272–4.
66 KF, 'Det kooperativa programmet' (1921); cited and translated in Örne, *Co-operative Ideals*, p. 2.
67 A. Örne, *Kooperativa idéer och spörsmål* (Stockholm: Kooperativa Förbundets bokförlag, 1924), pp. 19–20.
68 H. Kylebäck, *Konsumentkooperation och industrikarteller* (Stockholm: Rabén & Sjögren, 1974), p. 43, for the margarine conflict pp. 88–107; A. Gjöres, *Konsumentkooperationen i Sverige* (Stockholm: Tidens förlag, 1925), pp. 101–2. Margarine manufacturers also boycotted NKL in 1911. See: E. Lange (ed.), *Organisert kjøpekraft. Forbrukersamvirkets historie i Norge* (Oslo: Pax forlag, 2006), p. 200.
69 I. Millbourn, 'Kooperatismen – ett alternativ till kapitalismen och socialdemokrati 1900–1920', *Scandia*, 57:1 (1991), 89–112: 105; Kylebäck, *Konsumentkooperation*, p. 107.
70 Kylebäck, *Konsumentkooperation*, pp. 72–4.
71 Kylebäck, *Konsumentkooperation*, p. 78.
72 'Kooperasjonen og monopolerne i Sverige', *Kooperatøren*, 1929, pp. 6–7. This was translated from an article by Herman Stolpe in *International Labour Review*.
73 H. Stolpe, 'K. Albin A. Johansson', *Svenskt biografiskt lexikon*, available at https://sok.riksarkivet.se/Sbl/Presentation.aspx?id=12127, last accessed 3 July

2017; also: M. W. Childs, 'Sweden: Where Capitalism Is Controlled', *Harper's Monthly Magazine*, 167:1002 (November 1933), p. 757.

74 J. Brazda and R. Schediwy, 'Consumer Co-operatives on the Defensive: a Short Overview', in J. Brazda and R. Schediwy (eds), *A Time of Crises: Consumer Co-operatives and Their Problems Around 1990* (Vienna: Fachbereichs für Genossenschaftswesen, 2011), pp. 18–19; on Johansson, see also: H. Stolpe and S. Stolpe, *Boken om Albin Johansson*, 2 vols (Stockholm: Rabén & Sjögren, 1969).

75 A. Johansson, 'Private Enterprise and International Co-operation', *Review of International Co-operation*, June 1928, pp. 212–16.

76 Kooperativa Förbundets arkiv: Albin Johanssons personarkiv: Diverse XIII: 'Utdrag ur International Co-operative Wholesale Societys handlingar', n.d. (*c*.1936), pp. 9, 12–14; TA: 334.5 KOL, Box 0.4: Report on proceedings of ICA Executive meeting, Liège, 26–27 July 1928.

77 TA: HNA 14: Minutes of meeting of margarine experts, 13 February 1931; minutes of joint meeting of ICWS and ICA executives, 14 April 1931.

78 TA: 334.5 KOL, Box 10: ICA, 'Private monopolies', pp. 5, 27.

79 TA: 334.5 KOL, Box 10: ICA, 'Private monopolies', p. 6.

80 Työväen kirjasto, Helsinki: NAF aarsberetning, 1932; M. Bonow, 'Developments in the Swedish Production of Margarine, 1919–1935', *Review of International Co-operation*, July 1936, pp. 249–55.

81 Kylebäck, *Konsumentkooperation*, p. 86.

82 H. Friedmann, 'Food', in A. Iriye and P.-Y. Saunier (eds), *The Palgrave Dictionary of Transnational History: From the Mid-19th-Century to the Present Day* (Basingstoke: Palgrave Macmillan, 2009), p. 419.

83 For the importance of margarine in British working-class diets – and ambivalence towards it – see: A. Levene, 'The Meanings of Margarine in England: Class, Consumption and Material Culture from 1918 to 1953', *Contemporary British History*, 28:2 (2014), 145–65.

84 TA: 334.5 KOL, Box 10: ICA, 'Private monopolies in the production and distribution of essential commodities', memorandum no. 2 on margarine (1936).

85 A. Hedberg, 'Luma: An International Venture', *Review of International Co-operation*, August 1932, pp. 309–11; P. L. M., 'Et Lyspalads. Kooperativa Förbundet begynder Fabrikationen af Glødelamper', *Andelsbladet*, 27:9, February 1931, p. 285.

86 'en merkepel i kooperasjonens kamp mot trustene.' 'Kooperativa Förbundet i kamp mot den internasjonale glødelamptrust', *Kooperatøren*, 11, 1928, pp. 122–3.

87 C. K., 'Luma-Lampen', *Andelsbladet*, 25 September 1931, pp. 1336–41.

88 A. Hedberg, 'Lumas födelse', *Kooperatören*, 1932, pp. 3–9; Hedberg, 'Luma: An International Venture'.

89 'Norges kooperative Landsforening køber Glødelampfabrik i Oslo', *Andelsbladet*, 8 June 1934, pp. 904–5; 'The Luma Factory in Scotland', *Review of International Co-operation*, September 1939, pp. 441–3.

90 Hedberg, 'Luma: An International Venture'.

91 H. J. May, 'Luma – The First International Co-operative Factory', *Review of International Co-operation*, January 1933, pp. 8–9.

92 On the modernity of electric lighting, see: J. B. Chadaga, 'Light in Captivity: Spectacular Glass and Soviet Power in the 1920s and 1930s', *Slavic Review*, 66:1 (2007), 82–105; J. Garnert, 'Upplysningens århundrade', in Y. Hirdman, U. Lundberg and J. Björkman (eds), *Sveriges historia 1920–1965*, vol. 7 of *Norstedts Sveriges historia* (Stockholm: Norstedts, 2012), pp. 373–8.

93 C. K., 'Luma-lampen', pp. 1336–41; 'Nordens Andelsfolks Fællesfront mod Lampe-kartellet', *Andelsbladet*, 15 September 1933, pp. 1424–6.

94 'Gennem Glasvæggene strømmer Luma-Lyset ud over Stockholm og fortæller enhver, der har Øjne i Hovedet, at Forbrugernes Forsvarskamp mod det internationale Glødelampekartel er i fuld Gang.' C.K., 'Luma-lampen', pp. 1336–1341;

95 'Nordens Andelsfolks Fællesfront mod Lampe-kartellet', *Andelsbladet*, 15 September 1933, pp. 1424–6. See also: Hilson, 'Consumers' International?', 203–33: 230.

96 On the 'symbolic capital' of buildings, see: I. S. Black, 'Spaces of Capital: Bank Office Building in the City of London, 1830–1870', *Journal of Historical Geography*, 26:3 (2000), 351–75.

97 T. Odhe, *The Place of Co-operation in World Economy* (London: ICA, 1947), p. 13.

98 T. Odhe, *Finland: A Nation of Co-operators*, trans. J. Downie (London: Williams & Norgate, 1931), p. 87.

99 'Suurleipomo ja siihen liittyvä mylly ovat nyt täydessä kunnossa', *Elanto*, 5, March 1925; 'Pohjois-Euroopan suurin leipomo työssä', *Elanto*, 6, March 1925.

100 'Näyttely ja suurjuhlat Messuhallissa', *Elanto*, 4 October 1935; 'Elannon näyttely ja suurjuhlat', *Elanto*, 1 November 1935. The paper reported that 105,000 had attended the exhibition.

101 P. Jonsson, 'From Commercial Trickery to Social Responsibility: Marketing in the Swedish Co-operative Movement in the Early Twentieth Century', in M. Hilson, S. Neunsinger and G. Patmore (eds), *A Global History of Consumer Co-operation since 1850: Movements and Businesses* (Leiden: Brill, 2017). For examples, see: R. Molin, 'Varorna i butiken', *Kooperatören*, August 1923, pp. 249–54; A. Hedberg, 'Behovet av dåliga varor', *Kooperatören*, October 1923, pp. 317–19.

102 Aléx, *Den rationella konsumenten*.

103 Johansson, *Aktuella kooperativa problem*, pp. 5, 9–11; also: Odhe, *Place of Co-operation*, p. 3.

104 Musiał, *Scandinavian Model*; P. Stadius and C. Marklund, 'Acceptance and Conformity: Merging Modernity with Nationalism in the Stockholm Exhibition in 1930', *Culture Unbound: Journal of Current Cultural Research*, 2 (2010), 609–34.

105 P. Stadius, 'Happy Countries', pp. 242–3.

106 Stadius, 'Happy Countries', p. 259.

107 Musiał, *Scandinavian Model*, p. 197.

108 P. Teeboom, 'Searching for the Middle Way: Consumer Co-operation and the Co-operative Movement in New Deal America' (PhD dissertation, University of Amsterdam, 2009), ch. 3, p. 53.

109 Childs justified his inclusion of the Danish co-operatives 'because of the great influence it has exerted upon Sweden', which was debatable. M. W. Childs, *Sweden – the Middle Way* (revised edn, New York: Penguin Books, 1948; first published 1936), p. 129.
110 Childs, *Sweden*, pp. 30–6.
111 Childs, *Sweden*, p. 44.
112 Howe, *Cooperative Commonwealth*, pp. 29–30.
113 Howe, *Cooperative Commonwealth*, pp. vi–vii.
114 Teeboom, 'Searching for the Middle Way', ch. 4, pp. 1–2. The following also draws on Hilson, 'Consumer Co-operation and Economic Crisis'.
115 US Government, *Report of the Inquiry on Cooperative Enterprise in Europe 1937* (Washington, DC: United States Government Printing Office, 1937).
116 Teeboom, 'Searching for the Middle Way', ch. 4.
117 'Notes and Comments', *Review of International Co-operation*, August 1936, pp. 282–3; TA: 334.5 KOL, Box 11: Report on proceedings of ICA Executive meeting, Warsaw, 27 September 1936. See also Hilson, 'Consumer Co-operation and Economic Crisis', 189.
118 J. Hampden Jackson, *Finland* (revised 2nd edn, London: George Allen & Unwin Ltd, 1940; first published 1938), p. 15.
119 Hampden Jackson, *Finland*, p. 132.
120 O. B. Grimley, *The New Norway: A People with the Spirit of Co-operation* (Oslo: Johan Grundt Tanum, 1939), p. 107.
121 Franklin D. Roosevelt Presidential Library: President's Committee on an Inquiry on Cooperative Enterprise in Europe Records, 1936–37: Box 6: Preliminary Report on Scandinavia; Box 5: Guest list for KF dinner 15 July 1936. See also: Hilson, 'Consumer Co-operation and Economic Crisis', 192.
122 Reviews of Childs, *Sweden* by Sune Carlsson in *Journal of Political Economy*, 45:2 (1937), 273–5 and John H. Vuorinen in *Political Science Quarterly*, 52:2 (1937), 283–4; also: G. R. Mitchinson, 'Retail Trade and the Co-operative Movement', in M. Cole and C. Smith (eds), *Democratic Sweden: A Volume of Studies Prepared by Members of the New Fabian Research Bureau* (London: George Routledge and Sons, 1938), pp. 208–25.
123 Childs, *Sweden*, pp. 4, 10.
124 Childs, *Sweden*, p. 23.
125 C. Marklund, 'The Social Laboratory, the Middle Way and the Swedish Model: Three Frames for the Image of Sweden', *Scandinavian Journal of History*, 34:3 (2009), 264–85.
126 Aléx, *Den rationella konsumenten*, pp. 115–21.
127 Aléx, *Den rationella konsumenten*, pp. 112–15.
128 'Vi anse rätten till möjligast fri företagsverksamhet vara ett fundamentalt villkor för ett sunt ekonomiskt liv.' Gjöres, *Konsumentkooperationen*, pp. 108–9.
129 A. Johansson, *Frihetsgaranti – skapande samverkan* (Stockholm: Kooperativa Förbundets bokförlag, 1945), p. 17.
130 'Forbrugerne lærer at forstaa, hvilket Forsvarsvaaben de har i Brugsforeningerne.' F. Nielsen, 'Den kooperative Produktions Betydning i Kampen mod Truster og

Karteller', *Kooperationen*, 9, September 1929, pp. 122–8; continued in 10, October 1929, pp. 135–40.

131 'Trustkampen', *Kooperatøren*, 4 1924, pp. 37–8; 'Kampen mot trustveldet', *Kooperatøren*, 2 February 1928, pp. 13–14.

132 'åpner i virkeligheten døren for et økonomisk diktatur efter de aller beste opskrifter.' TA: HNA 16 KK/OTK 1932–1940 NAF correspondence: Trustloven i Norge: Foredrag av sekretær Randolf Arnesen ved Det Nordiske Kooperative Kursus i Middelfart, 29/8–1/9 1938. See also: Lange, *Organisert kjøpekraft*, p. 198.

133 Lange, *Organisert kjøpekraft*, p. 201.

134 Lange, *Organisert kjøpekraft*, pp. 202–3.

135 J. W. Ames, *Co-operative Sweden Today* (Manchester: Co-operative Union, 1956), p. 9.

136 C. C. Thomson and M. Hilson, 'Beauty in Bacon: "The Pattern of Co-operation" and the Export of Postwar Danish democracy', *Kosmorama*, 255 (2014), available at www.kosmorama.org/Artikler/Beauty-in-Bacon.aspx, accessed 4 July 2017; M. Hilson, P. Markkola and A.-C. Östman, 'Introduction: Co-operatives and the Social Question', in Hilson, Markkola and Östman (eds), *Co-operatives and the Social Question*, pp. 14–15.

137 See, for example: G. R. Nelson et al. (eds), *Freedom and Welfare: Social Patterns in The Northern Countries of Europe* (Copenhagen: Ministries of Social Affairs of Denmark, Finland, Iceland, Norway, Sweden, 1953), pp. 191–234.

Conclusion

The six members of the official US Inquiry on Co-operative Enterprise in Europe, reporting their preliminary findings to President Roosevelt in August 1936, presented a highly favourable picture of the Nordic co-operative movements. At this stage of their travels they had spent a month in the Nordic region and had interviewed about 120 individuals, both from within the co-operative movement and outside it. They reported that co-operative enterprise was universally recognised as having an important role in national economic life, and that it was acknowledged to have had a stabilising influence since the depression.[1] A significant proportion of the Nordic population lived in households where there was at least one member of a consumer co-operative: over 20 per cent in Norway, over 30 per cent in Denmark and Sweden and over 50 per cent in Finland.[2] They also estimated that co-operatives accounted for approximately 10 per cent of the retail trade in Denmark and Sweden and more than a third in Finland.[3] Statistics on co-operation are difficult to verify and must be treated with care, but the raw data on membership collected by the Inquiry do seem to correspond with other available data (see table C.1). The Inquiry members tried hard to present an impartial and sober assessment of Nordic co-operation as a corrective to some of the more hyperbolic accounts. Their assessment of the significance of co-operative retail trade in Sweden also corresponds to the findings of a team of Fabian Society researchers who visited in the summer of 1937.[4]

By the eve of the Second World War, the co-operative movements of the Nordic countries could certainly celebrate some conspicuous successes. Most visible were the successful challenges to the trusts, such as the Luma factory, but consumer co-operatives also drew international praise for the modernity and efficiency of their operations, and for their role in the successful defence of democracy against authoritarian challenge. An official English-language guide to Nordic society, produced in 1953 under the collaborative sponsorship of the Nordic Ministries of Social Welfare, devoted a whole section to the co-operative movement, noting that it was 'one of the major factors influencing the level of education and culture of the population as well as the forms

Table C.1 Membership of consumer co-operative societies, as percentage of population in selected countries, 1935–39

Country	Population		Number of consumer co-operative societies		Members of consumer co-operative societies		Members as percentage of population	
	1935	1939	1935	1939	1935	1939	1935	1939
Denmark	3,705,559	3,749,000	1,939	1,851	354,000	380,000	9.6	10.1
Finland	3,762,026	3,660,000	532	542	517,763	606,000	13.8	16.6
France	41,228,000	41,906,000	2,908*	1,176	2,540,290*	1,695,000	6.2	4.0
Britain	46,082,000	50,232,000	1,118	1,133	7,483,976	8,023,000	16.2	16.0
Norway	2,817,124	2,911,000	497	626	138,557	169,000	4.9	5.8
Sweden	6,211,566	6,285,000	719	715	568,161	635,000	9.1	10.1
Switzerland	4,066,400	4,176,000	585*	916	402,535*	450,000	9.9	10.8

*1934.

Note: 1935 figures for Britain include Northern Ireland and the Irish Free State. It is not specified whether this is the case for the 1939 source.

Sources: (1935) US Government, *Report of the Inquiry on Cooperative Enterprise in Europe 1937* (Washington, DC: United States Government Printing Office, 1937), p. 7, table I; (1939) H. Gebhard and I. Rahola, *Huvuddraget av andelsrörelsen i Finland*, trans. A. Lagus (Helsinki: Sällskapet Pellervo, 1939), p. 36.

and contents of public life'. For this reason, it had 'long been among those aspects of Northern life which have attracted most interest in the outside world'.[5]

Co-operation has thus often been ascribed a special role in histories of the Nordic countries and the distinctive Nordic 'paths to modernity'.[6] The emphasis on co-operation in its broadest sense seems to chime with perceptions of the Nordic region as one that came to be characterised by compromise, consensus and social harmony in the twentieth century. But at the same time, with the possible exceptions of Denmark and Finland where the agricultural co-operative movement played a much greater role in the national consciousness, the co-operative *movement* has often been curiously invisible in accounts of the Nordic model.[7] From the 1960s Nordic exceptionalism came to be understood largely in terms of the strong state as the means to manage capitalism and mitigate its negative impacts, aided by a voluntary system of collective bargaining in the labour market.[8] Less attention has been paid to the role of consumer co-operatives in the Nordic model of capitalism, even though co-operative businesses outperformed many of their European counterparts in the competitive retailing sector of the late twentieth century.[9]

The same paradox – of success and invisibility – also applies to the ICA. Historian Patricia Clavin has shown how the economic crisis of the 1930s highlighted the interdependence of economic and political affairs, forcing the League of Nations to grapple with questions of nutrition, housing, employment and social inequality in its international diplomacy.[10] With its claims to represent the interests of over 70 million individual members in 1930,[11] a large proportion of whom were the working-class members of consumer co-operatives, the ICA felt itself well-placed to play a leading role in these international debates. ICA activists were convinced of the distinctiveness of their movement and the opportunities it offered to tackle 'the great and varied changes in the economic life of the world which have been brought about by the world war', while acknowledging that they were faced with 'a new orientation of economic life which demands a new outlook and new methods', very different to the laissez-faire liberalism under which the Rochdale Pioneers had founded their famous society.[12]

Despite this, and despite its undisputed presence in everyday life as the supplier of essential groceries, the international co-operative movement is curiously absent from accounts of interwar internationalism. The ICA has received scant attention in the histories of international organisations of this period, but this neglect also mirrors the frustrations of co-operators at that time, as they struggled to persuade the League of Nations to give formal recognition to the ICA in its activities. Any discussion of ICA history therefore needs to give attention not only to explaining its apparent successes but also to its failures and difficulties in making a greater impact on international debates.

It is possible that part of the explanation, at least, lies in the fact that, as Katarina Friberg has suggested, the co-operative movement was simply 'too big to be visible'.[13] Co-operators liked to think of their movement as embodying ideas and principles that were universal – after all, who would not want to be thought of as co-operative? – but at the same time this meant that it was sometimes difficult to define what co-operation actually was. Throughout this book, I have tried to acknowledge that there was always a duality in the meaning of co-operation.[14] It was both a social movement and a business; motivated by ideological principle and steered by commercial pragmatism; opposed to capitalism but forced to compete for market share and willing to learn practical lessons from capitalist businesses.

For most of the period covered by this book, the ICA was an organisation mostly – though never exclusively – of consumer co-operatives. For these organisations the Rochdale Equitable Pioneers Society was a common reference point, and it was therefore to Rochdale that the ICA turned when it attempted to establish a set of definitive co-operative principles in the 1930s. These were eventually agreed in 1937, but not without some controversy. There were those – especially in the Soviet Union but also in Austria, Britain and elsewhere – who wished the ICA to adopt an explicitly socialist position as the third pillar of the international working-class movement alongside socialist parties and trade unions. Against this position, another group championed the commitment to political neutrality, and it was in defence of this that the Nordic co-operative organisations emerged as an influential force during the interwar period. Such was the significance of these different national positions, and the difficulties that these presented to attempts to reach agreement, that it may be hard to speak of co-operative internationalism at all.

At the same time it could also be argued that the appeal of co-operation lay in its ideological ambivalence. In the wake of the Great Depression and the political extremism of the 1930s, co-operation was cited as a 'middle way', between capitalism and state socialism.[15] As Anthony Webster and colleagues have noted, the attractiveness of co-operation as a 'hidden alternative' within the capitalist economy lay not so much in its ideology as in its 'instrumental practicability': its ability to offer concrete, tangible solutions to acute problems in times of crisis.[16] It should not be forgotten, of course, that consumer co-operatives also attracted hostility in many parts of Europe, especially from those representing the interests of private traders – a measure perhaps of the extent of co-operative influence. In some instances this led to the adoption of anti-co-operative legislation.[17] But despite KF's well-publicised struggles against the trusts, these tensions seemed to be much less prominent in the Nordic region. Indeed, a report on attacks on co-operatives to the ICA's special congress in June 1933 noted the absence of conflicts between co-operators and the representatives of private trade, or indeed the state, in the Nordic countries.[18]

From the mid-1930s, interest in co-operatives converged with interest in the Scandinavian or Nordic middle way, in a process that was mutually reinforcing. The middle way concept was most famously stated in Marquis W. Childs' 1936 book on Sweden, which devoted many pages to the achievements of co-operation not only in Sweden but also in Denmark and through NAF in the Nordic region more generally. As Carl Marklund has noted, the key term in Childs' account was pragmatism.[19] For Childs, the success of Swedish consumer co-operation could be explained by its focus on practical action over idealism: 'the cost of bread and galoshes and housing and automobile tires and insurance and electricity'.[20] In this it contrasted with the much more politically motivated English consumer co-operatives.[21] At the same time, however, NAF was cited approvingly as 'a brake to halt the excesses of capitalism; to prevent monopoly and the narrow concentration of wealth; in short to check the very tendencies by which capitalism tends to destroy itself'.[22]

Childs' best-selling book stands out for the interest it generated among contemporaries and scholars alike, but it also needs to be understood in the wider context of the emerging foreign interest in the region. First, the idea of the Nordic middle way was seen as attractive not only in the US but also in other parts of Europe. For example, Katalin Miklóssy has shown how Hungarian intellectuals cited Finnish co-operatives as a potential 'third way' towards modernisation during the 1930s.[23] Second, the middle way also formed part of the self-understanding of co-operators, for example in Sweden and Norway during this period.[24] During the 1920s and especially the 1930s the leaders of the Nordic co-operative movements became increasingly forthright in asserting a distinctive position within the international co-operative movement and the ICA. They defended the principle of co-operative political neutrality, and in doing so argued for a vision of co-operation that was defined above all by its focus on practical, commercial aims. Typical of this was Albin Johansson's comment to the ICA's Central Committee on the subject of disarmament in 1931. Following his Danish colleague A. Axelsen Drejer, who had argued that the topic was irrelevant to the ICA, Johansson stated: 'In Sweden we never put the question of peace in the agenda of our Congresses; we do not have time for that; we are quite busy discussing about shoes, about margarine, about local stores, and such problems of internal organisation, and to those who are interested in the problem of peace we say, "Why don't you join a pacifist society?"'[25]

The growing prominence of the Nordic co-operative organisations within the ICA was due partly to their undoubted strength, measured in terms of both membership and trade. The loss of the German co-operative federation after 1933 shifted the balance of power within the Alliance, and although the Nordic federations could never match the size – in membership or trade – of the two giants, the English CWS/Co-operative Union and the Soviet Union's

Tsentrosouiz, they could certainly hold their own in terms of influence. There were also growing signs that they were prepared to act together as a bloc, adopting common positions on matters of importance. Nordic co-operation (*kooperation)* was shaped by regional Nordic collaboration (*nordiskt samarbete*), within the ICA and in other specifically Nordic organisations such as NAF. This regional collaboration was largely motivated by pragmatism, but it was not entirely devoid of idealism. On the eve of the 1939–40 crisis, leading co-operators including Albin Johansson and Väinö Tanner referred to NAF as an example of the potential for closer regional unity.[26]

Like other forms of Nordic co-operation, these inter-regional relationships were nominally a partnership among equals, but there were also inequalities in resources and ambitions. In terms of foreign interest in Nordic co-operation Denmark has to be considered a pioneer, but from the end of the First World War, Sweden's KF sought to take a leading role in international co-operative initiatives. The two Finnish federations also grew in influence, especially from 1927 when Väinö Tanner became president of the ICA. Participation in international co-operation could serve not only to reinforce national divisions within the co-operative movement but also to help overcome them. The Norwegian co-operative union was the smallest of all the organisations considered here and the least prominent within the ICA, though NKL's founder O. Dehli was also one of the prime movers behind the initiatives that led to NAF.

This reminds us that the influence of certain individuals – who in this period were almost exclusively men – was very significant in shaping the development of the Nordic co-operative movements and through them the ICA. Participation in international co-operative congresses and meetings was an experience reserved for relatively few co-operators, who also generated most of the sources used in this study. What we still know relatively little about is the impact of the international co-operative movement on its members. Consumer co-operation was a mass movement and for the vast majority of men and women it was about the stores and the goods that were sold there. The statements of co-operative leaders about the need to concentrate on practical matters were never empty rhetoric, but forged by the experience of managing the production and distribution of essential groceries. It was this dual nature of co-operation – between idealism and practice, between economics and politics – that was one of its weaknesses, but also one of its great strengths.

Notes

1 Franklin D. Roosevelt Library: President's Committee on an Inquiry on Co-operative Enterprise in Europe, Records 1936–1937: Box 6: Preliminary report on Scandinavia, submitted to the President 10 August 1936, pp. 4–5.

2 FDR Library: Preliminary report on Scandinavia, pp. 13–15; US Government, *Report of the Inquiry on Cooperative Enterprise in Europe 1937* (Washington, DC: United States Government Printing Office, 1937), pp. 6–18. The Inquiry calculated the percentage of the population affected by co-operative membership based on an estimated average of four individuals per household or family membership.
3 FDR Library: Preliminary report on Scandinavia, pp. 13–14.
4 G. R. Mitchinson, 'Retail Trade and the Co-operative Movement', in M. Cole and C. Smith (eds), *Democratic Sweden: A Volume of Studies Prepared by Members of the New Fabian Research Bureau* (London: George Routledge & Sons Ltd, 1938), pp. 208–25.
5 G. R. Nelson et al. (eds), *Freedom and Welfare: Social Patterns in The Northern Countries of Europe* (Copenhagen: Ministries of Social Affairs of Denmark, Finland, Iceland, Norway, Sweden, 1953), p. 191. The co-operative movement was also cited in J. A. Lauwerys (ed.), *Scandinavian Democracy: Development of Democratic Thought and Institutions in Denmark, Norway and Sweden* (Copenhagen, etc.: Det Danske Selskab, 1958).
6 J. P. Árnason and B. Wittrock, 'Introduction', in J. P. Árnason and B. Wittrock (eds), *Nordic Paths to Modernity* (New York: Berghahn Books, 2012).
7 I include here my own work on the Nordic model: M. Hilson, *The Nordic Model: Scandinavia since 1945* (London: Reaktion, 2008).
8 M. Hilson, P. Markkola and A.-C. Östman, 'Introduction: Co-operatives and the social question', in M. Hilson, P. Markkola and A.-C. Östman (eds), *Co-operatives and the Social Question: The Co-operative Movement in Northern and Eastern* Europe *(1880–1950)* (Cardiff: Welsh Academic Press, 2012), pp. 14–15.
9 E. Ekberg, 'Against the Tide: Understanding the Commercial Success of Nordic Consumer Co-operatives, 1950–2010', in M. Hilson, S. Neunsinger and G. Patmore (eds), *A Global History of Consumer Co-operation since 1850: Movements and Businesses* (Leiden: Brill, 2017).
10 P. Clavin, *Securing the World Economy: The Reinvention of the League of Nations, 1920–1946* (Oxford: Oxford University Press, 2013), pp. 8–9.
11 H. J. M., 'The International Co-operative Alliance in 1930', *Review of International Co-operation*, February 1931, pp. 41–7.
12 Työväen arkisto, Helsinki (hereafter TA): 334.5 Kansainvälinen Osuustoimintaliito (KOL), Box 7: ICA International Co-operative Economic Policy.
13 K. Friberg, 'A Co-operative Take on Free Trade – International Ambitions and Regional Initiatives in International Co-operative Trade', in Hilson, Neunsinger and Patmore (eds), *Global History*, p. 205.
14 See also: Hilson, Neunsinger and Patmore (eds), *Global History*; K. Jensen (ed.), *Brugsen – en anderledes forretning? Dansk brugsbevægelse fra pastor Sonne til det moderne Coop 1866–2016* (Albertslund: Samvirke, 2016), pp. 13–16.
15 P. Teeboom, 'Searching for the Middle Way: Consumer Co-operation and the Co-operative Movement in New Deal America' (PhD dissertation, University of Amsterdam, 2009); E. Furlough and C. Strikwerda, 'Economics, Consumer Culture and Gender: An Introduction to the Politics of Consumer Co-operation', in E. Furlough and C. Strikwerda (eds), *Consumers against Capitalism? Consumer*

Co-operation in Europe, North America and Japan, 1840–1990 (Lanham: Rowman and Littlefield, 1999), p. 3.

16 A. Webster et al., 'The Hidden Alternative?', in A. Webster et al. (eds), *The Hidden Alternative: Co-operative Values Past, Present and Future* (Manchester: Manchester University Press, 2012), pp. 8–9. Webster and colleagues refer to the revival of interest in co-operatives in the wake of the 2007–8 global financial crisis, which led to the United Nations' designation of 2012 as International Year of Co-operatives.

17 H. J. May, 'Co-operation on the Defensive', *Review of International Co-operation*, April 1933, pp. 121–4; P. Gurney, '"The Curse of the Co-ops": Co-operation, the Mass Press and the Market in Interwar Britain', *English Historical Review*, 130:547 (2015), 1479–512.

18 TA: 334.5 KOL, Box 6: H. J. May, 'The Present Position of the Co-operative Movement in Various Countries', paper to ICA Special Conference, June 1933.

19 C. Marklund, 'The Social Laboratory, the Middle Way and the Swedish Model: Three Frames for the Image of Sweden', *Scandinavian Journal of History*, 34:3 (2009), 264–85: 270–2; J. Logue, 'The Swedish Model: Visions of Sweden in American Politics and Political Science', *Swedish-American Historical Quarterly*, 50:3 (1999), 162–72: 164–5.

20 M. W. Childs, *Sweden – the Middle Way* (revised edn, New York: Penguin Books, 1948; first published 1936), p. 12.

21 M. W. Childs, 'Sweden: Where Capitalism Is Controlled', *Harper's Monthly Magazine*, 167:1002 (November 1933), 754–5.

22 Childs, *Sweden*, p. 12.

23 K. Miklóssy, 'The Nordic Ideal of a Central European Third Way: The Finnish model of Hungarian Modernisation in the 1930s', in M. Hilson, P. Markkola and A.-C. Östman (eds), *Co-operatives and the Social Question: The Co-operative Movement in Northern and Eastern Europe (1880–1950)* (Cardiff: Welsh Academic Press, 2012).

24 P. Aléx, 'Swedish Consumer Co-operation as an Educational Endeavour', in E. Furlough and C. Strikwerda (eds), *Consumers against Capitalism? Consumer Co-operation in Europe, North America and Japan, 1840–1990* (Lanham: Rowman and Littlefield, 1999), p. 260; E. Lange (ed.), *Organisert kjøpekraft. Forbrukersamvirkets historie i Norge* (Oslo: Pax forlag, 2006), p. 198.

25 TA: 334.5 KOL, Box 1: Report on proceedings of ICA Central Committee meeting, Paris, 30 September – 1 October 1931.

26 Kooperativa Förbundets arkiv: Albin Johanssons personarkiv: Referat av direktör Albin Johanssons föredrag på Auditorium tisdagen den 8 November 1938 i ABF:s och Konsums föreläsningskurs om 'Nordisk samhörighet'; V. Tanner, 'Fyra länder – ett hushåll', *Kooperatören*, 22–23, 1938, pp. 526–9; 545–8 (text of a lecture to the same course as Johansson).

Bibliography

Unpublished archive materials

Denmark

Arbejderbevægelsens bibliotek og arkiv, Copenhagen: Det kooperative Fællesforbund, 1129
Div. Korrespondance, modtagne breve, internationale 1922–26
Rigsarkivet, Aarhus (now in Viborg) (DRA)
Erhvervsarkivet: 06156 Andelsudvalget, 1910–64 Mødereferater mv vedr deltagelsen i ICA 1910 mm
Erhvervsarkivet: 02042 Nordisk Andelsforbund: 1918–76 Korrespondance, almindelig

Finland

Työväen kirjasto, Helsinki: NAF aarsberetning (TK)
Työväen arkisto, Helsinki (TA)
334.5 Kansainvälinen Osuustoimintaliito, Boxes 0.1–11
HNA 14/15/16 Keskusosuusliike OTK: Ulkomaiset osuuskunnat
92 Väinö Tannerin osuustoimintaa kosk. puheita ja artikkeleita 1928–61
Pellervo-seuran arkisto, Helsinki (Pellervo)
Lehtileikk. ulkom. leht. kirjoituksia
Pellervo-Seura ulkomaankirjeenvaihtoa 1911–25
Kansallisarkisto, Helsinki (KA)
Hannes Gebhardin arkisto: Saapuneet kirjeet I 1882–1932
Hedvig Gebhardin arkisto

Norway

Riksarkivet, Oslo (NRA)
PA 1394 Coop/NKL BA: Aaa L0001 Kongressprotokoller 1906–52
Serie K Nordisk og internasjonalt samarbeid L0011 Nordisk Andelsförbund 0004 Korrespondance mm 1916–43

Sweden

Kungliga Biblioteket, Stockholm (KB)
  Acc. 1980/8:2: G. H. von Kochs arkiv
Kooperativa Förbundets arkiv, Stockholm (KF)
  ICWS handlingar 1919–22
  ICWS 1919–25
  ICWS 1926–46
  Albin Johanssons personarkiv

United States of America

Franklin D. Roosevelt Library, Hyde Park, NY
  President's Committee on an Inquiry on Cooperative Enterprise in Europe; Records, 1936–37; Boxes 1–6.

Published sources

Newspapers and congress proceedings

Arbejderbevægelsens bibliotek og arkiv, Copenhagen: Høje Taastrup: *Kooperationen*, 1923–39
Det Kongelige Bibliotek, Copenhagen. *Andelsbladet*, 1918–39
Työväen arkisto, Helsinki: *Konsumentbladet* (Finland), 1921–28
Kansalliskirjasto, Helsinki: *Elanto*, 1922–39; *Kuluttajain Lehti*, 1919–36; *Samarbete*, 1932–34; *Yhteishyvä*, 1917–37
Arbeiderbevegelsens arkiv og bibliotek, Oslo: *Kooperatøren*, 1918–39
Kooperativa Förbundets arkiv, Stockholm: *Kooperatören*, 1918–39
National Co-operative Archives (UK), Manchester
  ICA Congress reports, 1902–37
  International Co-operative Bulletin, 1909–27
  Review of International Co-operation, 1927–39
  Co-operative News, 1922

Books, journal articles and pamphlets

Ames, J. W., *Co-operative Sweden Today* (Manchester: Co-operative Union, 1956).

Arnesen, R., *Co-operation in Norway* (Oslo: Norges Kooperative Landsforenings forlag, 1937).

Arnfred, J. Th., 'Dansk Andelsbevægelse', in A. Axelsen Drejer (ed.), *Den danske Andelsbevægelse* (3rd edn, Copenhagen: Martins forlag, 1934).

Bremer, F., *England om hösten 1851. Utgiven och kommenterad av Klara Johanson* (Stockholm: Norstedt, 1922).

Childs, M. W., 'Sweden: Where Capitalism Is Controlled', *Harper's Monthly Magazine*, 167:1002 (November 1933), 749–58.

Childs, M. W., *Sweden – the Middle Way* (revised edn, New York: Penguin Books, 1948; first published 1936).

Cole, M., and C. Smith (eds), *Democratic Sweden: A Volume of Studies Prepared by Members of the New Fabian Research Bureau* (London: George Routledge and Sons, 1938).

'Den kooperativa rörelsen. Från det kooperativa Belgien', *Social Tidskrift*, 11 May 1902.

Drejer, A. Axelsen (ed.), *Den danske Andelsbevægelse* (3rd edn, Copenhagen: Martins forlag, 1934).

Dyke Acland, A. H., and B. Jones, *Arbetarnes cooperations-föreningar i Storbritannien – hvad de uträttat och hvad de åsyfta*, trans. P. D., foreword by O. Lamm (Stockholm: Nordin & Josephson, 1894).

Gebhard, Han., *Andelsvärksamhet bland jordbrukarna! Tre föredrag* (Helsinki: Otava, 1899).

Gebhard, Han., *Co-operation in Finland* (London: Williams and Norgate, 1916).

Gebhard, Han., and I. Rahola, *Huvuddraget av andelsrörelsen i Finland*, trans. Allan Lagus (Helsinki: Sällskapet Pellervo, 1939).

Gebhard, Hed., 'Kooperationen. En social rörelse, som står kvinnorna nära', *Nutid: Tidskrift för sociala frågor och hemmets intressen*, 3 (March 1905), 89–97, and 4 (April 1905), 129–42.

Gide, C., *The International Co-operative Alliance*, trans. H. J. May (London: ICA, n.d. [*c*.1919]).

Gide, C., *Consumers' Co-operative Societies*, trans. staff of the Co-operative Reference Library, Dublin (Manchester: Co-operative Union, 1921).

Gjöres, A., *Konsumentkooperationen i Sverige* (Stockholm: Tidens förlag, 1925).

Granström, A., *Om kooperativa självhjälpsföreningar* (Mariehamn: Förf., 1898).

Grimley, O. B., *The New Norway: A People with the Spirit of Co-operation* (Oslo: Johan Grundt Tanum, 1939).

Hampden Jackson, J., *Finland* (revised 2nd edn, London: George Allen & Unwin Ltd, 1940; first published 1938).

Hedberg, A., *Samköp i Norden. Konsumentkooperation i fem länder* (Stockholm: Kooperativa Förbundets bokförlag, 1956).

Howe, F. C., *Denmark: A Cooperative Commonwealth* (New York: Harcourt, Brace and Company, 1921).

Howe, F. C., 'The Most Complete Agricultural Recovery in History', *Annals of the American Academy of Political and Social Science*, 172 (March 1934), 123–9.

Howe, F. C., *Denmark: The Coöperative Way* (New York: Coward-McCann, 1936).

Johansson, A., *Aktuella kooperativa problem* (Stockholm: Kooperativa Förbundets bokförlag, 1927).

Johansson, A., *Frihetsgaranti – skapande samverkan* (Stockholm: Kooperativa Förbundets bokförlag, 1945).

Kallen, H. M., *The Decline and Rise of the Consumer: A Philosophy of Consumer Co-operation* (New York: D. Appleton-Century, 1936).

Kallen, H. M., 'Philosophical and Ethical Aspects of Consumer Co-operation', *Annals of American Academy of Political and Social Science*, 191 (May 1937), 1–6.

Koch, G. H. von, 'Om arbetarnas konsumtionsföreningar i England', *Studentföreningen Verdandis småskrifter*, 78 (Stockholm: Albert Bonniers förlag, 1899).

Lauwerys, J. A. (ed.), *Scandinavian Democracy: Development of Democratic Thought and Institutions in Denmark, Norway and Sweden* (Copenhagen, etc.: Det Danske Selskab, 1958).

Mitchinson, G. R., 'Retail Trade and the Co-operative Movement', in M. Cole and C. Smith (eds), *Democratic Sweden: A Volume of Studies Prepared by Members of the New Fabian Research Bureau* (London: George Routledge & Sons Ltd, 1938).

Nelson, G. R. et al. (eds), *Freedom and Welfare: Social Patterns in the Northern Countries of Europe* (Copenhagen: Ministries of Social Affairs of Denmark, Finland, Iceland, Norway, Sweden, 1953).

Odhe, T., *Kooperationen i Finland* (Stockholm: Kooperativa Förbundets bokförlag, 1929).

Odhe, T., *Finland: A Nation of Co-operators*, trans. J. Downie (London: Williams & Norgate, 1931).

Odhe, T., *The Place of Co-operation in World Economy* (London: ICA, 1947).

Odhe, T., *Scandinavian Co-operative Wholesale Society 1918–1958* (Copenhagen: NAF/Det danske forlag, 1960).

Örne, A., *Kooperativa idéer och spörsmål* (Stockholm: Kooperativa Förbundets bokförlag, 1924).

Örne, A., *Co-operative Ideals and Problems*, trans. J. Downie (Manchester: Co-operative Union, 1926).

Örne, A., *De sju grundsatserna. Kooperationens program i kort sammanfattning* (Stockholm: Kooperativa Förbundets bokförlag, 1934; first published 1919).

Örne, A., *'Det internationella varuutbytet från konsumentsynpunkt'. Föredrag vid IKA:s sextonde kongress i Zürich den 10 oktober 1946* (Stockholm: Kooperativa Förbundets bokförlag, 1946).

Rylander, A., 'Kunna konsumtions och produktionsföreningar gagna arbetarrörelsen?', *Social-Demokraten*, 8 October 1894; 16 October 1894; 22 October 1894.

Sonne, H. Chr., *Om Arbeiderforeninger. Til Oplysning og Veiledning* (Copenhagen: H. Hagerups Boghandel, 1867).

US Government, *Report of the Inquiry on Cooperative Enterprise in Europe 1937* (Washington, DC: United States Government Printing Office, 1937).

Webb, S., and B. Webb, *The Consumers' Co-operative Movement* (published by authors, 1921).

Wedenoja, K. J., 'Osuuskaupat', in L. Harmaja et al. (eds), *Valtiotieteiden käsikirja. Aakkosellinen tietoteos*, vol. 2 (Helsinki: Tietosanakirja Osakeyhtiö, 1922).

Secondary material

Aaltonen, E., *Finlands konsumenter i samarbete*, trans. S. Malmström (Helsinki: KK, 1954).

Albrecht, C., 'Nationalism in the Cooperative Movement in Bohemia before 1914', in T. Lorenz (ed.), *Cooperatives in Ethnic Conflicts: Eastern Europe in the 19th and Early 20th Century* (Berlin: Berliner Wissenschafts-Verlag, 2006).

Aléx, P., *Den rationella konsumenten. KF som folkuppfostrare 1899–1939* (Stockholm/Stehag: Brutus Östlings Bokförlag Symposion, 1994).

Aléx, P., 'Swedish Consumer Co-operation as an Educational Endeavour', in E. Furlough and C. Strikwerda (eds), *Consumers against Capitalism? Consumer Co-operation in Europe, North America and Japan, 1840–1990* (Lanham: Rowman and Littlefield, 1999).

Árnason, J. P., and B. Wittrock, 'Introduction', in J. P. Árnason and B. Wittrock (eds), *Nordic Paths to Modernity* (New York: Berghahn Books, 2012).

Arsan, A., S. L. Lewis and A.-I. Richard, 'Editorial – The Roots of Global Civil Society and the Interwar Moment', *Journal of Global History*, 7:2 (2012), 157–65.

Balnave, N., and G. Patmore, 'The Politics of Consumption and Co-operation: An Overview', *Labour History*, 91 (2006), 1–12.

Bayly, C. A. et al., 'AHR Conversation: On Transnational History', *American Historical Review*, 111:5 (2006), 1440–64.

Berg, M., 'Global History: Approaches and New Directions', in M. Berg (ed.), *Writing the History of the Global: Challenges for the Twenty-first Century* (Oxford: Oxford University Press/British Academy, 2013).

Bergholm, T., 'Masculinity, Violence and Disunity: Waterfront Strikes and Strikebreakers in Finnish Ports in the 1920s and 1930s', *International Journal of Maritime History*, 8:1 (1996), 23–42.

Birchall, J., *The International Co-operative Movement* (Manchester: Manchester University Press, 1997).

Birchall, J., *People-Centred Businesses: Co-operatives, Mutuals and the Idea of Membership* (Basingstoke: Palgrave Macmillan, 2011).

Bjørn, C. (ed.), *Dansk mejeribrug 1882–2000* (n.p.: De danske Mejeriers Fællesorganisation, 1982).

Bjørn, C., *Anders Nielsen Svejstrup Østergaard* (Odense: Landbohistorisk selskab, 1993).

Bjørn, C., *Fortid med fremtid: Danske Andelsselskaber 100 år 1899–1999* (Copenhagen: Danske Andelsselskaber, 1999).

Black, I. S., 'Spaces of Capital: Bank Office Building in the City of London, 1830–1870', *Journal of Historical Geography*, 26:3 (2000), 351–75.

Black, L., and N. Robertson, 'Taking Stock: An Introduction', in L. Black and N. Robertson (eds), *Consumerism and the Co-operative Movement in Modern British History: Taking Stock* (Manchester: Manchester University Press, 2009).

Black, N., 'The Mothers' International: The Women's Co-operative Guild and Feminist Pacifism', *Women's Studies International Forum*, 7:6 (1984), 467–76.

Bonner, A., *British Co-operation: The History, Principles and Organisation of the British Co-operative Movement* (Manchester: Co-operative Union, 1961).

Borrero, M., *Hungry Moscow: Scarcity and Urban Society in the Russian Civil War, 1917–1921* (New York: Peter Lang, 2003).

Boyce, R., *The Great Interwar Crisis and the Collapse of Globalization* (Basingstoke: Palgrave Macmillan, 2009).

Brandesten, O., *Lantbrukarnas organisationer. Agrart och kooperativt 1830–1930* (Stockholm: Kungliga Skogs- och Lantbruksakademien, 2005).

Braunthal, J., *History of the International 1864–1914*, trans. H. Collins and K. Mitchell (London and Edinburgh: Thomas Nelson and Sons Ltd, 1966).

Brazda, J., and R. Schediwy (eds), *A Time of Crises: Consumer Co-operatives and Their Problems Around 1990* (Vienna: Fachbereich für Genossenschaftswesen, Universität Wien, 2011; first published 1989), available at https://genos.univie.ac.at/veroeffentlichungen/, accessed 10 August 2016.

Brazda, J., and R. Schediwy, 'Consumer Co-operatives on the Defensive: A Short Overview', in J. Brazda and R. Schediwy (eds), *A Time of Crises: Consumer Co-operatives and Their Problems Around 1990* (Vienna: Fachbereichs für Genossenschaftswesen, 2011), available at https://genos.univie.ac.at/fileadmin/user_upload/genossenschaftswesen/Genos/consum.pdf, accessed 3 February 2017.

Brazda, J., F. Jagschitz, S. Rom and R. Schediwy, 'The Rise and Fall of Austria's Consumer Co-operatives', in M. Hilson, S. Neunsinger and G. Patmore (eds), *A Global History of Consumer Co-operation since 1850: Movements and Businesses* (Leiden: Brill, 2017).

Bryld, C., 'Kooperationen – et stridspunkt i den socialdemokratiske strategiudvikling 1871–1923', *Arbejderhistorie*, 4 (December 2003), 3–22.

Bull, E. and E. Jansen (eds), *Norsk biografisk leksikon*, vol. 3 (Oslo: H. Aschehoug, 1926).

Burton, A., *The People's Cinema: Film and the Co-operative Movement* (London: National Film Theatre, 1994).

Callahan, K., 'Performing "Inter-Nationalism" in Stuttgart in 1907: French and German Socialist Nationalism and the Political Culture of an International Socialist Congress', *International Review of Social History*, 45:1 (2000), 51–87.

Callahan, K., *Demonstration Culture: European Socialism and the Second International, 1889–1914* (Leicester: Troubadour Publishing Ltd, 2010).

Carbery, T. F., *Consumers in Politics: A History and General Review of the Co-operative Party* (Manchester: Manchester University Press, 1969).

Carpelan, T., and L. O. Th. Tudeer, *Helsingfors universitet. Lärare och tjänstemän från år 1828* (Helsinki: Söderström, 1925).

Chadaga, J. B., 'Light in Captivity: Spectacular Glass and Soviet Power in the 1920s and 1930s', *Slavic Review*, 66:1 (2007), 82–105.

Christiansen, N. F., 'Denmark's Road to Modernity and Welfare: The Co-operative Way', in M. Hilson, P. Markkola and A.-C. Östman (eds), *Co-operatives and the Social Question: The Co-operative Movement in Northern and Eastern Europe (1880–1950)* (Cardiff: Welsh Academic Press, 2012).

Clavin, P., 'Defining Transnationalism', *Contemporary European History*, 14:4 (2005), 421–39.

Clavin, P., *Securing the World Economy: The Reinvention of the League of Nations, 1920–1946* (Oxford: Oxford University Press, 2013).

Cohen, D., and M. O'Connor, 'Introduction: Comparative History, Cross-National History, Transnational History – Definitions', in D. Cohen and M. O'Connor (eds), *Comparison and History: Europe in Cross-National Perspective* (Abingdon and New York: Routledge, 2004).

Cole, G. D. H., *A Century of Co-operation* (Manchester: Co-operative Union, 1944).

Conrad, S., 'Double Marginalization: A Plea for a Transnational Perspective on German History', in J. Kocka and H.-G. Haupt (eds), *Comparative and Transnational History: Central European Approaches and New Perspectives* (New York: Berghahn Books, 2009).

Co-operative College (2012), 'Mainstreaming Co-operation', available at www.co-op.ac.uk/2012/07/mainstreaming-co-operation/, accessed 10 August 2016.

David-Fox, M., *Showcasing the Great Experiment: Cultural Diplomacy and Western Visitors to the Soviet Union 1921–1941* (Oxford: Oxford University Press, 2012).

Defoort, H., 'The Strongest Socialist Party in the World? The Influence of Belgian Social Democracy in International Socialism prior to 1914 as a Means to Study the Relations between Socialism and Co-operation', in P. Verbruggen and L. Soubry (eds), *Consumerism versus Capitalism? Co-operatives Seen from an International Comparative Perspective* (Ghent: Amsab-Institute of Social History, 2003).

Doyle, P., '"Better Farming, Better Business, Better Living": The Irish Co-operative Movement and the Construction of the Irish Nation-State, 1894–1932' (PhD thesis, University of Manchester, 2013).

Duedahl, P., and K. Gram-Skjoldager, 'De international organisationers Danmarkshistorie: En introduktion', *Temp*, 10 (2015), 5–15.

Earle, J., *The Italian Co-operative Movement: A Portrait of the Lega Nazionale delle Cooperative e Mutue* (London: Allen & Unwin, 1986).

Ekberg, E., 'Confronting Three Revolutions: Western European Consumer Co-operatives and Their Divergent Development', *Business History*, 54:6 (2012), 1004–21.

Ekberg, E., 'Against the Tide: Understanding the Commercial Success of Nordic Consumer Co-operatives, 1950–2010', in M. Hilson, S. Neunsinger and G. Patmore (eds), *A Global History of Consumer Co-operation since 1850: Movements and Businesses* (Leiden: Brill, 2017).

Eley, G., *Forging Democracy: The History of the Left in Europe, 1850–2000* (Oxford: Oxford University Press, 2002).

Eriksson, F., 'Modernity, Rationality and Citizenship: Swedish Agrarian Organisations as Seen through the Lens of the Agrarian Press, circa 1880–1917', in P. Wawrzeniuk (ed.), *Societal Change and Ideological Formation among the Rural Population of the Baltic Area 1880–1939* (Huddinge: Södertörns Högskola, 2008).

Eriksson, F., 'Swedish Agrarian Press: Co-operatives and the Social Question c.1880–1917', in M. Hilson, P. Markkola and A.-C. Östman (eds), *Co-operatives and the Social Question: The Co-operative Movement in Northern and Eastern Europe (1880–1950)* (Cardiff: Welsh Academic Press, 2012).

Espeli, H., T. Bergh and A. Rønning, *Melkens pris. Perspektiver på meierisamvirkets historie* (Oslo: Tun forlag, 2006).

Fairbairn, B., 'The Rise and Fall of Consumer Co-operation in Germany', in E. Furlough and C. Strikwerda (eds), *Consumers against Capitalism? Consumer Co-operation in Europe, North America and Japan, 1840–1990* (Lanham: Rowman and Littlefield, 1999).

Fellman, S., 'Growth and Investment: Finnish Capitalism, 1850s-2005', in S. Fellman et al. (eds), *Creating Nordic Capitalism: The Business History of a Competitive Periphery* (Basingstoke: Palgrave Macmillan, 2008).

Figes, O., *A People's Tragedy: The Russian Revolution 1891–1924* (New York: Penguin Books, 1997; first published 1996).

Friberg, K., *The Workings of Co-operation: A Comparative Study of Consumer Co-operative Organisation in Britain and Sweden 1860 to 1970* (Växjö: Växjö University Press, 2005).

Friberg, K., 'Visions and Organisation: Kooperativa Förbundet and the Social Question in Sweden', in M. Hilson, P. Markkola and A.-C. Östman (eds), *Co-operatives and the Social Question: The Co-operative Movement in Northern and Eastern Europe (1880–1950)* (Cardiff: Welsh Academic Press, 2012).

Friberg, K., 'A Co-operative Take on Free Trade – International Ambitions and Regional Initiatives in International Co-operative Trade', in M. Hilson, S. Neunsinger and G. Patmore (eds), *A Global History of Consumer Co-operation since 1850: Movements and Businesses* (Leiden: Brill, 2017).

Friedmann, H., 'Food', in A. Iriye and P.-Y. Saunier (eds), *The Palgrave Dictionary of Transnational History: From the Mid-19th-Century to the Present Day* (Basingstoke: Palgrave Macmillan, 2009).

Furlough, E., *Consumer Cooperation in France: The Politics of Consumption 1834–1930* (Ithaca: Cornell University Press, 1991).

Furlough, E., 'Consumer Cooperation', in A. Iriye and P.-Y. Saunier (eds), *The Palgrave Dictionary of Transnational History: From the Mid-19th-Century to the Present Day* (Basingstoke: Palgrave Macmillan, 2009).

Furlough, E., and C. Strikwerda (eds), *Consumers against Capitalism? Consumer Co-operation in Europe, North America and Japan, 1840–1990* (Lanham: Rowman and Littlefield, 1999).

Furlough, E., and C. Strikwerda, 'Economics, Consumer Culture and Gender: An Introduction to the Politics of Consumer Co-operation', in E. Furlough and C. Strikwerda (eds), *Consumers against Capitalism? Consumer Co-operation in Europe, North America and Japan, 1840–1990* (Lanham: Rowman and Littlefield, 1999).

Garnert, J., 'Upplysningens århundrade', in Y. Hirdman, U. Lundberg and J. Björkman (eds), *Sveriges historia 1920–1965*, vol. 7 of *Norstedts Sveriges historia* (Stockholm: Norstedts, 2012).

Glenny, M. V., 'The Anglo-Soviet Trade Agreement, March 1921', *Journal of Contemporary History*, 5:2 (1970), 63–82.

Gorman, D., *The Emergence of International Society in the 1920s* (Cambridge: Cambridge University Press, 2012).

Götz, N., 'On the Origins of Parliamentary Diplomacy: Scandinavian "Bloc Politics" and Delegation Policy in the League of Nations', *Cooperation and Conflict*, 40:3 (2005), 263–79.

Götz, N., 'Blue-Eyed Angels at the League of Nations: The Genevese Construction of Norden', in N. Götz and H. Haggrén (eds), *Regional Cooperation and International Organizations: The Nordic Model in Transnational Alignment* (London: Routledge, 2009).

Götz, N., 'Parliamentary Democracy Going Global: The Fading Nordic Model', in J. Kurunmäki and J. Strang (eds), *Rhetorics of Nordic Democracy* (Helsinki: Finnish Literature Society, 2010).

Götz, N., and H. Haggrén, 'Introduction: Transnational Nordic Alignment in Stormy Waters', in N. Götz and H. Haggrén (eds), *Regional Cooperation and International Organizations: The Nordic Model in Transnational Alignment* (London: Routledge, 2009).

Götz, N., H. Haggrén and M. Hilson, 'Nordic Cooperation in the Voluntary Sector', in J. Strang (ed.), *Nordic Cooperation: A European Region in Transition* (London: Routledge, 2016).

Grelle, H., *Det kooperative alternativ: Arbejderkooperationen i Danmark 1852–2012* (Copenhagen: Arbejdermuseet/ABA, 2012).

Grytten, O. H., and K. B. Minde, 'The Demand for Consumer Goods in the Modernisation of the Norwegian Economy, 1850–1920', *Scandinavian Economic History Review*, 46:1 (1998), 42–58.

Gurney, P., *Co-operative Culture and the Politics of Consumption in England, 1870–1930* (Manchester: Manchester University Press, 1996).

Gurney, P., '"The Curse of the Co-ops": Co-operation, the Mass Press and the Market in Interwar Britain', *English Historical Review*, 130:547 (2015), 1479–512.

Hansen, S. O., 'Nordisk kooperativt samarbeid. Et lite kjenr felleskals.' Unpublished manuscript, 2005.

Harvard, J., and P. Stadius, 'A Communicative Perspective on the Formation of the North: Contexts, Channels and Concepts', in J. Harvard and P. Stadius (eds), *Communicating the North: Media Structures and Images in the Making of the Nordic Region* (Farnham: Ashgate, 2013).

Heikkinen, S., 'Major Necessities and Minor Luxuries: Workers as Consumers in Finland at the Turn of the Twentieth Century', *Scandinavian Economic History Review*, 46:1 (1998), 59–70.

Heldal, H., 'Norway in the International Labour Organisation 1919–1939', *Scandinavian Journal of History*, 21:4 (1996), 255–83.

Hemstad, R., *Fra Indian Summer til nordisk vinter. Skandinavisk samarbeid, skandinavisme og unionsoppløsningen* (Oslo: Akademisk Publisering, 2008).

Henriksen, I., 'Avoiding Lock-In: Co-operative Creameries in Denmark 1882–1903', *European Review of Economic History*, 3:1 (1999), 57–78.

Higgins, D. M., and M. Mordhorst, 'Reputation and Export Performance: Danish Butter Exports and the British Market, c.1880–c.1914', *Business History*, 50:2 (2008), 185–204.

Hilson, M. K., 'Working-Class Politics in Plymouth, c.1890–1920' (PhD dissertation, University of Exeter, 1998).

Hilson, M., 'Consumers and Politics: The Co-operative Movement in Plymouth, 1890–1920', *Labour History Review*, 67:1 (2002), 7–27.

Hilson, M., 'Co-operation and Consumer Politics in Comparative Perspective: Britain and Sweden during the First World War', in P. Verbruggen and L. Soubry (eds), *Consumerism versus Capitalism? Co-operatives seen from an International Comparative Perspective* (Ghent: Amsab-Institute of Social History, 2003).

Hilson, M., *The Nordic Model: Scandinavia since 1945* (London: Reaktion, 2008).

Hilson, M., 'The Consumer Co-operative Movement in Cross-National Perspective: Britain and Sweden, c.1860–1939', in L. Black and N. Robertson (eds), *Consumerism and the Co-operative Movement in Modern British History: Taking Stock* (Manchester: Manchester University Press, 2009).

Hilson, M., 'The Nordic Consumer Co-operative Movements in International Perspective, 1890–1939', in R. Alapuro and H. Stenius (eds), *Nordic Associations in a European Perspective* (Baden-Baden: Nomos, 2010).

Hilson, M., 'A Consumers' International? The International Cooperative Alliance and Cooperative Internationalism, 1918–1939: A Nordic Perspective', *International Review of Social History*, 56:2 (2011), 203–33.

Hilson, M., 'Transnational Networks in the Development of the Co-operative Movement in the Early Twentieth Century: Finland in the Nordic Context', in M. Hilson, P. Markkola and A.-C. Östman (eds), *Co-operatives and the Social Question: The Co-operative Movement in Northern and Eastern Europe (1880–1950)* (Cardiff: Welsh Academic Press, 2012).

Hilson, M., 'Consumer Co-operation and Economic Crisis: The 1936 Roosevelt Inquiry on Co-operative Enterprise and the Emergence of the Nordic "Middle Way"', *Contemporary European History*, 22:2 (2013), 181–98.

Hilson, M., 'Consumer Co-operation in the Nordic Countries, c.1860–1939', in M. Hilson, S. Neunsinger and G. Patmore (eds), *A Global History of Consumer Co-operation since 1850: Movements and Businesses* (Leiden: Brill, 2017).

Hilson, M., '"A Model Co-operative Country": Irish-Finnish Contacts at the Turn of the Twentieth Century', *Irish Historical Studies*, 41:160 (2017), 227–43.

Hilson, M., and S. Neunsinger, 'Samarbete over gränser. Reflektioner och erfarenheter från ett kollektivt forskningsprojekt om konsumentkooperationens globala historia', *Historisk Tidskrift*, 133:3 (2013), 450–71.

Hilson, M., P. Markkola and A.-C. Östman (eds), *Co-operatives and the Social Question: The Co-operative Movement in Northern and Eastern Europe (1880–1950)* (Cardiff: Welsh Academic Press, 2012).

Hilson, M., P. Markkola and A.-C. Östman, 'Introduction: Co-operatives and the Social Question', in M. Hilson, P. Markkola and A.-C. Östman (eds), *Co-operatives and the Social Question: The Co-operative Movement in Northern and Eastern Europe (1880–1950)* (Cardiff: Welsh Academic Press, 2012).

Hilson, M., S. Neunsinger and G. Patmore (eds), *A Global History of Consumer Co-operation since 1850: Movements and Businesses* (Leiden: Brill, 2017).

Hilson, M., S. Neunsinger and G. Patmore, 'A Global History of Consumer Co-operation', in M. Hilson, S. Neunsinger and G. Patmore (eds), *A Global History of Consumer Co-operation since 1850: Movements and Businesses* (Leiden: Brill, 2017).

Hilton, M., *Consumerism in Twentieth-Century Britain* (Cambridge: Cambridge University Press, 2003).

Hilton, M., and M. Daunton, 'Material Politics: An Introduction', in M. Hilton and M. Daunton (eds), *The Politics of Consumption: Material Culture and Citizenship in Europe and America* (Oxford: Berg, 2001).

Hobsbawm, E., *Age of Extremes: The Short Twentieth Century 1914–1994* (London: Michael Joseph, 1994).

Hummelin, K., *Nordisk Andelsforbund NAF 1918–1993: Konsumentkooperativt samarbete i Norden*, trans. J. and N. Degerman (Copenhagen: Nordisk Andelsforbund, 1998).

International Co-operative Alliance, 'Co-operative Identity, Values and Principles', available at http://ica.coop/en/whats-co-op/co-operative-identity-values-principles, last accessed 3 February 2017.

Iriye, A., *Global Community: The Role of International Organizations in the Making of the Contemporary World* (Berkeley: University of California Press, 2002).

Iversen, M. J., and S. Andersen, 'Co-operative Liberalism: Denmark from 1857 to 2007', in S. Fellman et al. (eds), *Creating Nordic Capitalism: The Business History of a Competitive Periphery* (Basingstoke: Palgrave Macmillan, 2008).

Janfelt, M., *Att leva i den bästa av världar. Föreningen Nordens syn på Norden 1919–1933* (Stockholm: Carlssons bokförlag, 2005).

Jensen, K. (ed.), *Brugsen – en anderledes forretning? 1866–2016: Dansk brugsbevægelse fra pastor Sonne til det moderne Coop* (Albertslund: Samvirke, 2016).

Jonsson, P., 'From Commercial Trickery to Social Responsibility: Marketing in the Swedish Co-operative Movement in the Early Twentieth Century', in M. Hilson, S. Neunsinger and G. Patmore (eds), *A Global History of Consumer Co-operation since 1850: Movements and Businesses* (Leiden: Brill, 2017).

Jonsson, P., and S. Neunsinger, 'Comparison and Transfer – A Fruitful Approach to National History?' *Scandinavian Journal of History*, 32:3 (2007), 258–80.

Kaeble, H., 'Between Comparison and Transfers – and What Now? A French-German Debate', in J. Kocka and H.-G. Haupt (eds), *Comparative and Transnational History: Central European Approaches and New Perspectives* (New York: Berghahn Books, 2009).

Kaukiainen, L., 'From Reluctancy to Activity: Finland's Way to the Nordic Family during 1920s and 1930s', *Scandinavian Journal of History*, 9:2–3 (1984), 201–19.

Kayser Nielsen, N., *Bonde, stat og hjem. Nordisk demokrati og nationalisme – fra pietismen til 2. verdenskrig* (Aarhus: Aarhus Universitetsforlag, 2009).

Kayser Nielsen, N., and J. Bale, 'Associations and Democracy: Sport and Popular Mobilization in Nordic Societies c.1850–1900', *Scandinavian Journal of History*, 37:1 (2012), 69–86.

Kettunen, P., 'The Transnational Construction of National Challenges: The Ambiguous Nordic Model of Welfare and Competitiveness', in P. Kettunen and K. Petersen (eds), *Beyond Welfare State Models: Transnational Historical Perspectives on Social Policy* (Cheltenham: Edward Elgar, 2011).

Kettunen, P., and T. Tuomisto, 'Från enhetlighet till inre kamp. Revolutionära och reformistiska tendenser i den finländska arbetarrörelsen på 1910- och 1920-talet', in J. Christensen (ed.), *Nordisk arbejderbevægelse i mellemkrigstiden. Stat, parti og fagbevægelse* (Copenhagen: SFAH, 1980).

Kjærgaard, T., 'Gårdmandslinien i dansk historieskrivning', in C. Bjørn (ed.), *Fra fortid og nutid: En antologi* (Copenhagen: Dansk historisk fællesforening, 1984).

Kocka, J., and H.-G. Haupt (eds), *Comparative and Transnational History: Central European Approaches and New Perspectives* (New York: Berghahn Books, 2009).

Kocka, J., and H.-G. Haupt, 'Comparison and Beyond: Traditions, Scope and Perspective of Comparative History', in J. Kocka and H.-G. Haupt (eds), *Comparative and Transnational History: Central European Approaches and New Perspectives* (New York: Berghahn Books, 2009).

Korsager, E. M., 'Severin Jørgensen', in K. Jensen (ed.), *Brugsen – en anderledes forretning?* (Albertslund: Samvirke, 2016).

Kuisma, M. et al., *The Pellervo Story: A Century of Finnish Co-operation, 1899–1999*, trans. M. Wynne-Ellis (Helsinki: Pellervo/Kirjayhtymä, 1999).

Kurunmäki, J., and J. Strang, 'Nordic Democracy in a World of Tensions', in J. Kurunmäki and J. Strang (eds), *Rhetorics of Nordic Democracy* (Helsinki: Finnish Literature Society, 2010).

Kylebäck, H., *Konsumentkooperation och industrikarteller* (Stockholm: Rabén & Sjögren, 1974).

Lambersens, S. et al., 'History of Consumer Co-operatives in France: From the Conquest of Consumption by the Masses to the Challenge of Mass Consumption', in M. Hilson, S. Neunsinger and G. Patmore (eds), *A Global History of Consumer Co-operation since 1850: Movements and Businesses* (Leiden: Brill, 2017).

Lancaster, B., and P. Maguire, 'The Cooperative Movement in Historical Perspective', in B. Lancaster and P. Maguire (eds), *Towards the Co-operative Commonwealth: Essays in the History of Co-operation* (Manchester: Co-operative College/History Workshop Trust, 1996).

Lange, E. (ed.), *Organisert kjøpekraft. Forbrukersamvirkets historie i Norge* (Oslo: Pax forlag, 2006).

Laqua, D., 'Transnational Intellectual Cooperation, the League of Nations and the Problem of Order', *Journal of Global History*, 6:2 (2011), 223–47.

Laqua, D., *The Age of Internationalism and Belgium 1880–1930: Peace, Progress and Prestige* (Manchester: Manchester University Press, 2013).

Levene, A., 'The Meanings of Margarine in England: Class, Consumption and Material Culture from 1918 to 1953', *Contemporary British History*, 28:2 (2014), 145–65.

Linden, M. van der, *Workers of the World: Essays Towards a Global Labour History* (Leiden: Brill, 2011).

Logue, J., 'The Swedish Model: Visions of Sweden in American Politics and Political Science', *Swedish-American Historical Quarterly*, 50:3 (1999), 162–72.

Lorenz, T., 'Introduction: Cooperatives in Ethnic Conflicts', in T. Lorenz (ed.), *Cooperatives in Ethnic Conflicts: Eastern Europe in the 19th and Early 20th Century* (Berlin: Berliner Wissenschafts-Verlag, 2006).

Lyons, F. S. L., *Internationalism in Europe 1815–1914* (Leyden: A. W. Sythoff, 1963).

Macdonald, S., 'Transnational History: A Review of Past and Present Scholarship' (working paper, UCL Centre for Transnational History, 2013), available at www.ucl.ac.uk/centre-transnational-history/objectives/simon_macdonald_tns_review, accessed 10 August 2016.

MacPherson, I., 'The International Co-operative Movement and Peace: Questions Drawn from Its Early History', in J. Emmanuel and I. MacPherson (eds), *Co-operatives and the Pursuit of Peace* (Victoria: British Colombia Institute for Co-operative Studies, 2007).

Mäkinen, R., 'Finska agronomers skandinaviska kontakter, deras alternative och bondens nationella roll', in H. Haggrén, R. Hemstad and J. Marjanen (eds), *Civilsamhällets Norden* (Helsinki: CENS, 2005).

Mäkinen, R., and A.-L. Syysiharju, *Eteenpäin ja ylöspäin: Hedvig Gebhardin osuus ja toiminta* (Helsinki: Otava, 2006).
Månsson, K., 'Stjernen – arbejderbevægelsens bryggeri', *Arbejderhistorie* (December 2003), 23–37.
Manton, K., 'The Labour Party and the Co-op, 1918–58', *Historical Research*, 82 (2009), 756–78.
Marklund, C., 'The Social Laboratory, the Middle Way and the Swedish Model: Three Frames for the Image of Sweden', *Scandinavian Journal of History*, 34:3 (2009), 264–85.
Mazlish, B., *The New Global History* (New York: Routledge, 2006).
McDermott, K., and J. Agnew, *The Comintern: A History of International Communism from Lenin to Stalin* (Basingstoke: Macmillan Press, 1996).
Michelsen, J., 'Nordiske landbrugskooperativer i politiske og økonomiske omgivelser under forandring', in K. K. Klausen and P. Selle (eds), *Frivillig organisering i Norden* (Oslo: Tano, 1995).
Miklóssy, K., 'The Nordic Ideal of a Central European Third Way: The Finnish Model of Hungarian Modernisation in the 1930s', in M. Hilson, P. Markkola and A.-C. Östman (eds), *Co-operatives and the Social Question: The Co-operative Movement in Northern and Eastern Europe (1880–1950)* (Cardiff: Welsh Academic Press, 2012).
Millbourn, I., 'Kooperatismen – ett alternativ till kapitalismen och socialdemokrati 1900–1920', *Scandia*, 57:1 (1991), 89–112.
Mordhorst, M., 'Arla: From a Decentralized Co-operation to an MNE', in S. Fellman et al. (eds), *Creating Nordic Capitalism: The Business History of a Competitive Periphery* (Basingstoke: Palgrave Macmillan, 2008).
Mordhorst, M., 'Arla and Danish National Identity: Business History as Cultural History', *Business History*, 56:1 (2014), 116–33.
Morgan, K., *The Webbs and Soviet Communism* (London: Lawrence & Wishart, 2006).
Müller, M. G., and C. Torp, 'Conceptualising Transnational Spaces in History', *European Review of History*, 16:5 (2009), 609–17.
Musiał, K., *Roots of the Scandinavian Model: Images of Progress in the Era of Modernisation* (Baden-Baden: Nomos Verlagsgesellschaft, 2002).
Nilsson, K., *Stockholms kooperation 1900–1915* (Stockholm: Kooperativa Förbundets bokförlag, 1952).
Nützenadel, A., and F. Trentmann, 'Introduction: Mapping Food and Globalization', in A. Nützenadel and F. Trentmann (eds), *Food and Globalization: Consumption, Markets and Politics in the Modern World* (Oxford: Berg, 2008).
Nyzell, S., *'Striden ägde rum i Malmö': Möllevångskravallerna 1926. En studie av politiskt våld i mellankrigstidens Sverige*, Skrifter med historiska perspektiv, 10 (Malmö: Malmö högskola, 2010).

O'Rourke, K. H., 'Late Nineteenth Century Denmark in an Irish Mirror: Land Tenure, Homogeneity and the Roots of Danish Success', in J. L. Campbell, J. A. Hall and O. Pedersen (eds), *National Identity and the Varieties of Capitalism: The Danish Experience* (Montreal: McGill-Queen's University Press, 2006).

O'Rourke, K. H., 'Property Rights, Politics and Innovation: Creamery Diffusion in pre-1914 Ireland', *European Review of Economic History*, 11 (2007), 359–417.

Osterhammel, J., 'A "Transnational" History of Society: Continuity or New Departure?' in J. Kocka and H.-G. Haupt (eds), *Comparative and Transnational History: Central European Approaches and New Perspectives* (New York: Berghahn Books, 2009).

Östman, A.-C., 'Civilising and Mobilising the Peasantry: Co-operative Organisation and Understandings of Progress and Gender in Finland, c.1899–1918', in M. Hilson, P. Markkola and A.-C. Östman (eds), *Co-operatives and the Social Question: The Co-operative Movement in Northern and Eastern Europe (1880–1950)* (Cardiff: Welsh Academic Press, 2012).

Paavolainen, J., *Nuori Tanner menestyvä sosialisti. Elämäkerta vuoteen 1911* (Helsinki: Tammi, 1977).

Paavolainen, J., *Väinö Tanner sillanrakentaja. Elämäkerta vuosilta 1924–1936* (Helsinki: Tammi, 1984).

Påhlman, A., *Pionjärerna* (Stockholm: Kooperativa Förbundets Bokförlag, 1944).

Påhlman, A., and W. Sjölin, *Kooperationen i Karlskrona 1869–1939* (Stockholm: Tiden, 1940).

Pedersen, E. H., 'Svenske og danske andelsorganisationer og deres virksomhed til 1930'ernes begyndelse', *Historisk Tidsskrift*, 82 (1982–3), 305–21.

Pedersen, E. H., J. Jensen, F. Just and L. Scheving, *De første hundrede år: Danske slagterier 1887–1987* (Copenhagen: Danske Slagterier, 1987).

Pollard, S., 'Nineteenth-Century Co-operation: From Community Building to Shopkeeping', in A. Briggs and J. Saville (eds), *Essays in Labour History, 1886–1923* (London: Macmillan, 1960).

Raleigh, D. J., *Experiencing Russia's Civil War: Politics, Society and Revolutionary Culture in Saratov, 1917–1922* (Princeton: Princeton University Press, 2002).

Rasila, V., 'Kauppa ja rahaliike', in J. Ahvenainen, E. Pihkala and V. Rasila (eds), *Suomen taloushistoria 2: Teollistuva Suomi* (Helsinki: Tammi, 1982).

Rasmussen, J. R., *Modernitet eller åndsdannelse? Engelsk i skole og samfund 1800–1935* (Copenhagen: Museum Tusculanums forlag, 2003).

Reich, A., 'Economic Interests and National Conflict: The Relationship between Czech and German Consumer Cooperatives in Czechoslovakia between 1918 and 1939', in T. Lorenz (ed.), *Cooperatives in Ethnic Conflicts:*

Eastern Europe in the 19th and Early 20th Century (Berlin: Berliner Wissenschafts-Verlag, 2006).

Rhodes, R., *The International Co-operative Alliance during War and Peace 1910–1950* (Geneva: ICA, 1995).

Rhodes, R., *An Arsenal for Labour: The Royal Arsenal Co-operative Society and Politics 1896–1996* (Manchester: Holyoake Books, 1998).

Riddell, J. (ed.), *To the Masses: Proceedings of the Third Congress of the Communist International, 1921* (Leiden: Brill, 2015).

Roalkvam, G., 'Ole Dehli', *Norsk biografisk leksikon* (2009), available at http://nbl.snl.no/Ole_Dehli, accessed 14 January 2014.

Robertson, N., 'The Political Dividend: Co-operative Parties in the Midlands, 1917–1939', in M. Worley (ed.), *Labour's Grass Roots: Essays on the Activities of Local Labour Parties and Members, 1918–1945* (Aldershot: Ashgate, 2005).

Robertson, N., *The Co-operative Movement and Communities in Britain 1914–1960: Minding Their Own Business* (Farnham: Ashgate, 2010).

Rodríguez García, M., 'Early Views on Internationalism: Marxist Socialists vs Liberals', *Revue belge de philology et d'histoire – Belgisch Tijdschrift voor filologie en geschiednis*, 84:4 (2006), 1049–73.

Ruin, O., *Kooperativa Förbundet 1899–1929: En organisationsstudie* (Lund: Rabén & Sjögren, 1960).

Rupp, L. J., *Worlds of Women: The Making of an International Women's Movement* (Princeton: Princeton University Press, 1997).

Salzman, C., 'Consumer Cooperative Societies in Russia, Goals v. Gains, 1900–1918', *Cahiers du Monde russe et soviétique*, 23:3–4 (1982), 351–69.

Sandell, M., 'Regional versus International: Women's Activism and Organizational Spaces in the Inter-War Period', *International History Review*, 33:4 (2011), 607–25.

Saunier, P.-Y., 'Learning by Doing: Notes about the Making of the *Palgrave Dictionary of Transnational History*', *Journal of Modern European History*, 6:2 (2008), 159–72.

Scholliers, P., 'The Social Democratic World of Consumption: The Path-Breaking Case of the Ghent Cooperative Vooruit Prior to 1914', *International Labor and Working-Class History*, 55 (1999), 71–91.

Schoultz, J. von, *Bidrag till belysande av Finlands socialdemokratiska partis history, del 1: Tiden före representationsreformen år 1906* (Helsinki: Söderström, 1924).

Scott, G., *Feminism and the Politics of Working Women: The Women's Co-operative Guild 1880s to the Second World War* (London: UCL Press, 1998).

Sennett, R., *Together: The Rituals, Pleasures and Politics of Co-operation* (London: Allen Lane, 2012).

Shaw, G., and A. Alexander, 'British Co-operative Societies as Retail Innovators: Interpreting the Early Stages of the Self-Service Revolution', *Business History*, 50:1 (2008), 62–78.

Sluga, G., 'Editorial – the Transnational History of International Institutions', *Journal of Global History*, 6:2 (2011), 219–22.

Stadius, P., 'Happy Countries: Appraisals of Interwar Nordic Societies', in J. Harvard and P. Stadius (eds), *Communicating the North: Media Structures and Images in the Making of the Nordic Region* (Farnham: Ashgate, 2013).

Stadius, P., and C. Marklund, 'Acceptance and Conformity: Merging Modernity with Nationalism in the Stockholm Exhibition in 1930', *Culture Unbound: Journal of Current Cultural Research*, 2 (2010), 609–34.

Stenius, H., *Frivilligt, jämlikt, samfällt: Föreningsväsendets utveckling i Finland fram till 1900-talets början med speciell hänsyn till massorganisationsprincipens genombrott* (Helsinki: Svenska litteratursällskapet i Finland, 1987).

Stenius, H., 'Nordic Associational Life in a European and an Inter-Nordic Perspective', in R. Alapuro and H. Stenius (eds), *Nordic Associations in a European Perspective* (Baden-Baden: Nomos Verlag, 2010).

Stolpe, H., 'K. Albin A. Johansson', *Svenskt biografiskt lexikon* (n.d.), available at https://sok.riksarkivet.se/Sbl/Presentation.aspx?id=12127, last accessed 3 July 2017.

Stolpe, H., and S. Stolpe, *Boken om Albin Johansson I* (Stockholm: Rabén & Sjögren, 1969).

Strang, J., 'Introduction: The Nordic Model of Transnational Cooperation?', in J. Strang (ed.), *Nordic Cooperation: A European Region in Transition* (London: Routledge, 2016).

Struck, B., K. Ferris and J. Revel, 'Introduction: Space and Scale in Transnational History', *International History Review*, 33:4 (2011), 573–84.

Sundin, B., 'Kooperationen som utopi: Martin Sundell och den kooperativa rörelsen', *Lychnos* (1991), 77–109.

Sysiharju, A.-L., 'Gebhard, Hannes', *Kansallisbiografia-verkkojulkaisu, Studia Biographica 4* (Helsinki: Suomalaisen Kirjallisuuden Seura, 1997), available at www.kansallisbiografia.fi/kansallisbiografia/henkilo/4278, accessed 6 July 2017.

Sysiharju, A.-L., 'Gebhard, Hedvig', *Biografiskt Lexikon för Finland 2: Ryskatiden* (2009), available at www.blf.fi/index.php, last accessed 12 December 2016.

Teeboom, P., 'Searching for the Middle Way: Consumer Co-operation and the Co-operative Movement in New Deal America' (PhD dissertation, University of Amsterdam, 2009).

Ther, P., 'Comparisons, Cultural Transfers and the Study of Networks: Toward a Transnational History of Europe', in J. Kocka and H.-G. Haupt (eds),

Comparative and Transnational History: Central European Approaches and New Perspectives (New York: Berghahn Books, 2009).

Theien, I., 'Two Phases of Consumer Co-operation in Scandinavia: Pre-war Pluralism and Post-war Unification under Social Democracy', in P. Verbruggen and L. Soubry (eds), *Consumerism versus Capitalism? Co-operatives seen from an International Comparative Perspective* (Ghent: Amsab-Institute of Social History, 2003).

Thestrup, P., *Nærbutik og næringslovs-omgåelse: En undersøgelse af brugsforeningerne og deres placering i innovationsprocessen i Danmark mellem 1850 og 1919* (Odense: Odense Universitetsforlag, 1986).

Thomson, C. C., and M. Hilson, 'Beauty in Bacon: "The Pattern of Co-operation" and the Export of Postwar Danish Democracy', *Kosmorama*, 255 (2014), available at www.kosmorama.org/Artikler/Beauty-in-Bacon.aspx, accessed 4 July 2017.

Tingsten, H., *Den svenska socialdemokratins idéutveckling* (Stockholm: Tidens förlag, 1941).

Trentmann, F., 'Beyond Consumerism: New Historical Perspectives on Consumption', *Journal of Contemporary History*, 39:3 (2004), 373–401.

Trentmann, F., 'The Modern Genealogy of the Consumer: Meanings, Identities and Political Synapses', in J. Brewer and F. Trentmann (eds), *Consuming Cultures, Global Perspectives: Historical Trajectories, Transnational Exchanges* (Oxford: Berg, 2006).

Trentmann, F., *Free Trade Nation: Commerce, Consumption and Civil Society in Modern Britain* (Oxford: Oxford University Press, 2008).

Trentmann, F., 'Before Fair Trade: Empire, Free Trade and the Moral Economies of Food in the Modern World', in A. Nützenadel and F. Trentmann (eds), *Food and Globalization: Consumption, Markets and Politics in the Modern World* (Oxford: Berg, 2008).

Troebst, S., 'Introduction: What's in a Historical Region?', *European Review of History – Revue européene d'histoire*, 10:2 (2003), 173–88.

Veselov, S. V., 'The Cooperative Movement and Soviet Rule: The Period of "War Communism"', *Russian Studies in History*, 33:1 (1994), 52–71.

Wallén, B., *Enighet ger styrka. Finlands Svenska Andelsförbund 80 år* (Helsinki: Finlands Svenska Andelsförbund, 1999).

Watkins, W. P., *The International Co-operative Alliance 1895–1970* (London: ICA, 1970).

Webster, A., and J. K. Walton, 'Introduction', in 'The Business of Co-operation: National and International Dimensions since the Nineteenth Century', *Business History*, 54:6 (2012), 825–32.

Webster, A., J. F. Wilson and R. Vorberg-Rugh, 'Going Global. The Rise of CWS as an International Commercial and Political Actor, 1863–1950: Scoping an Agenda for Future Research', in M. Hilson, S. Neunsinger and G. Patmore (eds), *A Global History of Consumer Co-operation 1850–2000: Movements and Businesses* (Leiden: Brill, 2017).

Webster, A., L. Shaw, D. Stewart, J. K. Walton and A. Brown, 'The Hidden Alternative?' in A. Webster et al. (eds), *The Hidden Alternative: Co-operative Values Past, Present and Future* (Manchester: Manchester University Press, 2012).

Wendt, F., *Cooperation in the Nordic Countries: Achievements and Obstacles* (Stockholm: Nordic Council, 1981).

Wilson, J. F., A. Webster and R. Vorberg-Rugh, *Building Co-operation: A Business History of the Co-operative Group, 1863–2013* (Oxford: Oxford University Press, 2013).

Wirén, A., *G. H. von Koch: Banbrytare i svensk socialvård* (Stockholm: Rabén & Sjögren, 1980).

Wrigley, C., 'The Co-operative Movement', *Mitteilungsblatt des Instituts für soziale Bewegungen*, 27 (2002), 103–16.

Yeo, S. (ed.), *New Views of Co-operation* (London: Routledge, 1988).

Zacher, M. W., and R. A. Matthew, 'Liberal International Theory: Common Threads, Divergent Strands', in C. W. Kegley, Jr. (ed.), *Controversies in International Relations Theory: Realism and the Neoliberal Challenge* (New York: St Martin's Press, 1995).

Index

agricultural co-operatives
in Denmark 12, 24–5, 137–8
in Finland 30–3, 86
in the ICA 6, 54–5, 56, 140
in Norway 28–9
in Sweden 33, 37, 143–4
relations with consumer co-operatives 138–41
Aléx, Peder 4, 38, 42, 73, 142–3, 149, 152
Allen, Thomas 94
Andelsudvalget (Denmark) 26, 27, 65, 87, 97, 98, 99, 141, 143
Anglo-Soviet Trade Agreement (1921) 88
Arnesen, Randolf 85
Arnfred, J. Th. 25
Austria, co-operative movement in 4, 10, 42, 58, 67, 75n.20, 82, 83, 87, 97, 98, 113, 165

Belgium, co-operative movement in 10, 35, 36, 41, 42, 50n.108, 53, 64–5, 87, 93, 97, 99
see also Vooruit
Black, Lawrence 5
Boyce, Robert 111, 119
Brandesten, Olof 33
Brazda, Johann 146
Britain, co-operative movement in 3, 4, 8, 26, 35, 42, 54, 64, 66, 67, 72, 78n.65, 84, 92, 111, 113, 145
and the ICA 6, 10, 11, 54–5, 56, 58, 59, 60, 69, 75n.18, 90, 91, 92, 96, 97, 113, 127, 165
see also Co-operative Wholesale Society (CWS); Rochdale co-operation

Callahan, Kevin 8, 54, 67
Canada, co-operative movement in 81n.118, 139, 140
cartels *see* trusts
Centrosoyus *see* Tsentrosoiuz
Childs, Marquis W. 2, 12, 136, 137, 150, 151, 152, 166
Clavin, Patricia 164
Cleuet, A. J. 118
coffee 110, 116, 117, 118, 120, 147
Cole, G. D. H. 92, 105n.82
Comintern 11, 90
consumption 2, 4–6, 38, 141–2, 150
co-operative internationalism 10, 53–4, 72, 73, 165
Co-operative Wholesale Society (CWS) 35, 64, 69, 90, 92, 109, 126–7, 166
and ICWS 112–19, 123–4, 125
trade with Denmark 115, 138
co-partnership 3, 54, 56–7

Danielsson, Axel 36
Davies, Margaret Llewellyn 32
de Boyve, Edouard 54
Dehli, Ole 28, 29, 35, 39, 40, 42, 85, 87, 112, 116, 167

Denmark, co-operative movement in 24–7, 137–8
as a model 137–8
relations with the ICA 65, 97, 141
see also Andelsudvalget (Denmark); Fællesforeningen for Danmarks Brugsforeninger (FDB); Hovedstadens Brugsforening; Det kooperative Fællesforbund (Denmark); Stjernen co-operative brewery; Thisted Kjøbstads Arbeiderforening
Det kooperative Fællesforbund (Denmark) 27, 65, 87–8, 141
Drejer, A. Axelsen 27, 98, 141, 166
dried fruit 117, 118, 123

Elanto 32, 40, 42, 86, 87, 149
electric lightbulbs 148–9
Eley, Geoff 92
Espeli, Harald 29

Finland
co-operative law (1901) 31
co-operative movement 29–33, 85–7
during civil war 86
language differences 33, 40, 86–7
and Nordisk Andelsforbund (NAF) 125–6
ICA meetings in 70
see also Elanto; Gebhard, Hannes; Gebhard, Hedvig; Hankkija; Kulutusosuuskuntien Keskusliitto (KK); Pellervo; Suomen Osuuskauppojen Keskuskunta (SOK); Tanner, Väinö
First World War 2, 5, 6, 9, 58, 84, 111, 127, 144–5
folk high schools 22, 25, 137
France, co-operative movement in 3, 4, 6, 8, 53, 54, 55, 59, 91, 97, 98, 142
Freundlich, Emmy 106n.103
Friberg, Katarina 36–7, 143, 165
Friedmann, Harriet 147
Furlough, Ellen 4
Fællesforeningen for Danmarks Brugsforeninger (FDB) 27, 29, 34, 40, 115, 116, 121

Gebhard, Hannes 13, 30–1, 35, 39, 40, 42, 55, 84
Gebhard, Hedvig 31–2, 39, 55
Germany, co-operative movement in 3, 4, 6, 10, 26, 35, 53, 55, 58, 59, 67, 82, 83, 94, 95, 98, 115, 124, 140–1, 166
see also Nazism and co-operation; Raiffeisen co-operatives; Schulze-Delitzsch co-operatives
Gide, Charles 32, 41, 55, 58, 92, 93, 111, 113, 142, 152
Gjöres, Axel 34, 73, 96, 152
Goedhart, G. J. D. C. 59, 70, 77n.47
Gorman, Daniel 9, 11
Great Depression 93–4, 144, 150, 164, 165
Greening, Edward Owen 54
Grelle, Henning 87
Grimley, O. B. 151
Gurney, Peter 3, 4, 6

Hampden Jackson, J. 151
Hankkija 32
Heckscher, Eli F. 146
Hedberg, Anders 95, 117
Hemstad, Ruth 38
Hovedstadens Brugsforening 27
Howe, Frederic C. 137, 138, 150–1
Hummelin, Keijo 116

Inquiry on Co-operative Enterprise in Europe (1936) 12, 136, 151, 162
International Co-operative Agency (INCALIM) 119

International Co-operative Alliance (ICA)
British dominance of 8, 10, 113
and First World War 58–60
historiography 9–10, 164
history and development 6, 8, 9, 39, 53, 54–7
ideology and principles 14n.1, 82–3, 84, 92–3, 93–7, 98–9, 111–12, 138–40, 142, 165
languages 66–8
national differences in 57–8, 60, 73
Nordic influence in 11–12, 24, 27, 29, 39, 40, 42, 65, 70, 87–8, 97–8, 136, 141, 142, 144
organisation 53, 56–7, 60–1, 64, 66–7, 68–71, 90, 104n.67, 165
International Co-operative Bulletin 57, 59, 77n.48, 99
international co-operative congresses 54, 63–8
Basle (1921) 56, 60, 61, 64, 88, 91–2, 111
Budapest (1904) 55, 56, 64
Cremona (1907) 112
Ghent (1924) 61, 64–5, 98
Glasgow (1913) 56, 58, 73–4, 138
Hamburg (1910) 56, 84, 112
London (1934) 82, 96
Manchester (1902) 56, 64
Paris (1937) 97
special conference Basle (1933) 94, 140
Stockholm (1927) 61, 64, 139
Vienna (1930) 61, 83, 93
International Co-operative Day 9, 72, 81n.118
international co-operative exhibition (Ghent 1924) 64–5
International Co-operative Wholesale Society (ICWS) 82, 110, 112–19, 120, 123–4, 125, 127
International Federation of Agricultural Co-operation 139
International Labour Organisation (ILO) 11, 121, 139
International Year of Co-operatives (2012) 4, 169n.16
internationalism 7–9, 11, 19n.55, 53–4, 58, 61, 71, 164
see also co-operative internationalism
Ireland 137, 138
as a model for Finnish co-operation 30
Italy, co-operative movement in 10, 65, 79n.79, 82

Jaeggi, Bernhard 66, 139, 141
Janfelt, Monika 121
Jensen, Kristoffer 27
Johansson, Albin 11, 70, 95, 112, 117, 118, 120, 124, 139, 142, 144, 146, 150, 151, 152, 166, 167
Jonsson, Pernilla 149
Juell, Andreas 85
Jørgensen, Severin 27, 39, 91, 139

Kaufmann, Heinrich 48n.81, 59, 67, 95, 106n.104, 113, 115, 138
Kettunen, Pauli 22
Koch, Gerhard Halfred von 35–7, 39, 42, 125
Kooperativa Förbundet (KF) 37–8, 39, 42, 73, 85, 87, 95, 98, 99, 110, 111–12, 116, 117, 121, 123, 124, 127, 142, 144, 167
campaigns against trusts 144–9, 166
as a model 150–3
relations with agricultural co-operatives 143–4
see also Johansson, Albin; Örne, Anders
Kristiania Arbeidersamfund 28
Kulutusosuuskuntien Keskusliitto (KK) 32–3, 70, 86–7, 125–6, 139

labour movement and co-operation 3–4, 10, 36, 40–1, 42, 83–5, 165
Lancaster, R. 120
Lange, Even 28
Laqua, Daniel 11, 71
League of Nations 9, 11, 82, 111, 112, 164
Lindblad, A. C. 36
Lloyd George, David 88
Luma 148–9, 150, 162
Lustig, Emil 118
Lyons, F. S. L. 53

Mäkinen, Riitta 39
margarine 37, 124, 145, 147, 166
Marklund, Carl 166
Maxwell, Sir William 68
May, Henry 59, 87, 89, 91, 94, 95, 96, 98, 99, 115, 124, 140, 148
middle way, co-operation as 2, 12, 136–7, 150–2, 165, 166
Miklóssy, Katalin 166
Millbourn, Ingrid 145
monopolies *see* trusts
Mordhorst, Mads 24
Morgan, Kevin 90–1, 92
Musiał, Kazimierz 137
Müller, Hans 57, 84, 92, 100–1n.15

Nazism and co-operation 94–5, 106n.103
Neale, Edward Vansittart 54
Nielsen, Anders 80n.98, 137
Nielsen, Frederik 116, 117, 118, 120, 123, 124, 126, 127, 136, 152
Nordic co-operative movements
  foreign interest in 162, 164
  in ICA *see* International Co-operative Alliance (ICA)
  regional contacts 8, 23, 38–41, 116
  similarities 22, 23, 38, 41–2, 119, 136–7, 162
Nordic model 2, 12, 41, 137, 164
Nordic regional co-operation 11–12, 23, 38, 97, 98, 110, 120, 121, 125, 126, 136–7, 153, 167
Nordisk Andelsforbund (NAF) 27, 40, 110, 116–18, 119–26, 147, 167
Norges Kooperative Landsforening (NKL) 28, 29, 40, 42, 68, 85, 110, 125, 148, 153
  see also Dehli, Ole
Norway, co-operation in 27–9
  see also Kristiania Arbeidersamfund; Norges Kooperative Landsforening (NKL)
Nützenadel, Alexander 111

Odhe, Thorsten 85, 149
Örne, Anders 11, 64, 98, 111–12, 124, 126, 127, 142–3, 145, 152
Osterhammel, Jürgen 8
Owen, Robert 41, 65

Palm, August 35
Pellervo 30–4, 39, 97, 143
Plunkett, Horace 30
Plymouth co-operative society 2
Poisson, Ernest 80n.100, 89, 90, 91, 95, 141
popular movements 22, 41
Primus-Nyman, K. E. 55

Raiffeisen co-operatives 30
Rhodes, Rita 9–10, 11–12, 89
Robertson, Nicole 5, 72, 92
Rochdale co-operation 12, 23, 25, 26, 28, 31, 34, 35, 36, 38, 42, 47n.72, 55, 64, 65, 83, 111, 116, 142, 164, 165
  ICA enquiry on the Rochdale principles 96–7, 140, 165
Rodríguez García, Magaly 7

Roosevelt commission *see* Inquiry on Co-operative Enterprise in Europe (1936)
Ruin, Olof 37
Rupp, Leila 8, 68
rural areas, consumer co-operation in 26, 29, 31, 32, 38, 86, 87
Russia *see* Comintern; Tsentrosoiuz
Rylander, Axel 36

Scandinavianism 38, 125, 127
Schediwy, Robert 146
Schulze-Delitzsch co-operatives 35, 143
Scottish Co-operative Wholesale Society (SCWS) 35, 148
Second International 3, 9, 54, 64, 67, 71, 84, 95
Serwy, Victor 89, 91, 98, 115–16, 119–20
Sonne, Hans Christian 25–6, 39
Soviet Union *see* Comintern; Tsentrosoiuz
Stadius, Peter 150
Stauning, Thorvald 87
Stenius, Henrik 31, 34, 58
Stjernen co-operative brewery 26
Stockholm Exhibition (1930) 150
Stolpe, Herman 146
Strikwerda, Carl 4
Sundell, Martin 37, 40
Suomen Osuuskauppojen Keskuskunta (SOK) 32–3, 66, 70, 85, 86–7, 97, 98, 125, 126, 139
Suomen Osuustukkukauppa (OTK) *see* Kulutusosuuskuntien Keskusliitto (KK)
Sweden, co-operative movement in 33–8
  see also Kooperativa Förbundet (KF)

Tanner, Väinö 11, 12, 13, 32, 48n.81, 61, 67–8, 70, 71, 82, 95, 124, 126, 167
Teeboom, Piebe 150
Ther, Philipp 8, 18n.48
Thestrup, Poul 25, 27
Thisted Kjøbstads Arbeiderforening 25–6
Thomas, Albert 57, 139, 140
Treaty of Versailles 9, 60, 67
Trentmann, Frank 5, 110, 111, 141
trusts 38, 73, 110, 136, 144–9, 152–3, 162, 165
Tsentrosoiuz 27, 61
  ICA delegation to 89–90
  membership of ICA 9, 61, 66–7, 77n.48, 88–93, 166–7

Vooruit 3, 64, 78n.68, 83
  see also Belgium, co-operative movement in

Walton, John K. 5
Watkins, W. P. 9, 10, 142
Webb, Beatrice and Sidney 113, 115, 145
Webster, Anthony 5, 165
Wolff, Henry 54–5
Women's Co-operative Guild (UK) 5, 32, 92
worker co-operation 26–7
  see also co-partnership